HARRIET TUBMAN

FIGHTER for FREEDOM!

BY
JAMES BUCKLEY JR.

ILLUSTRATED BY
IZEEK ESIDENE

LETTERING & DESIGN BY
COMICRAFT

COVER ART BY
IAN CHURCHILL

PORTABLE
PRESS

SAN DIEGO, CALIFORNIA

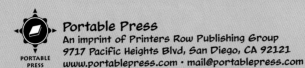

Portable Press
An imprint of Printers Row Publishing Group
9717 Pacific Heights Blvd, San Diego, CA 92121
www.portablepress.com • mail@portablepress.com

Portable Press hardcover edition 2020
Portable Press paperback edition 2022

Correspondence regarding the content of this book should be addressed to Portable Press, Editorial Department, at the above address. Author and illustrator inquiries should be addressed to Oomf, Inc., www.oomf.com.

Publisher: Peter Norton
Associate Publisher: Ana Parker
Developmental Editor: Vicki Jaeger
Production Team: Beno Chan, Julie Greene, Rusty von Dyl

Created at Oomf, Inc., www.Oomf.com
Director: Mark Shulman
Producer: James Buckley Jr.

Author: James Buckley Jr.
Illustrator: Izeek Esidene
Inkers: Cassie Anderson, Caitlin Like, Duddy & Rachmat Pratama
Colorists: Cassie Anderson, Azhar Fauzi, Shamsudeen Idris, Julius Stiawan
Lettering & design by Comicraft: John Roshell, Forest Dempsey, Sarah Jacobs
Cover illustrator: Ian Churchill
Special thanks to Chris Johnson at Anomalous Studios for his help.

The Library of Congress has cataloged the original edition of this title as follows:

Names: Buckley, James, Jr., 1963- author. | Esidene, Izeek, illustrator.
Title: Harriet Tubman: Fighter for Freedom! / by James Buckley, Jr.; illustrated by Izeek Esidene; Lettering & design by Comicraft; Cover art by Ian Churchill.
Description: San Diego, CA: Printers Row Publishing Group, 2020. | Series: Show Me History! | Audience: Grades 4-6. | Audience: Ages 8-12.
Identifiers: LCCN 2019018132 | ISBN 9781645170730 (hc)
Subjects: LCSH: Tubman, Harriet, 1822-1913--Juvenile literature. | Slaves--United States--Biography--Juvenile literature. | African American women--Biography--Juvenile literature. | Underground Railroad--Juvenile literature. | Tubman, Harriet, 1822-1913--Comic books, strips, etc. | Slaves--United States--Biography--Comic books, strips, etc. | African American women--Biography--Comic books, strips, etc. | Underground Railroad--Comic books, strips, etc. | Graphic novels.
Classification: LCC E444.T82 B83 2020 | DDC 326/.8092 [B]--dc23
LC record available at https://lccn.loc.gov/2019018132

ISBN: 978-1-6672-0300-3

Printed in China

26 25 24 23 22   1 2 3 4 5

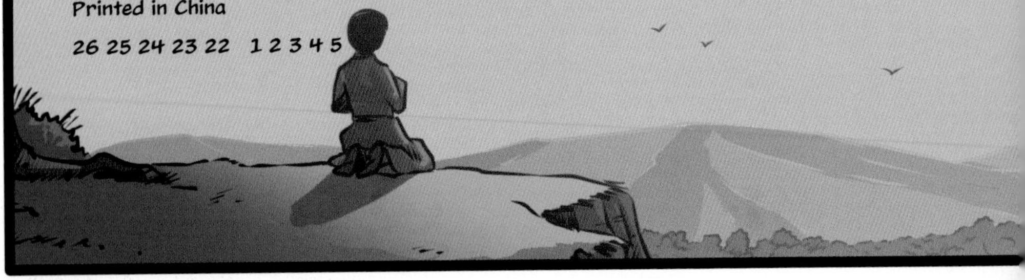

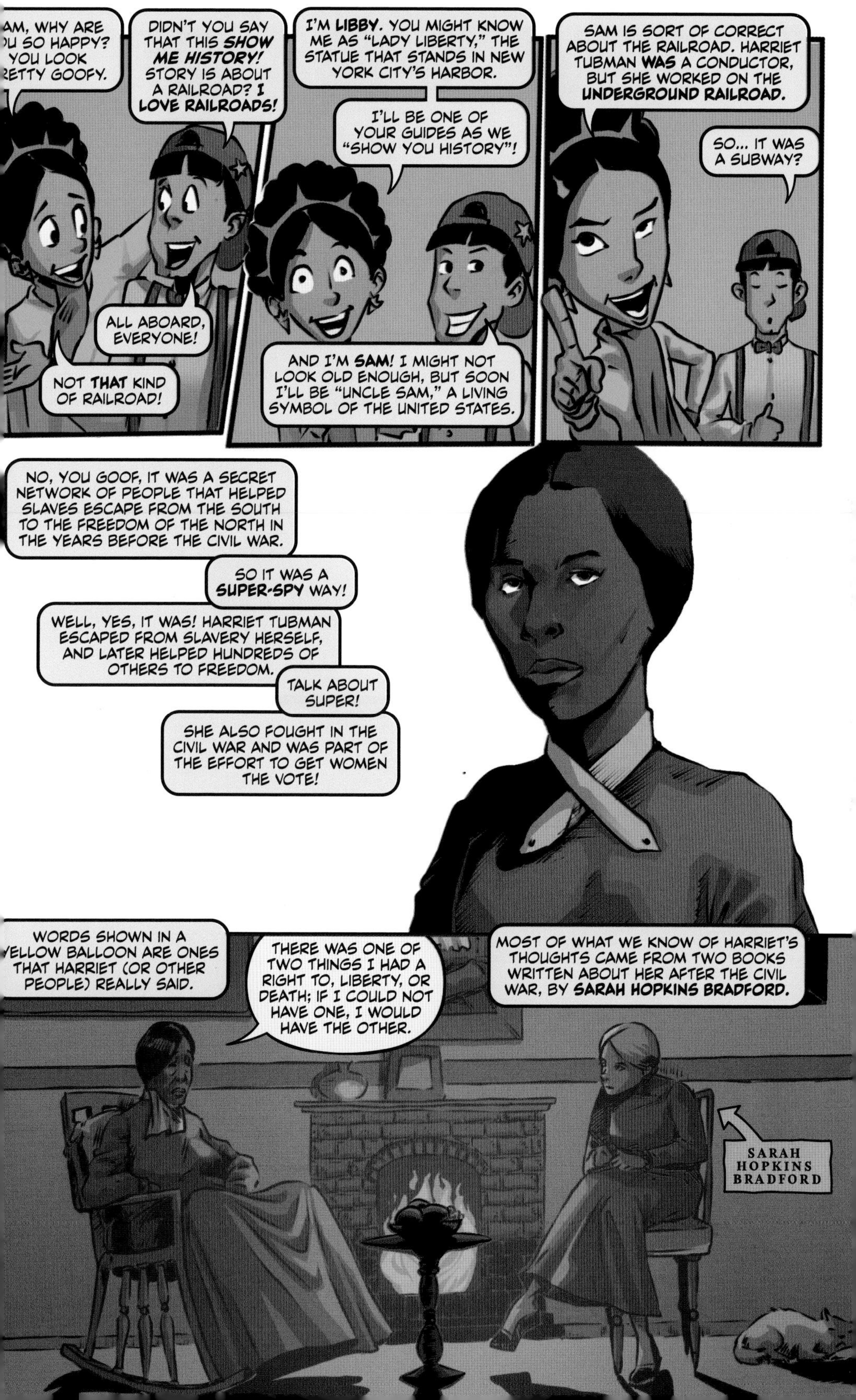
AM, WHY ARE
OU SO HAPPY? YOU LOOK
RETTY GOOFY.
DIDN'T YOU SAY THAT THIS SHOW ME HISTORY! STORY IS ABOUT A RAILROAD? I LOVE RAILROADS!
ALL ABOARD, EVERYONE!
NOT THAT KIND OF RAILROAD!
I'M LIBBY. YOU MIGHT KNOW ME AS "LADY LIBERTY," THE STATUE THAT STANDS IN NEW YORK CITY'S HARBOR.
I'LL BE ONE OF YOUR GUIDES AS WE "SHOW YOU HISTORY"!
AND I'M SAM! I MIGHT NOT LOOK OLD ENOUGH, BUT SOON I'LL BE "UNCLE SAM," A LIVING SYMBOL OF THE UNITED STATES.
SAM IS SORT OF CORRECT ABOUT THE RAILROAD. HARRIET TUBMAN WAS A CONDUCTOR, BUT SHE WORKED ON THE UNDERGROUND RAILROAD.
SO... IT WAS A SUBWAY?
NO, YOU GOOF, IT WAS A SECRET NETWORK OF PEOPLE THAT HELPED SLAVES ESCAPE FROM THE SOUTH TO THE FREEDOM OF THE NORTH IN THE YEARS BEFORE THE CIVIL WAR.
SO IT WAS A SUPER-SPY WAY!
WELL, YES, IT WAS! HARRIET TUBMAN ESCAPED FROM SLAVERY HERSELF, AND LATER HELPED HUNDREDS OF OTHERS TO FREEDOM.
TALK ABOUT SUPER!
SHE ALSO FOUGHT IN THE CIVIL WAR AND WAS PART OF THE EFFORT TO GET WOMEN THE VOTE!
WORDS SHOWN IN A
ELLOW BALLOON ARE ONES THAT HARRIET (OR OTHER PEOPLE) REALLY SAID.
THERE WAS ONE OF TWO THINGS I HAD A RIGHT TO, LIBERTY, OR DEATH; IF I COULD NOT HAVE ONE, I WOULD HAVE THE OTHER.
MOST OF WHAT WE KNOW OF HARRIET'S THOUGHTS CAME FROM TWO BOOKS WRITTEN ABOUT HER AFTER THE CIVIL WAR, BY SARAH HOPKINS BRADFORD.
SARAH HOPKINS BRADFORD

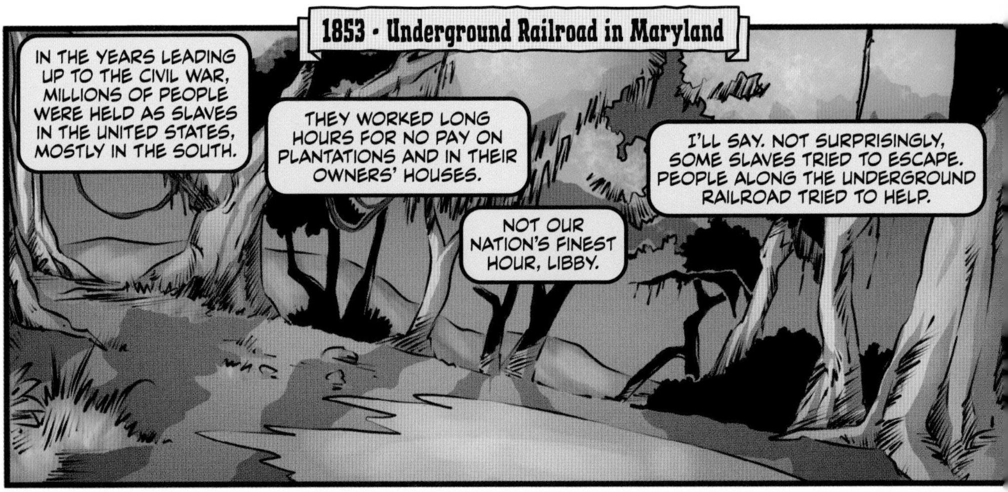
1853 - Underground Railroad in Maryland
IN THE YEARS LEADING UP TO THE CIVIL WAR, MILLIONS OF PEOPLE WERE HELD AS SLAVES IN THE UNITED STATES, MOSTLY IN THE SOUTH.
THEY WORKED LONG HOURS FOR NO PAY ON PLANTATIONS AND IN THEIR OWNERS' HOUSES.
NOT OUR NATION'S FINEST HOUR, LIBBY.
I'LL SAY. NOT SURPRISINGLY, SOME SLAVES TRIED TO ESCAPE. PEOPLE ALONG THE UNDERGROUND RAILROAD TRIED TO HELP.

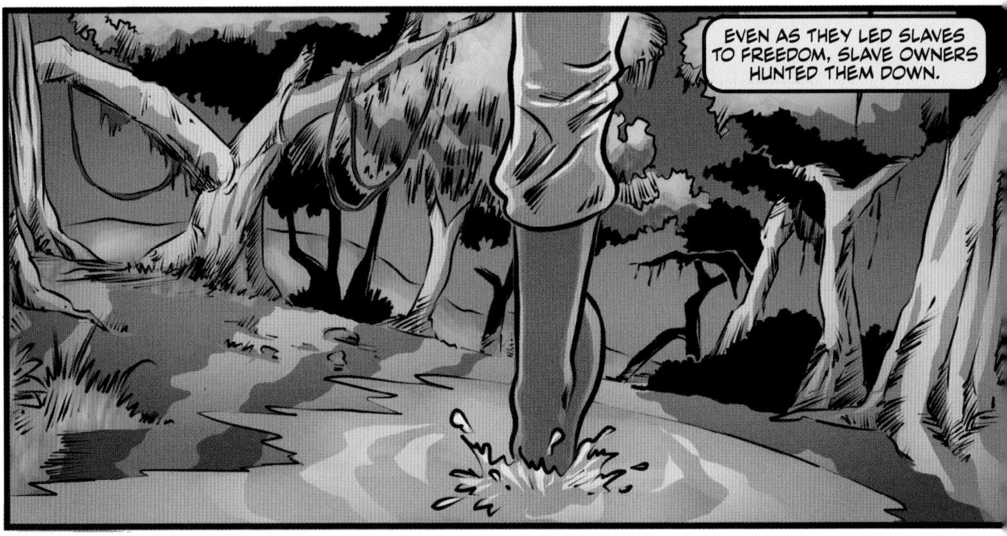
EVEN AS THEY LED SLAVES TO FREEDOM, SLAVE OWNERS HUNTED THEM DOWN.

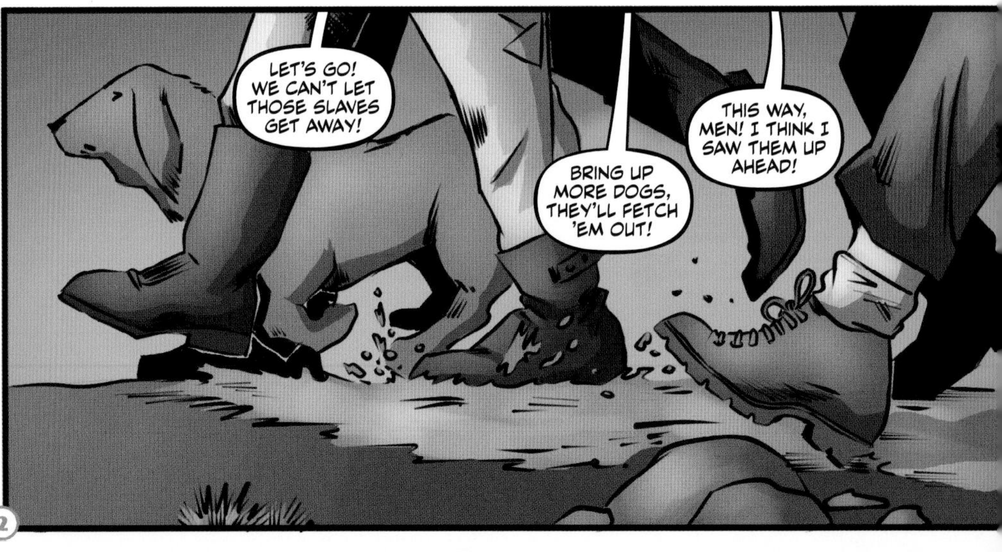
LET'S GO! WE CAN'T LET THOSE SLAVES GET AWAY!
BRING UP MORE DOGS, THEY'LL FETCH 'EM OUT!
THIS WAY, MEN! I THINK I SAW THEM UP AHEAD!

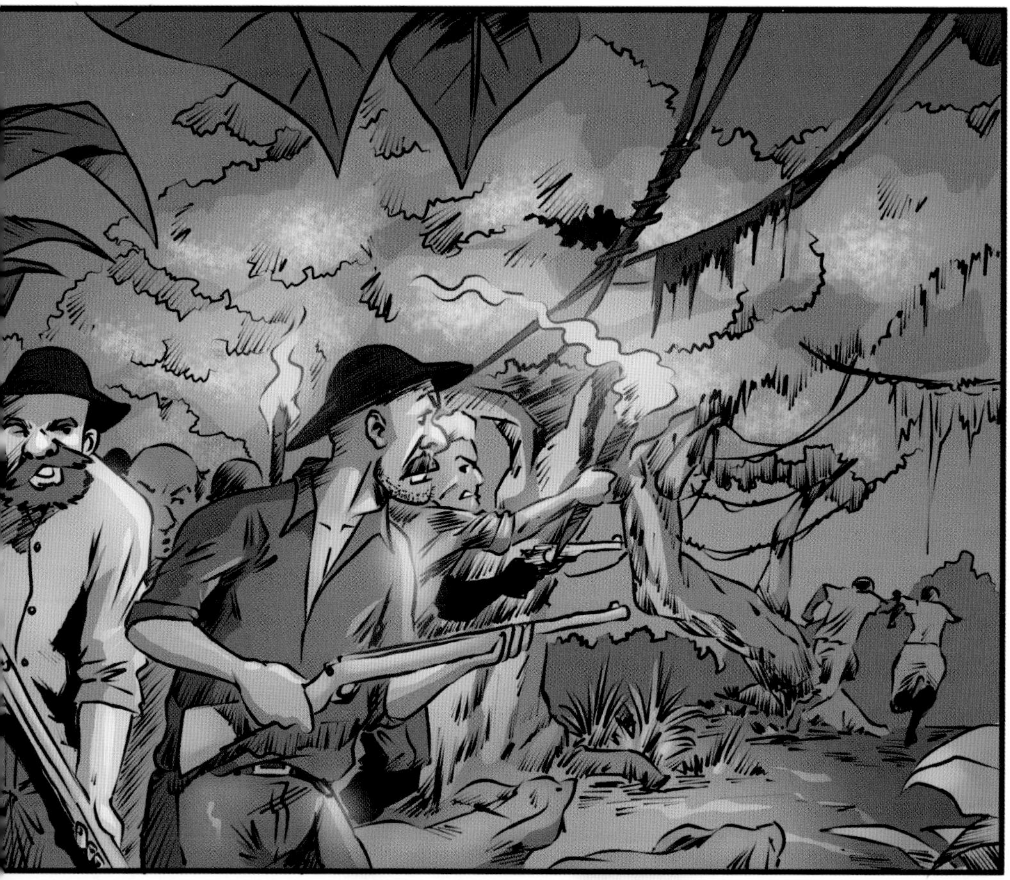

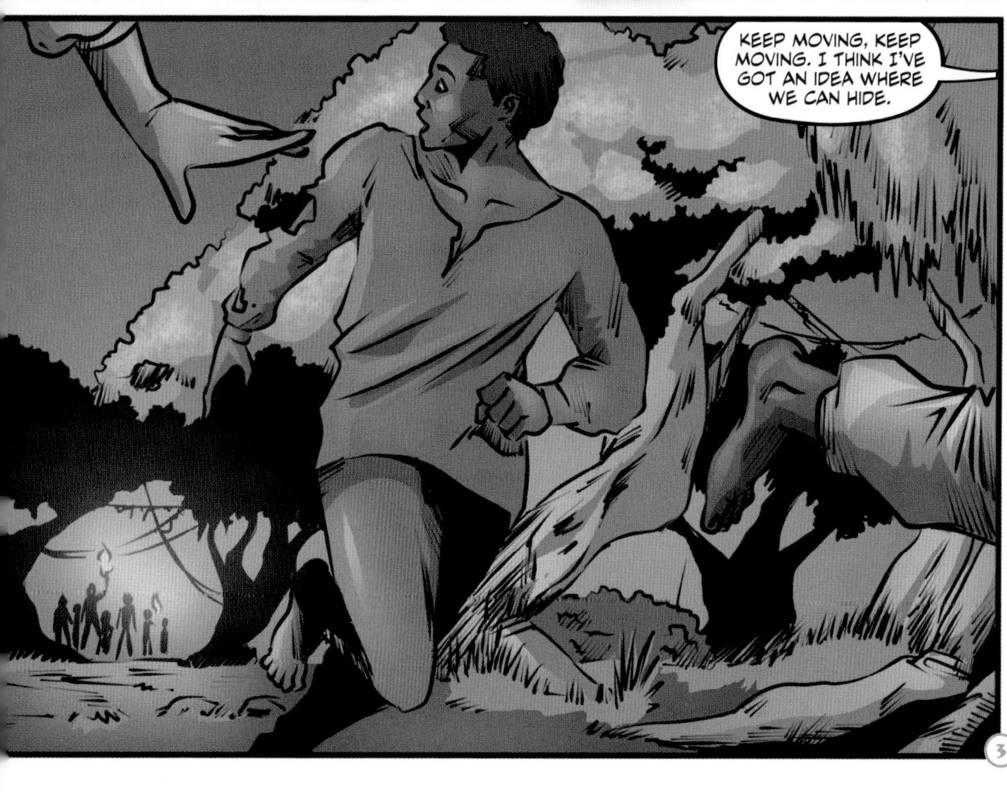
KEEP MOVING, KEEP MOVING. I THINK I'VE GOT AN IDEA WHERE WE CAN HIDE.

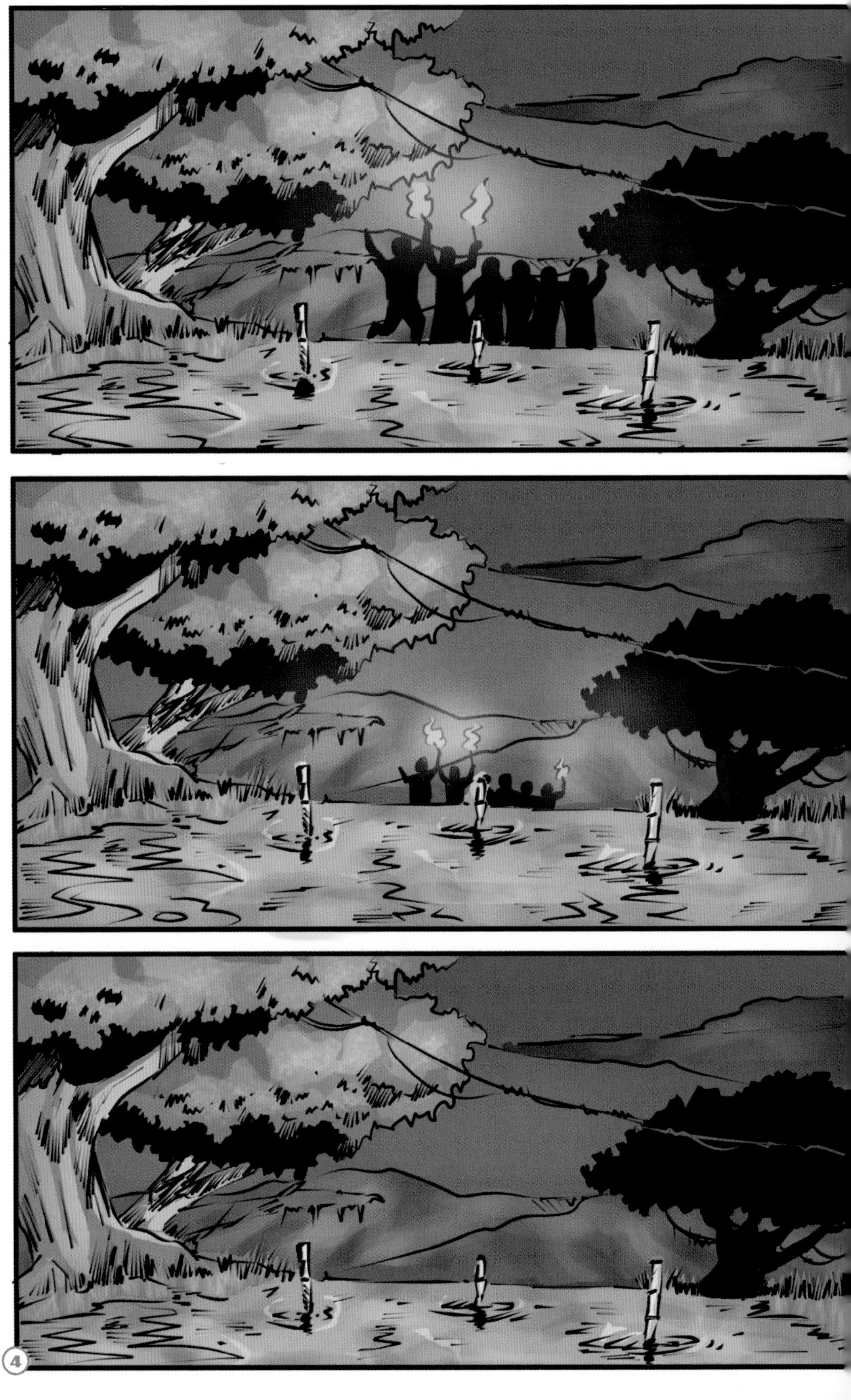

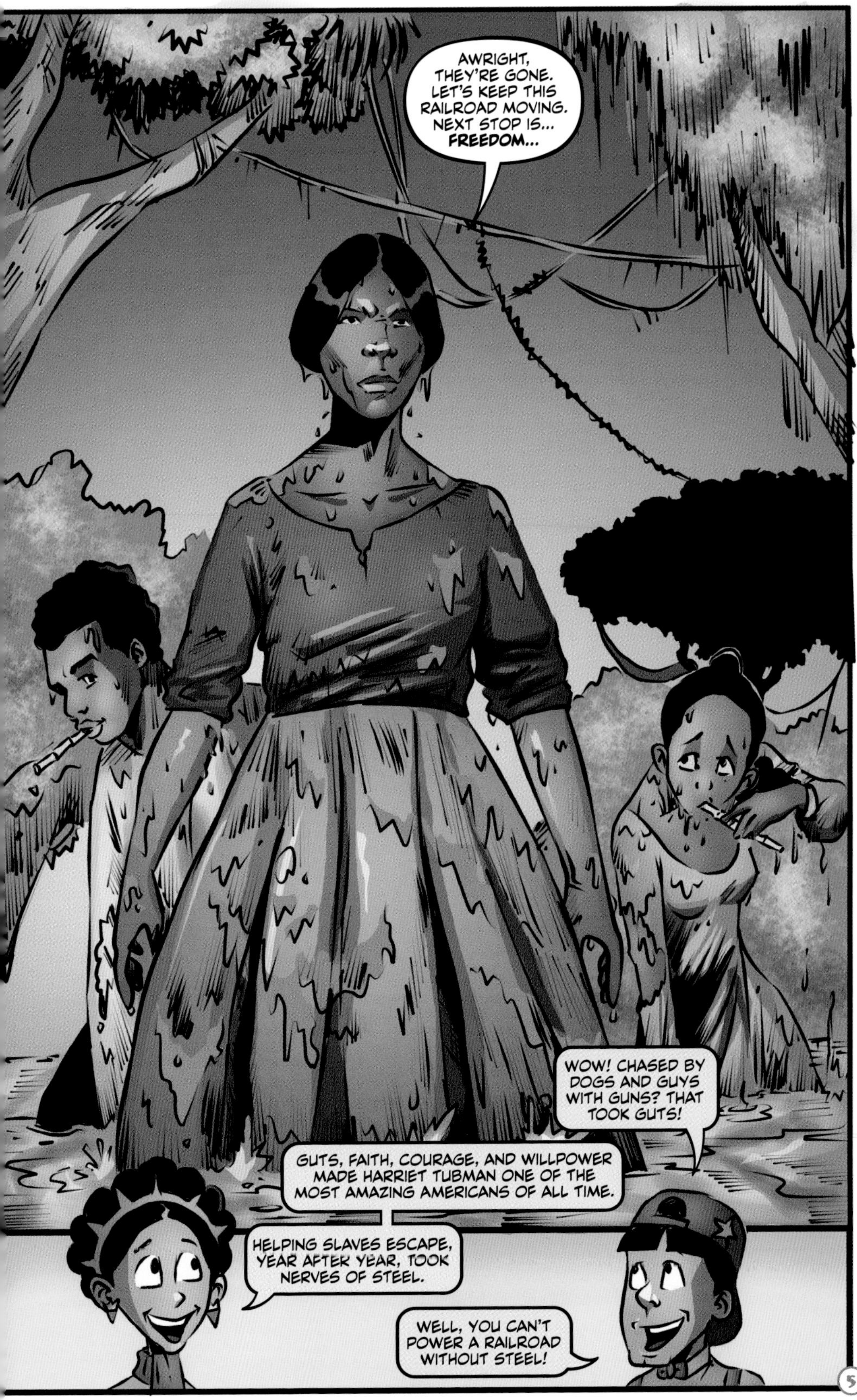
AWRIGHT, THEY'RE GONE. LET'S KEEP THIS RAILROAD MOVING. NEXT STOP IS... **FREEDOM...**
WOW! CHASED BY DOGS AND GUYS WITH GUNS? THAT TOOK GUTS!
GUTS, FAITH, COURAGE, AND WILLPOWER MADE HARRIET TUBMAN ONE OF THE MOST AMAZING AMERICANS OF ALL TIME.
HELPING SLAVES ESCAPE, YEAR AFTER YEAR, TOOK NERVES OF STEEL.
WELL, YOU CAN'T POWER A RAILROAD WITHOUT STEEL!

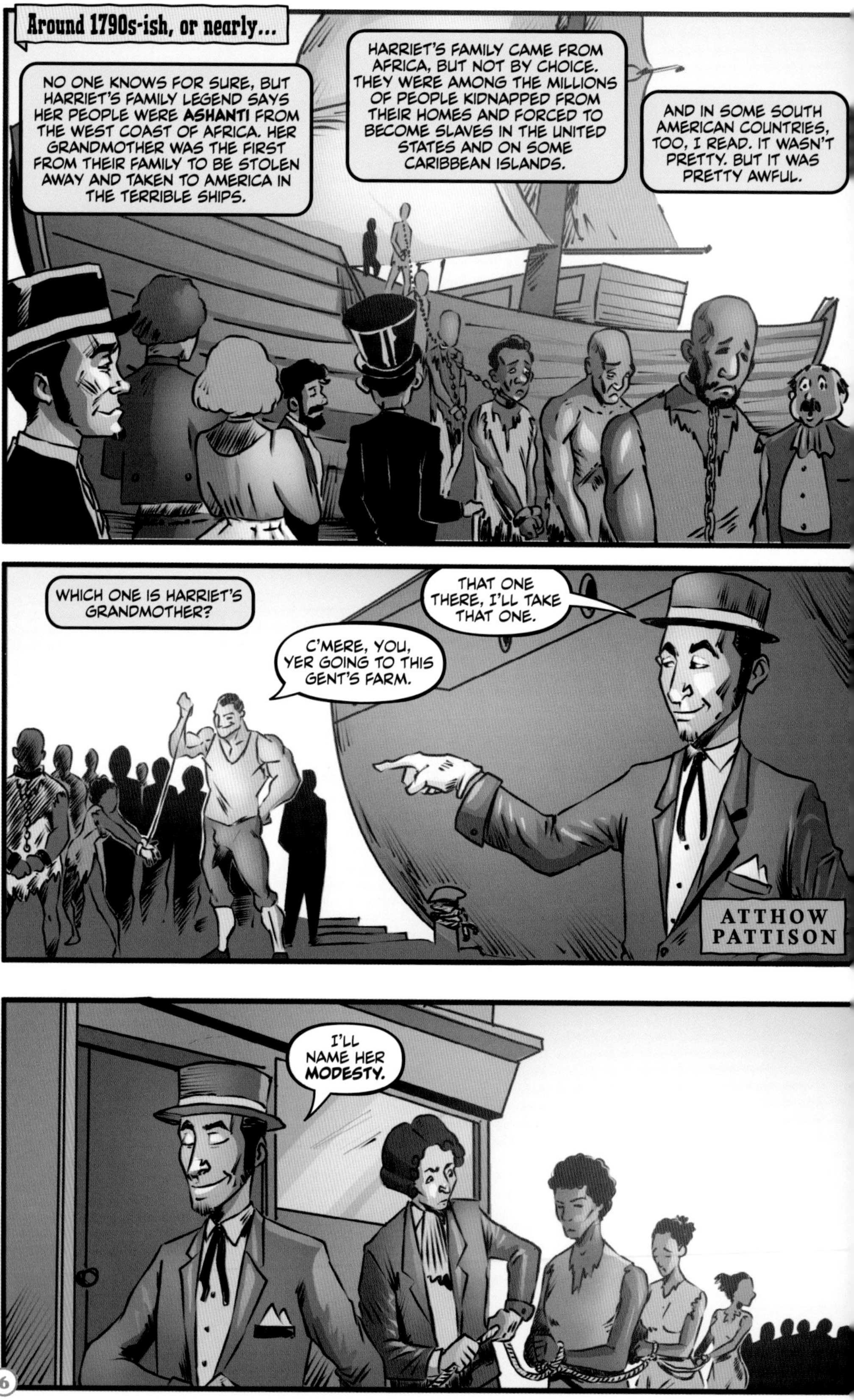
Around 1790s-ish, or nearly...
NO ONE KNOWS FOR SURE, BUT HARRIET'S FAMILY LEGEND SAYS HER PEOPLE WERE ASHANTI FROM THE WEST COAST OF AFRICA. HER GRANDMOTHER WAS THE FIRST FROM THEIR FAMILY TO BE STOLEN AWAY AND TAKEN TO AMERICA IN THE TERRIBLE SHIPS.
HARRIET'S FAMILY CAME FROM AFRICA, BUT NOT BY CHOICE. THEY WERE AMONG THE MILLIONS OF PEOPLE KIDNAPPED FROM THEIR HOMES AND FORCED TO BECOME SLAVES IN THE UNITED STATES AND ON SOME CARIBBEAN ISLANDS.
AND IN SOME SOUTH AMERICAN COUNTRIES, TOO, I READ. IT WASN'T PRETTY. BUT IT WAS PRETTY AWFUL.
WHICH ONE IS HARRIET'S GRANDMOTHER?
THAT ONE THERE, I'LL TAKE THAT ONE.
C'MERE, YOU, YER GOING TO THIS GENT'S FARM.
ATTHOW PATTISON
I'LL NAME HER MODESTY.

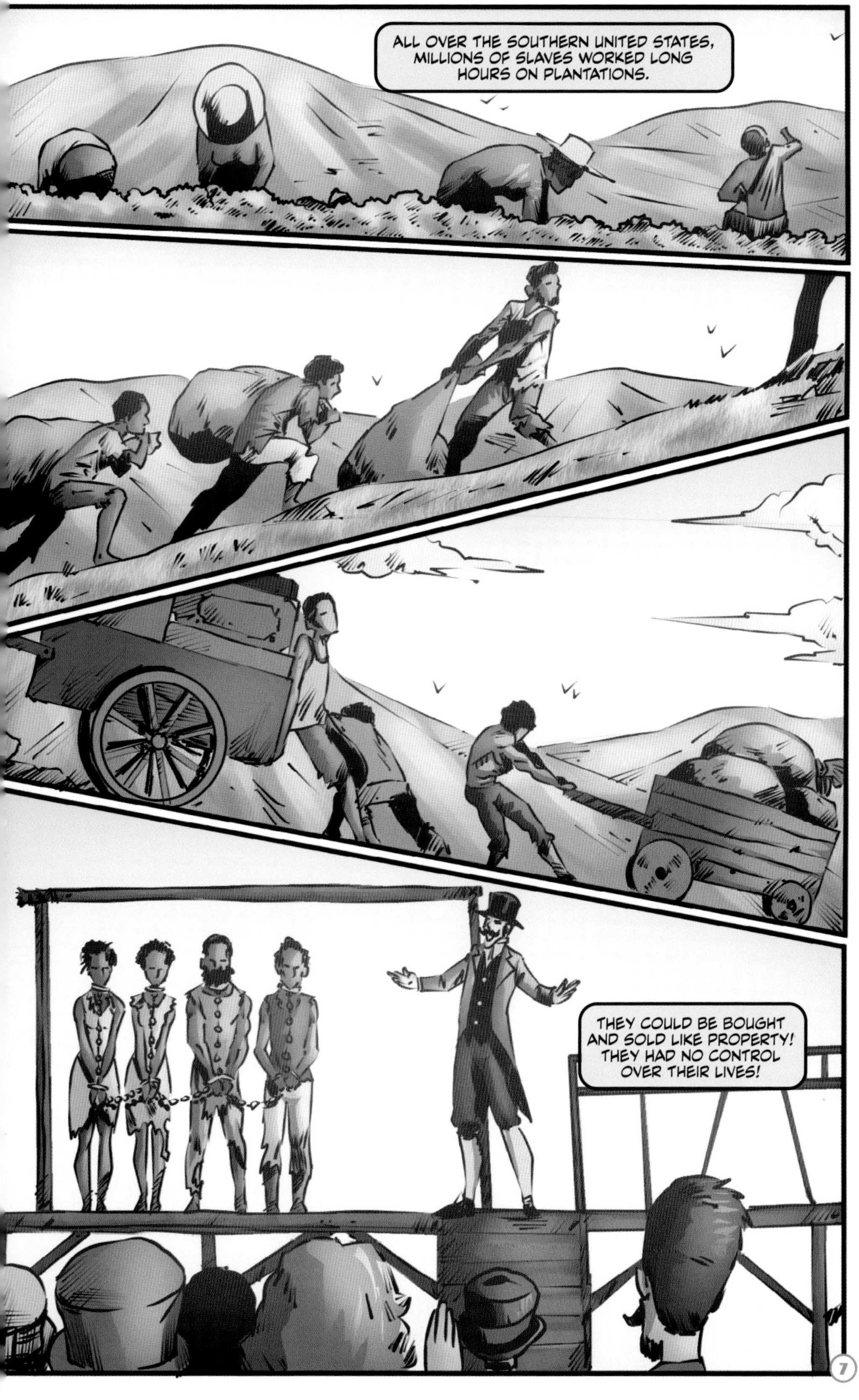
ALL OVER THE SOUTHERN UNITED STATES, MILLIONS OF SLAVES WORKED LONG HOURS ON PLANTATIONS.
THEY COULD BE BOUGHT AND SOLD LIKE PROPERTY! THEY HAD NO CONTROL OVER THEIR LIVES!

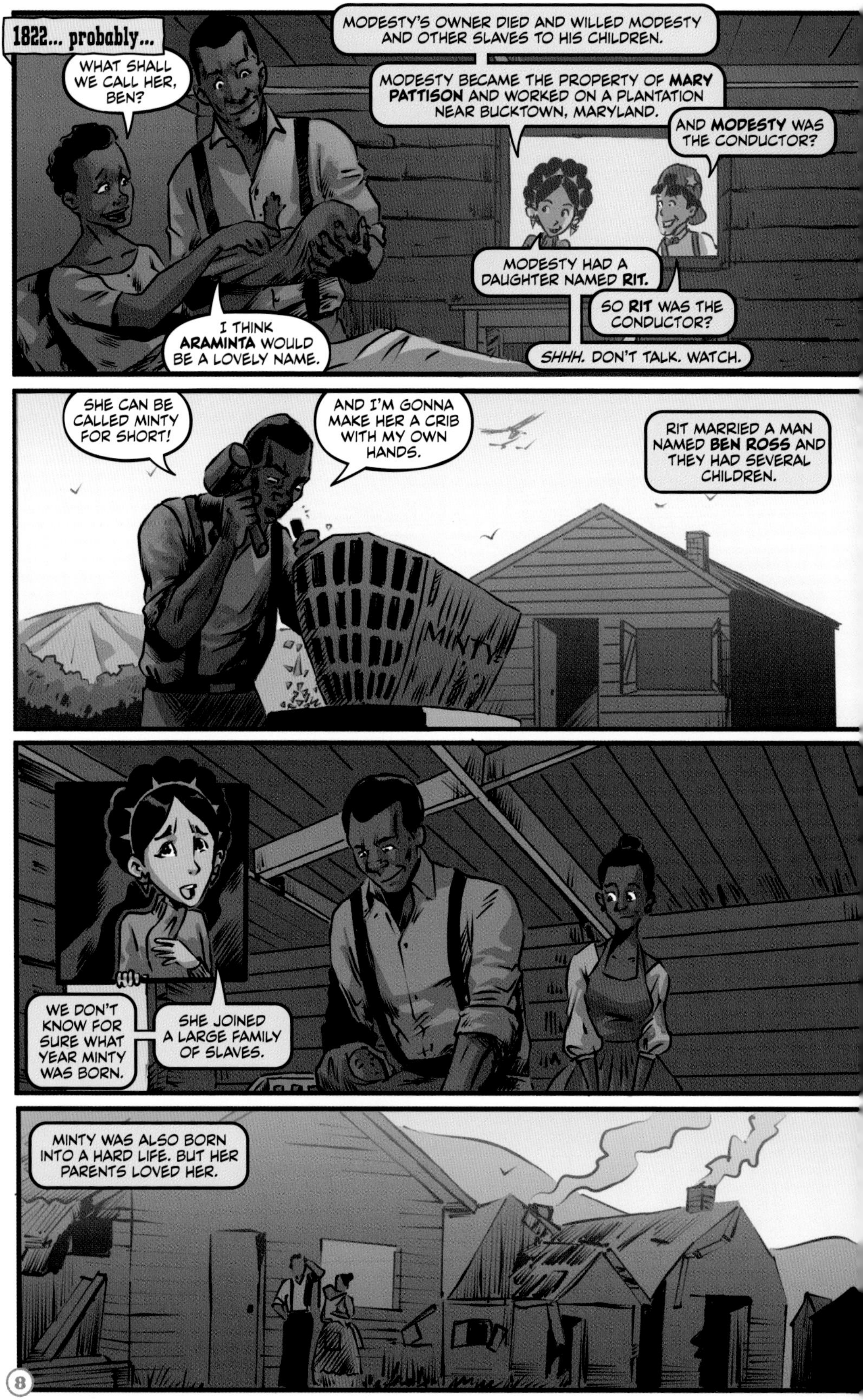
1822... probably...
WHAT SHALL WE CALL HER, BEN?
I THINK ARAMINTA WOULD BE A LOVELY NAME.
MODESTY'S OWNER DIED AND WILLED MODESTY AND OTHER SLAVES TO HIS CHILDREN.
MODESTY BECAME THE PROPERTY OF MARY PATTISON AND WORKED ON A PLANTATION NEAR BUCKTOWN, MARYLAND.
AND MODESTY WAS THE CONDUCTOR?
MODESTY HAD A DAUGHTER NAMED RIT.
SO RIT WAS THE CONDUCTOR?
SHHH. DON'T TALK. WATCH.
SHE CAN BE CALLED MINTY FOR SHORT!
AND I'M GONNA MAKE HER A CRIB WITH MY OWN HANDS.
RIT MARRIED A MAN NAMED BEN ROSS AND THEY HAD SEVERAL CHILDREN.
MINTY
WE DON'T KNOW FOR SURE WHAT YEAR MINTY WAS BORN.
SHE JOINED A LARGE FAMILY OF SLAVES.
MINTY WAS ALSO BORN INTO A HARD LIFE. BUT HER PARENTS LOVED HER.

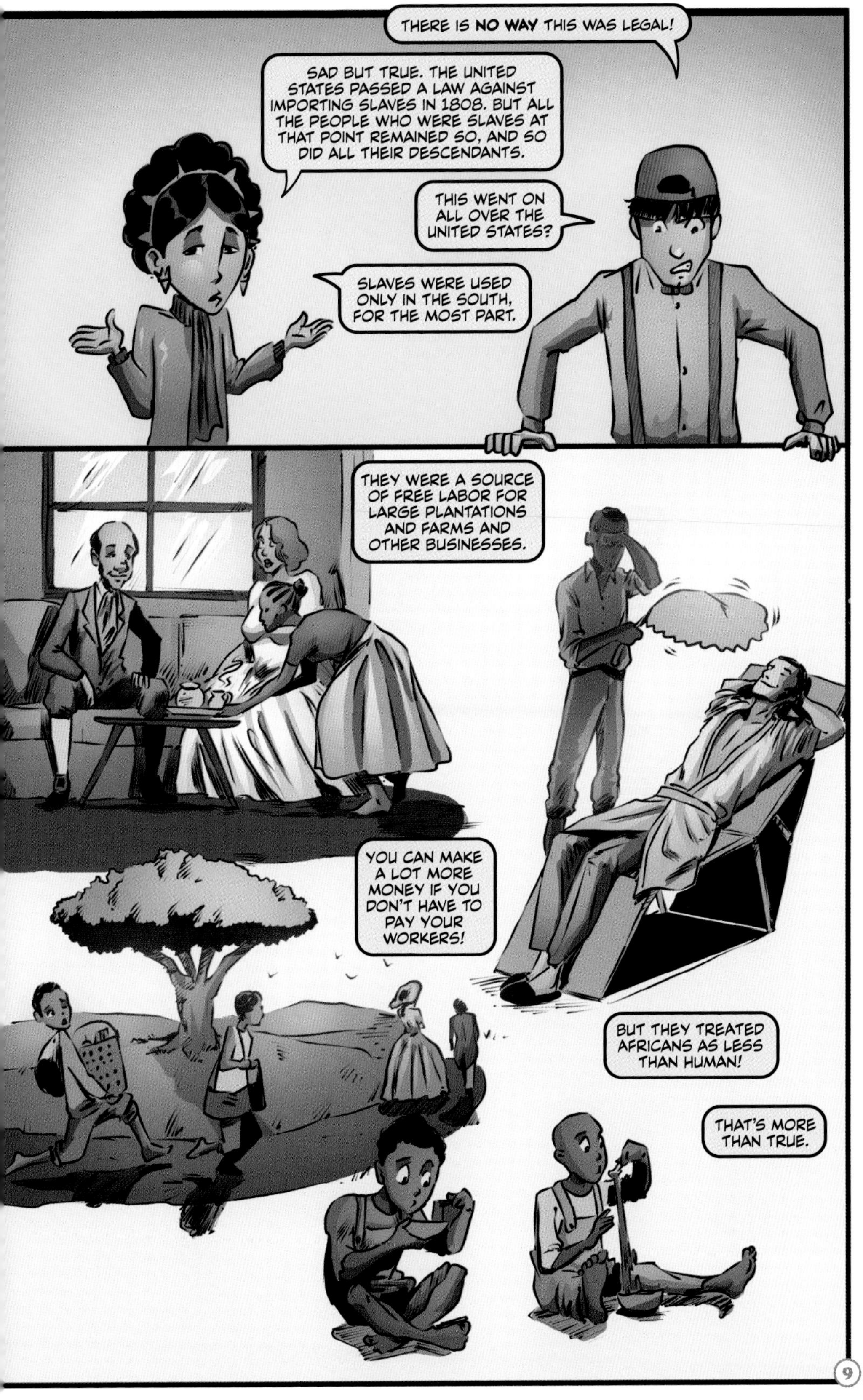
THERE IS **NO WAY** THIS WAS LEGAL!
SAD BUT TRUE. THE UNITED STATES PASSED A LAW AGAINST IMPORTING SLAVES IN 1808. BUT ALL THE PEOPLE WHO WERE SLAVES AT THAT POINT REMAINED SO, AND SO DID ALL THEIR DESCENDANTS.
THIS WENT ON ALL OVER THE UNITED STATES?
SLAVES WERE USED ONLY IN THE SOUTH, FOR THE MOST PART.
THEY WERE A SOURCE OF FREE LABOR FOR LARGE PLANTATIONS AND FARMS AND OTHER BUSINESSES.
YOU CAN MAKE A LOT MORE MONEY IF YOU DON'T HAVE TO PAY YOUR WORKERS!
BUT THEY TREATED AFRICANS AS LESS THAN HUMAN!
THAT'S MORE THAN TRUE.

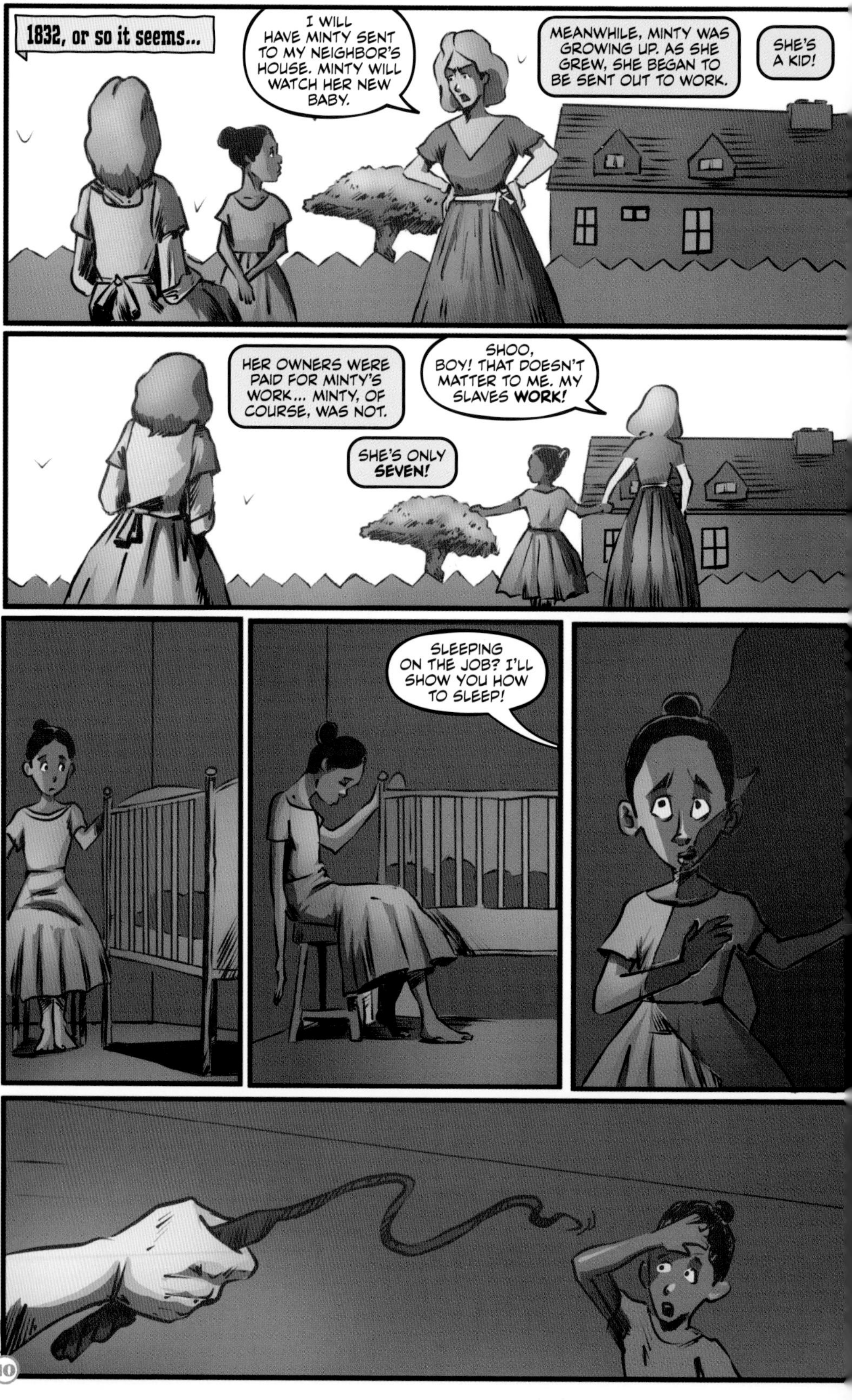
1832, or so it seems...
I WILL HAVE MINTY SENT TO MY NEIGHBOR'S HOUSE. MINTY WILL WATCH HER NEW BABY.
MEANWHILE, MINTY WAS GROWING UP. AS SHE GREW, SHE BEGAN TO BE SENT OUT TO WORK.
SHE'S A KID!
HER OWNERS WERE PAID FOR MINTY'S WORK... MINTY, OF COURSE, WAS NOT.
SHOO, BOY! THAT DOESN'T MATTER TO ME. MY SLAVES **WORK!**
SHE'S ONLY **SEVEN!**
SLEEPING ON THE JOB? I'LL SHOW YOU HOW TO SLEEP!

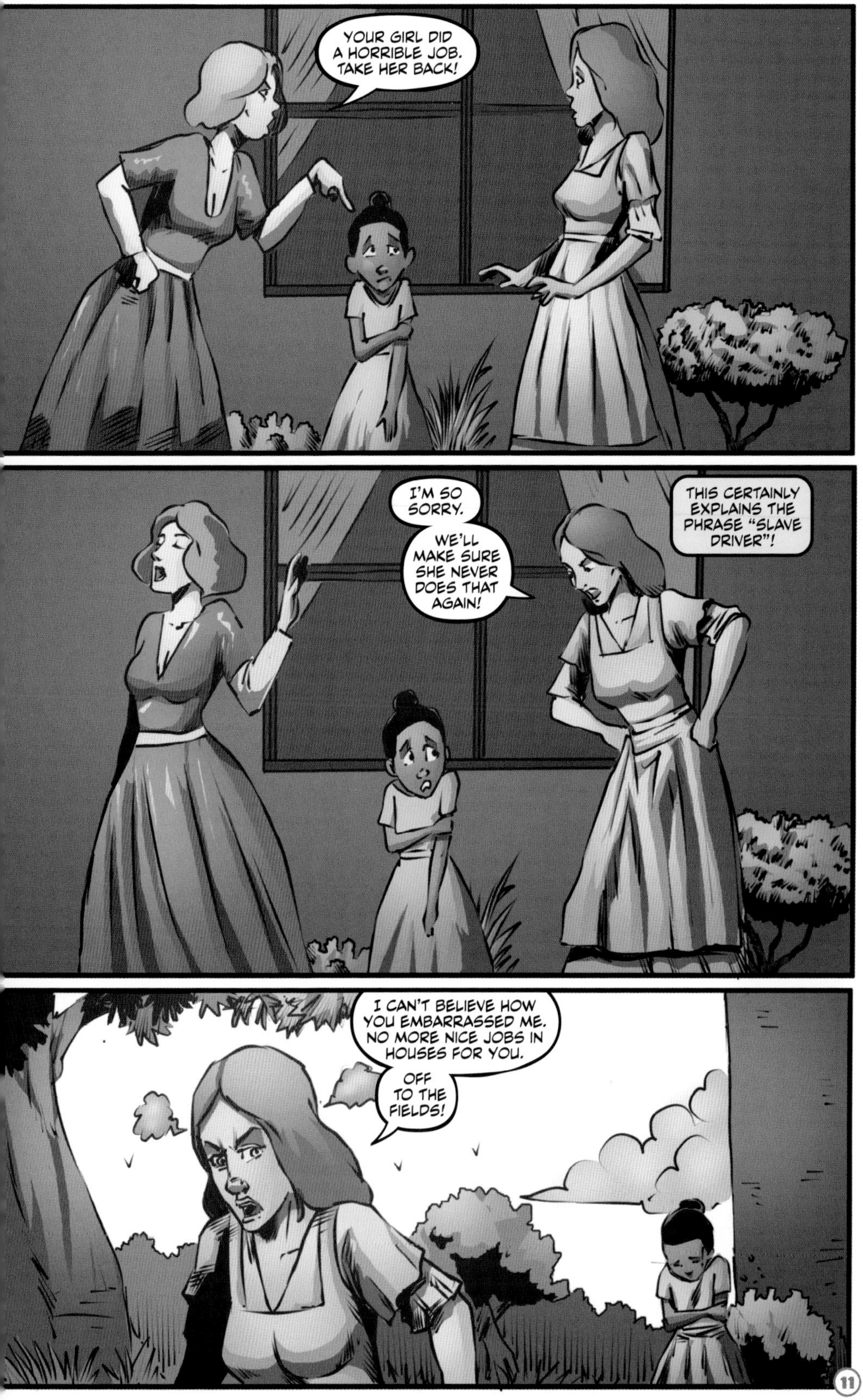
YOUR GIRL DID A HORRIBLE JOB. TAKE HER BACK!
I'M SO SORRY.
WE'LL MAKE SURE SHE NEVER DOES THAT AGAIN!
THIS CERTAINLY EXPLAINS THE PHRASE "SLAVE DRIVER"!
I CAN'T BELIEVE HOW YOU EMBARRASSED ME. NO MORE NICE JOBS IN HOUSES FOR YOU.
OFF TO THE FIELDS!

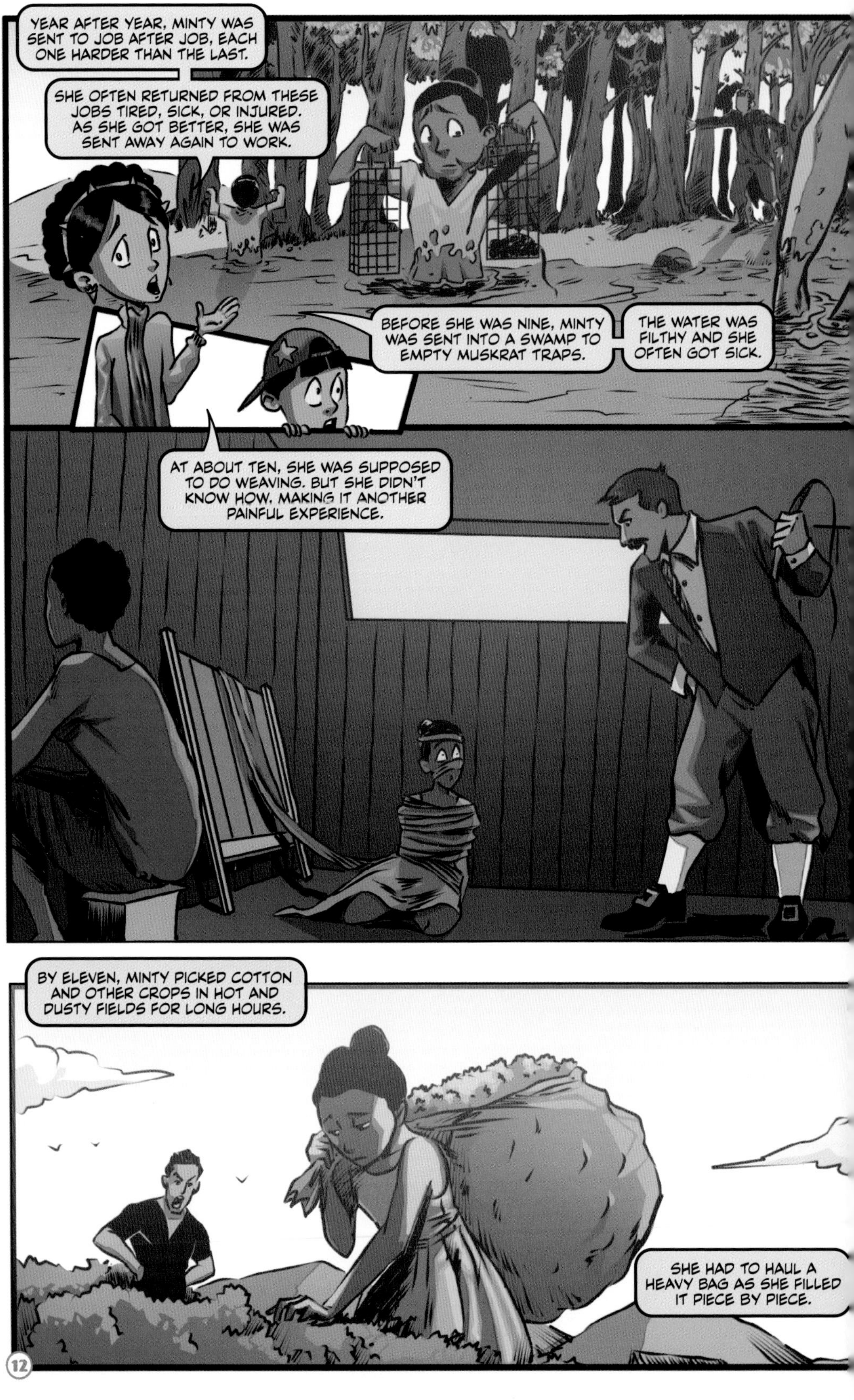

YEAR AFTER YEAR, MINTY WAS SENT TO JOB AFTER JOB, EACH ONE HARDER THAN THE LAST.
SHE OFTEN RETURNED FROM THESE JOBS TIRED, SICK, OR INJURED. AS SHE GOT BETTER, SHE WAS SENT AWAY AGAIN TO WORK.
BEFORE SHE WAS NINE, MINTY WAS SENT INTO A SWAMP TO EMPTY MUSKRAT TRAPS.
THE WATER WAS FILTHY AND SHE OFTEN GOT SICK.
AT ABOUT TEN, SHE WAS SUPPOSED TO DO WEAVING. BUT SHE DIDN'T KNOW HOW, MAKING IT ANOTHER PAINFUL EXPERIENCE.
BY ELEVEN, MINTY PICKED COTTON AND OTHER CROPS IN HOT AND DUSTY FIELDS FOR LONG HOURS.
SHE HAD TO HAUL A HEAVY BAG AS SHE FILLED IT PIECE BY PIECE.

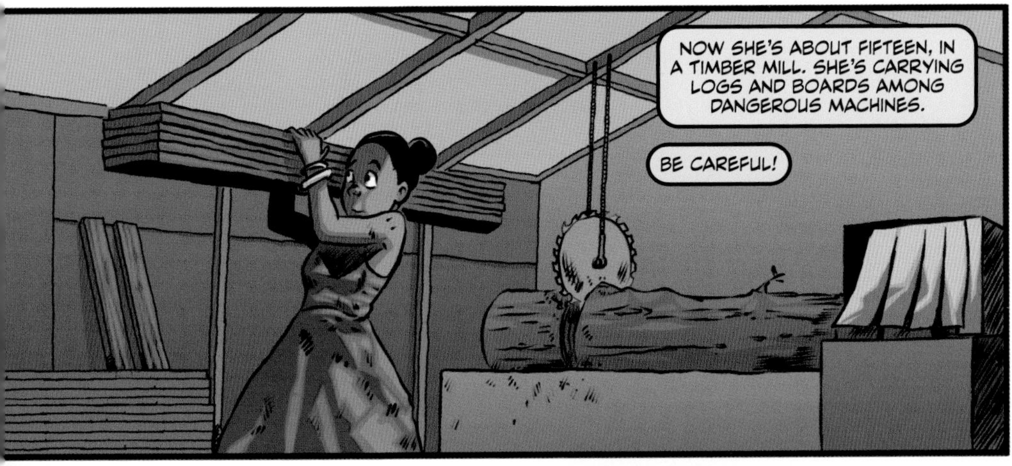
NOW SHE'S ABOUT FIFTEEN, IN A TIMBER MILL. SHE'S CARRYING LOGS AND BOARDS AMONG DANGEROUS MACHINES.
BE CAREFUL!

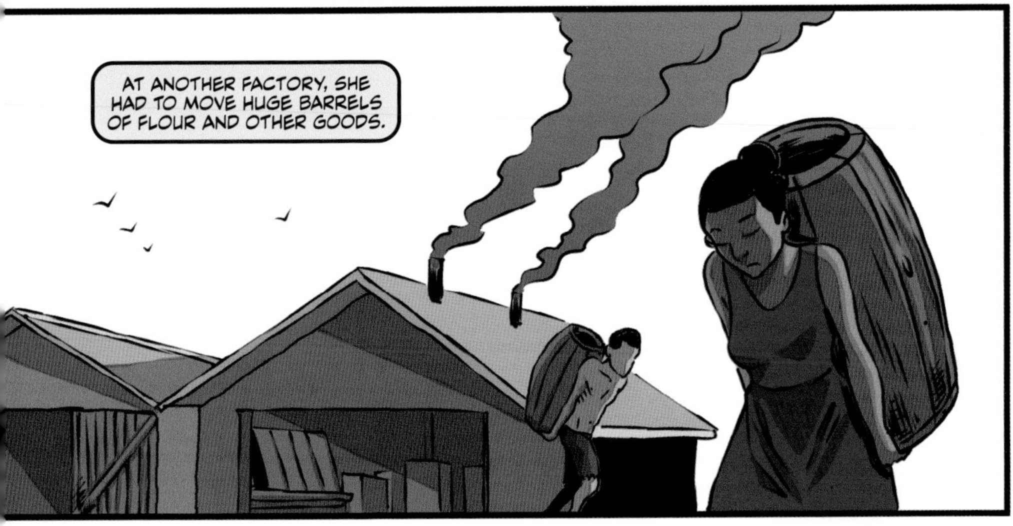
AT ANOTHER FACTORY, SHE HAD TO MOVE HUGE BARRELS OF FLOUR AND OTHER GOODS.

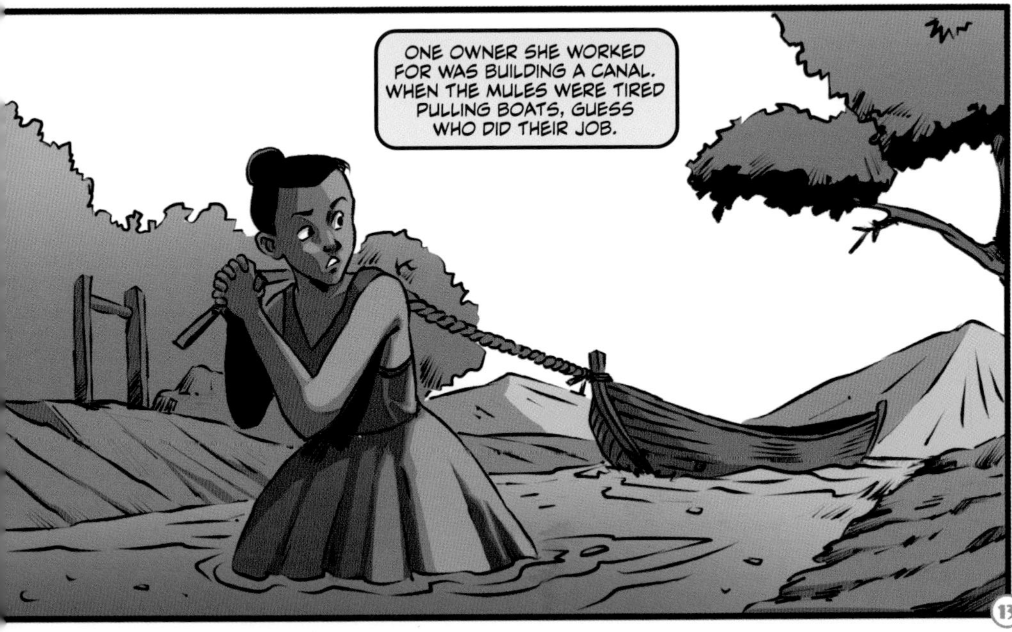
ONE OWNER SHE WORKED FOR WAS BUILDING A CANAL. WHEN THE MULES WERE TIRED PULLING BOATS, GUESS WHO DID THEIR JOB.

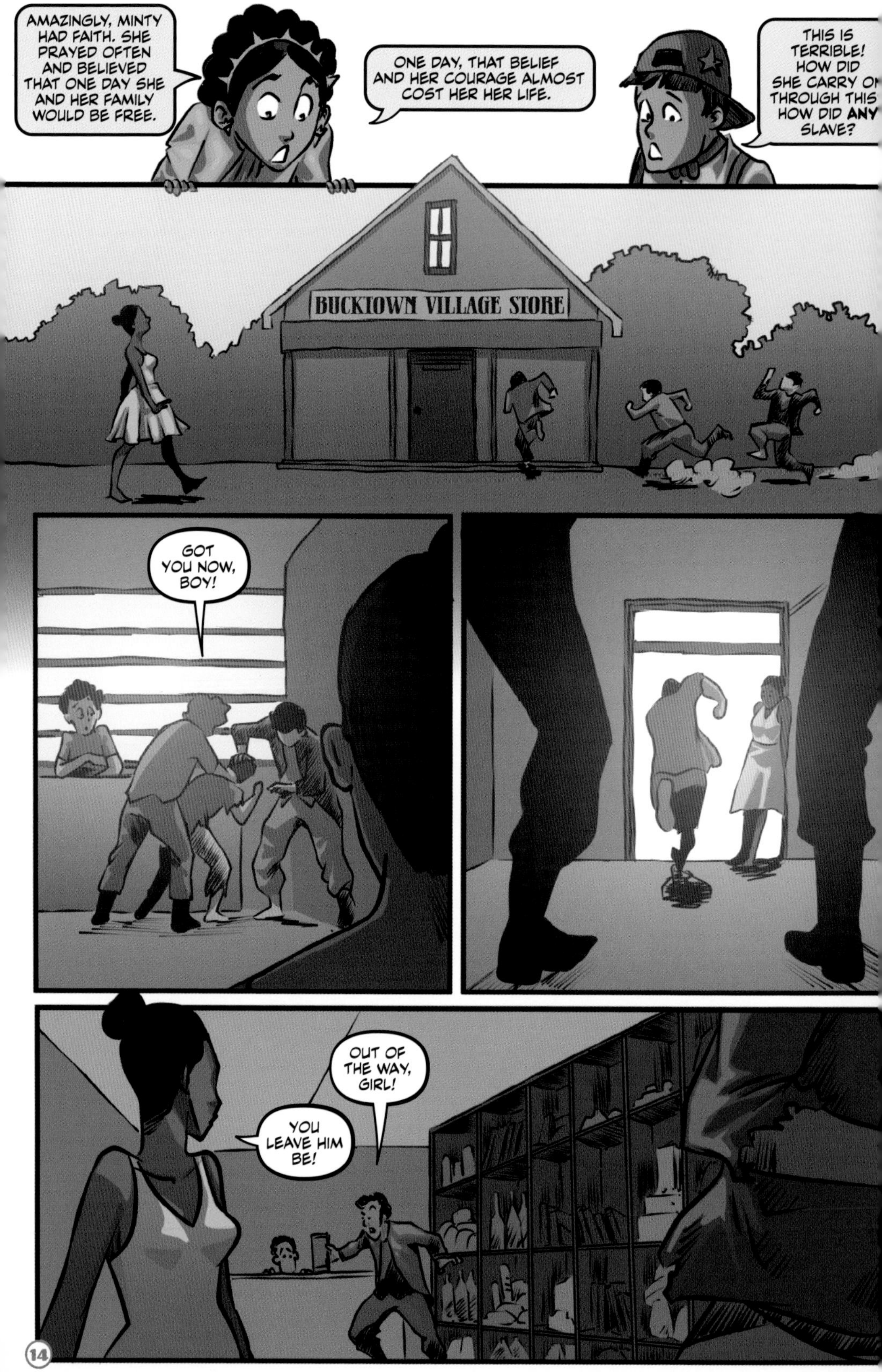
AMAZINGLY, MINTY HAD FAITH. SHE PRAYED OFTEN AND BELIEVED THAT ONE DAY SHE AND HER FAMILY WOULD BE FREE.
ONE DAY, THAT BELIEF AND HER COURAGE ALMOST COST HER HER LIFE.
THIS IS TERRIBLE! HOW DID SHE CARRY ON THROUGH THIS? HOW DID **ANY** SLAVE?
BUCKTOWN VILLAGE STORE
GOT YOU NOW, BOY!
OUT OF THE WAY, GIRL!
YOU LEAVE HIM BE!

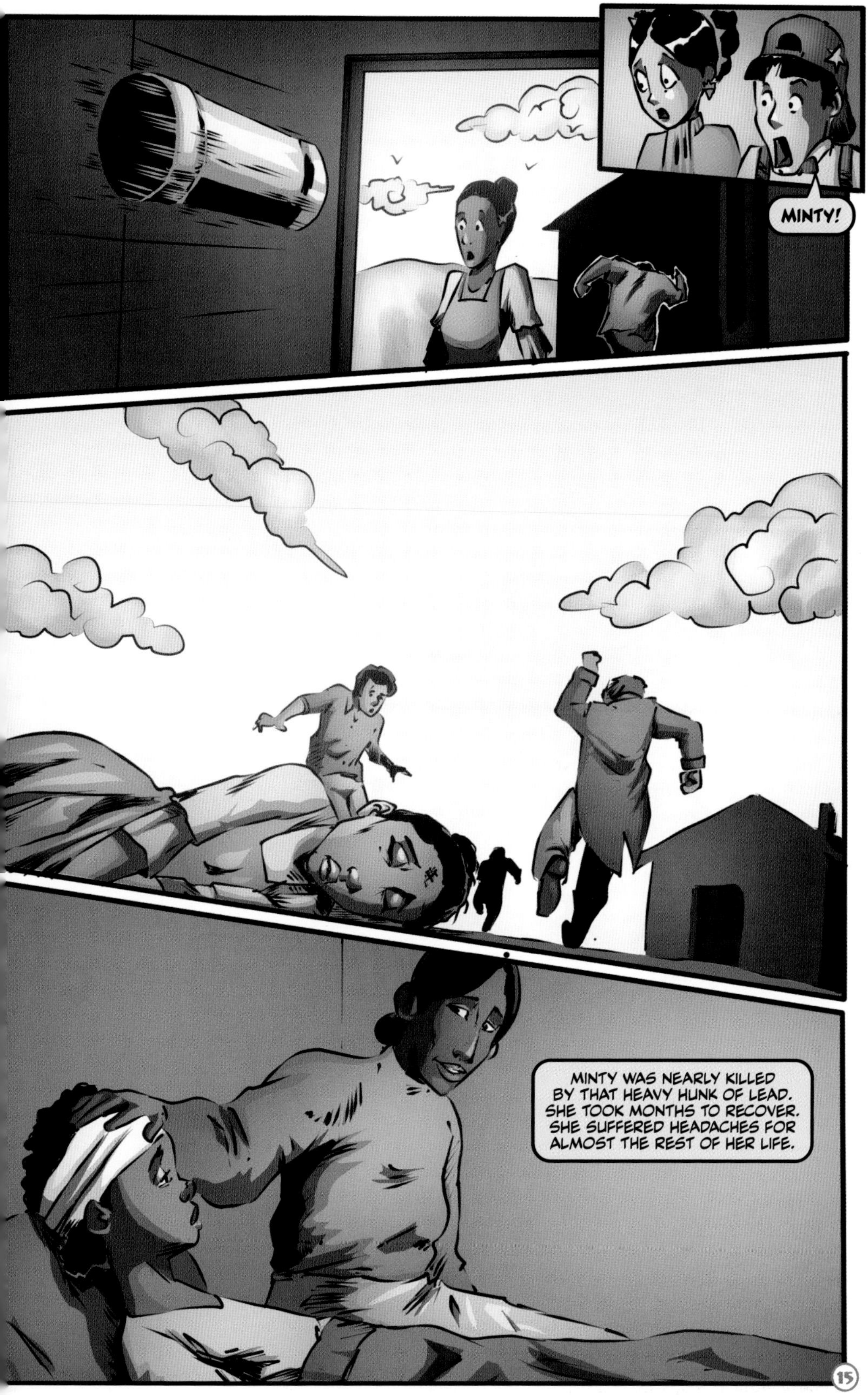
MINTY!
MINTY WAS NEARLY KILLED BY THAT HEAVY HUNK OF LEAD. SHE TOOK MONTHS TO RECOVER. SHE SUFFERED HEADACHES FOR ALMOST THE REST OF HER LIFE.

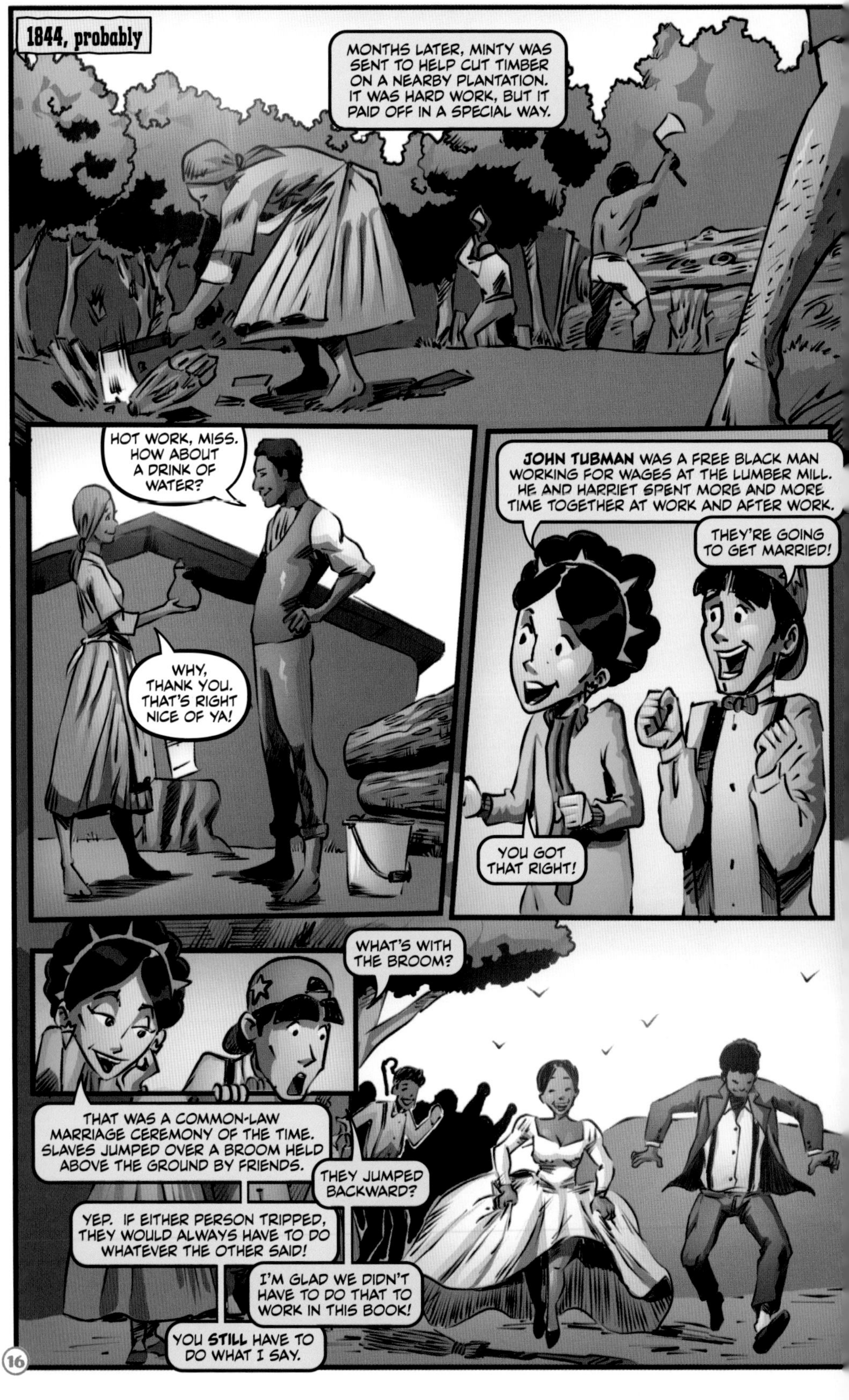
1844, probably
MONTHS LATER, MINTY WAS SENT TO HELP CUT TIMBER ON A NEARBY PLANTATION. IT WAS HARD WORK, BUT IT PAID OFF IN A SPECIAL WAY.
HOT WORK, MISS. HOW ABOUT A DRINK OF WATER?
WHY, THANK YOU. THAT'S RIGHT NICE OF YA!
JOHN TUBMAN WAS A FREE BLACK MAN WORKING FOR WAGES AT THE LUMBER MILL. HE AND HARRIET SPENT MORE AND MORE TIME TOGETHER AT WORK AND AFTER WORK.
THEY'RE GOING TO GET MARRIED!
YOU GOT THAT RIGHT!
WHAT'S WITH THE BROOM?
THAT WAS A COMMON-LAW MARRIAGE CEREMONY OF THE TIME. SLAVES JUMPED OVER A BROOM HELD ABOVE THE GROUND BY FRIENDS.
THEY JUMPED BACKWARD?
YEP. IF EITHER PERSON TRIPPED, THEY WOULD ALWAYS HAVE TO DO WHATEVER THE OTHER SAID!
I'M GLAD WE DIDN'T HAVE TO DO THAT TO WORK IN THIS BOOK!
YOU STILL HAVE TO DO WHAT I SAY.

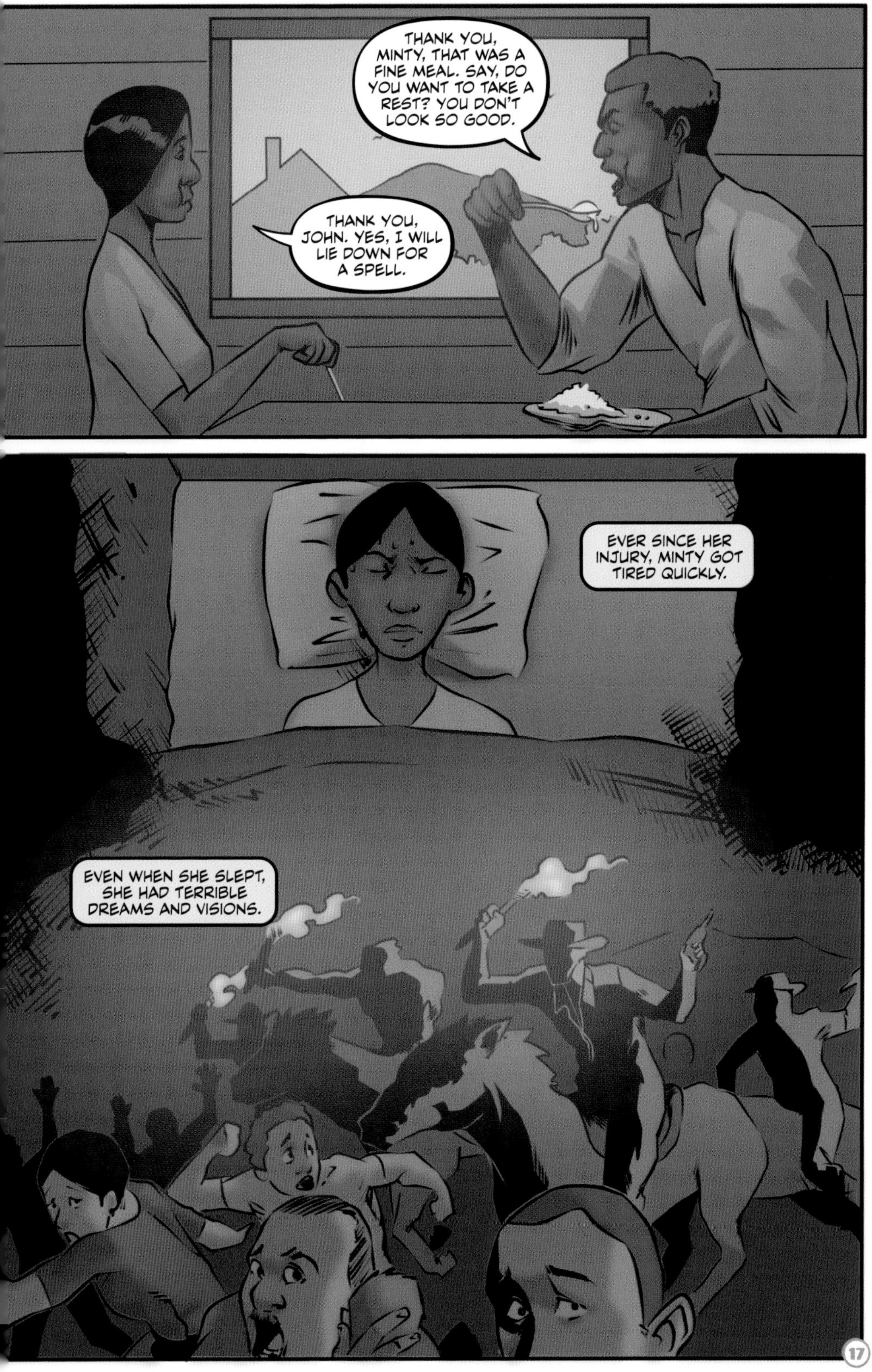
THANK YOU, MINTY, THAT WAS A FINE MEAL. SAY, DO YOU WANT TO TAKE A REST? YOU DON'T LOOK SO GOOD.
THANK YOU, JOHN. YES, I WILL LIE DOWN FOR A SPELL.
EVER SINCE HER INJURY, MINTY GOT TIRED QUICKLY.
EVEN WHEN SHE SLEPT, SHE HAD TERRIBLE DREAMS AND VISIONS.

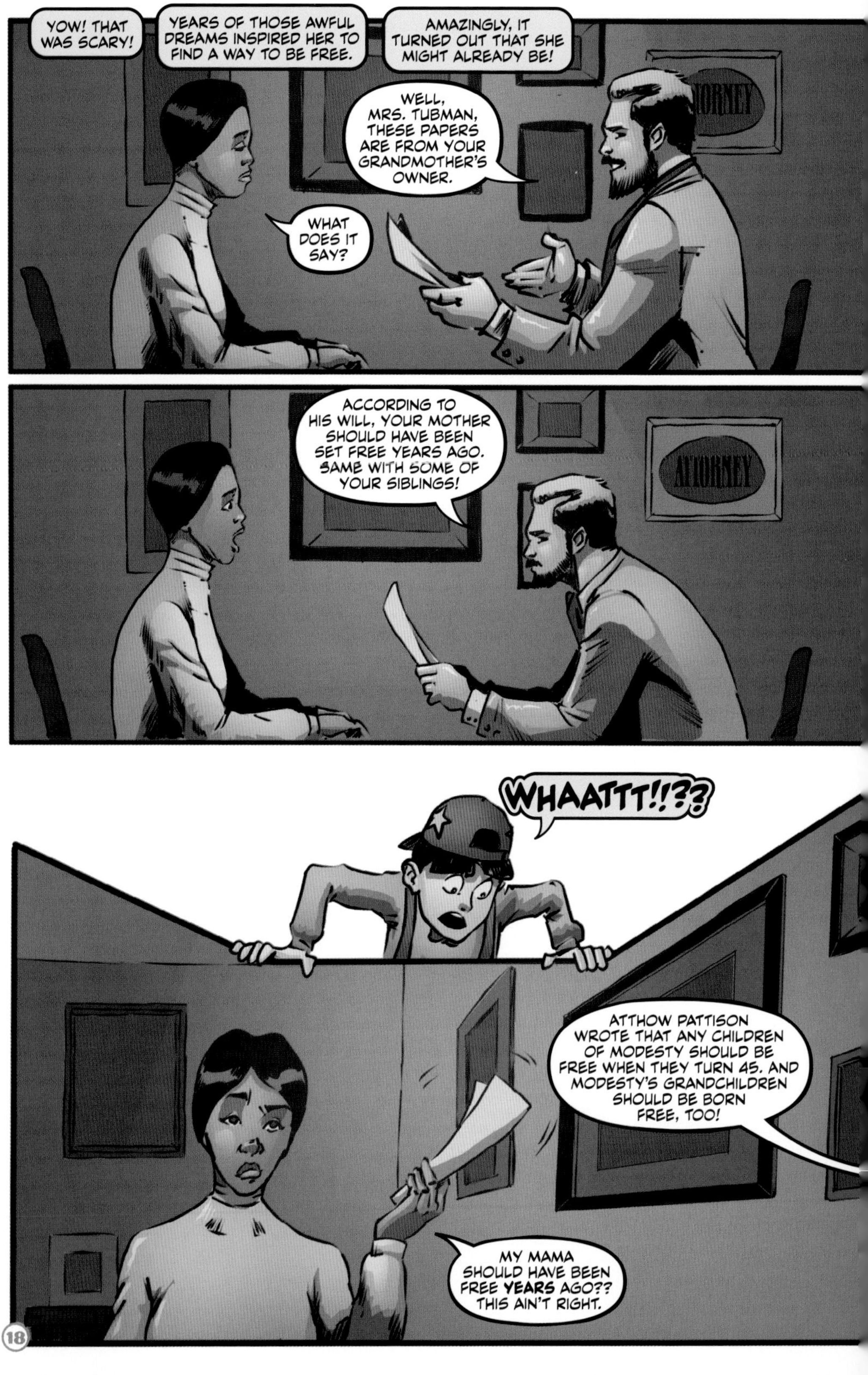
YOW! THAT WAS SCARY!
YEARS OF THOSE AWFUL DREAMS INSPIRED HER TO FIND A WAY TO BE FREE.
AMAZINGLY, IT TURNED OUT THAT SHE MIGHT ALREADY BE!
ATTORNEY
WELL, MRS. TUBMAN, THESE PAPERS ARE FROM YOUR GRANDMOTHER'S OWNER.
WHAT DOES IT SAY?
ACCORDING TO HIS WILL, YOUR MOTHER SHOULD HAVE BEEN SET FREE YEARS AGO. SAME WITH SOME OF YOUR SIBLINGS!
ATTORNEY
WHAATTT!!??
ATTHOW PATTISON WROTE THAT ANY CHILDREN OF MODESTY SHOULD BE FREE WHEN THEY TURN 45. AND MODESTY'S GRANDCHILDREN SHOULD BE BORN FREE, TOO!
MY MAMA SHOULD HAVE BEEN FREE **YEARS** AGO?? THIS AIN'T RIGHT.

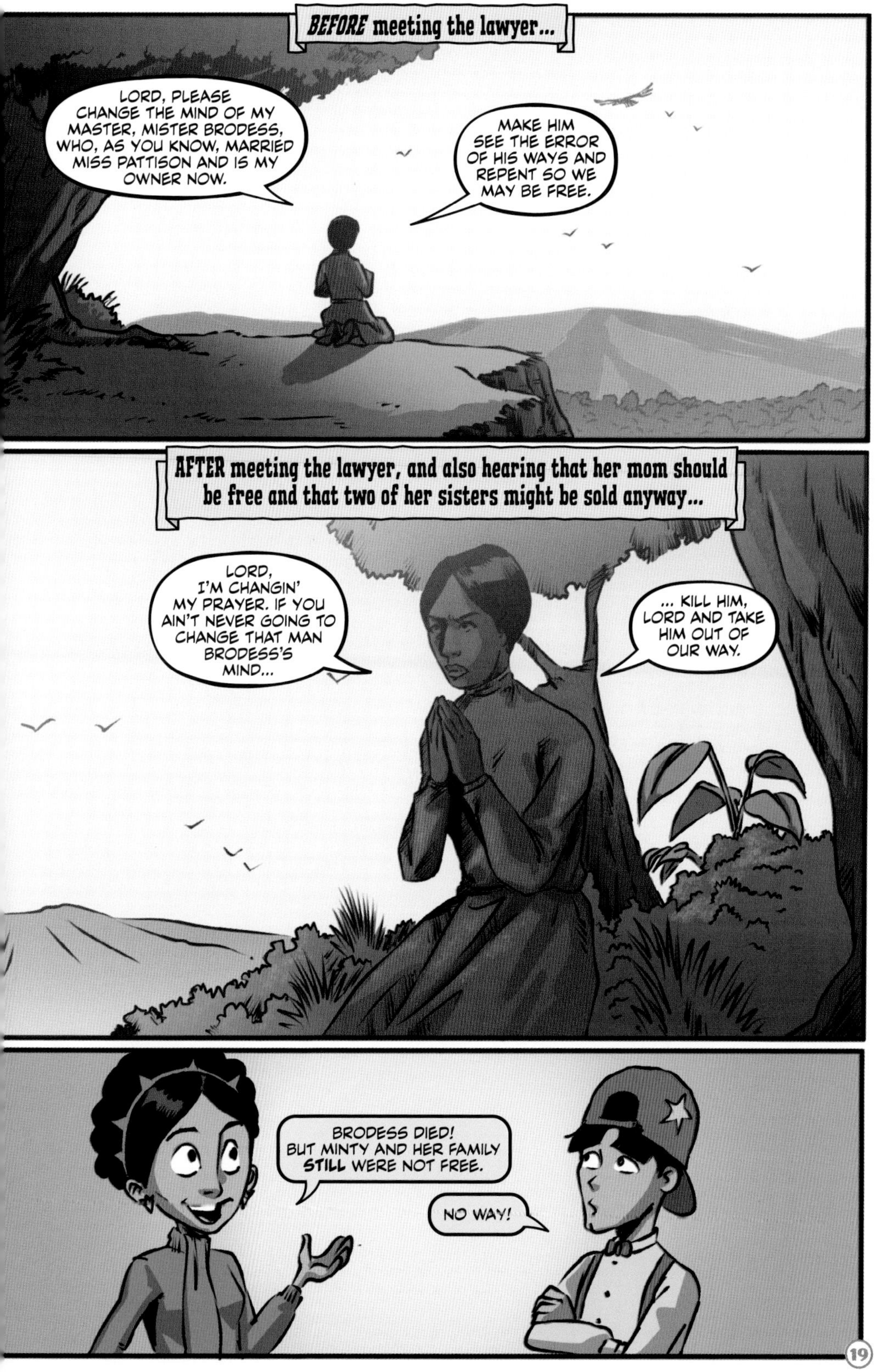
BEFORE meeting the lawyer...
LORD, PLEASE CHANGE THE MIND OF MY MASTER, MISTER BRODESS, WHO, AS YOU KNOW, MARRIED MISS PATTISON AND IS MY OWNER NOW.
MAKE HIM SEE THE ERROR OF HIS WAYS AND REPENT SO WE MAY BE FREE.
AFTER meeting the lawyer, and also hearing that her mom should be free and that two of her sisters might be sold anyway...
LORD, I'M CHANGIN' MY PRAYER. IF YOU AIN'T NEVER GOING TO CHANGE THAT MAN BRODESS'S MIND...
... KILL HIM, LORD AND TAKE HIM OUT OF OUR WAY.
BRODESS DIED! BUT MINTY AND HER FAMILY STILL WERE NOT FREE.
NO WAY!

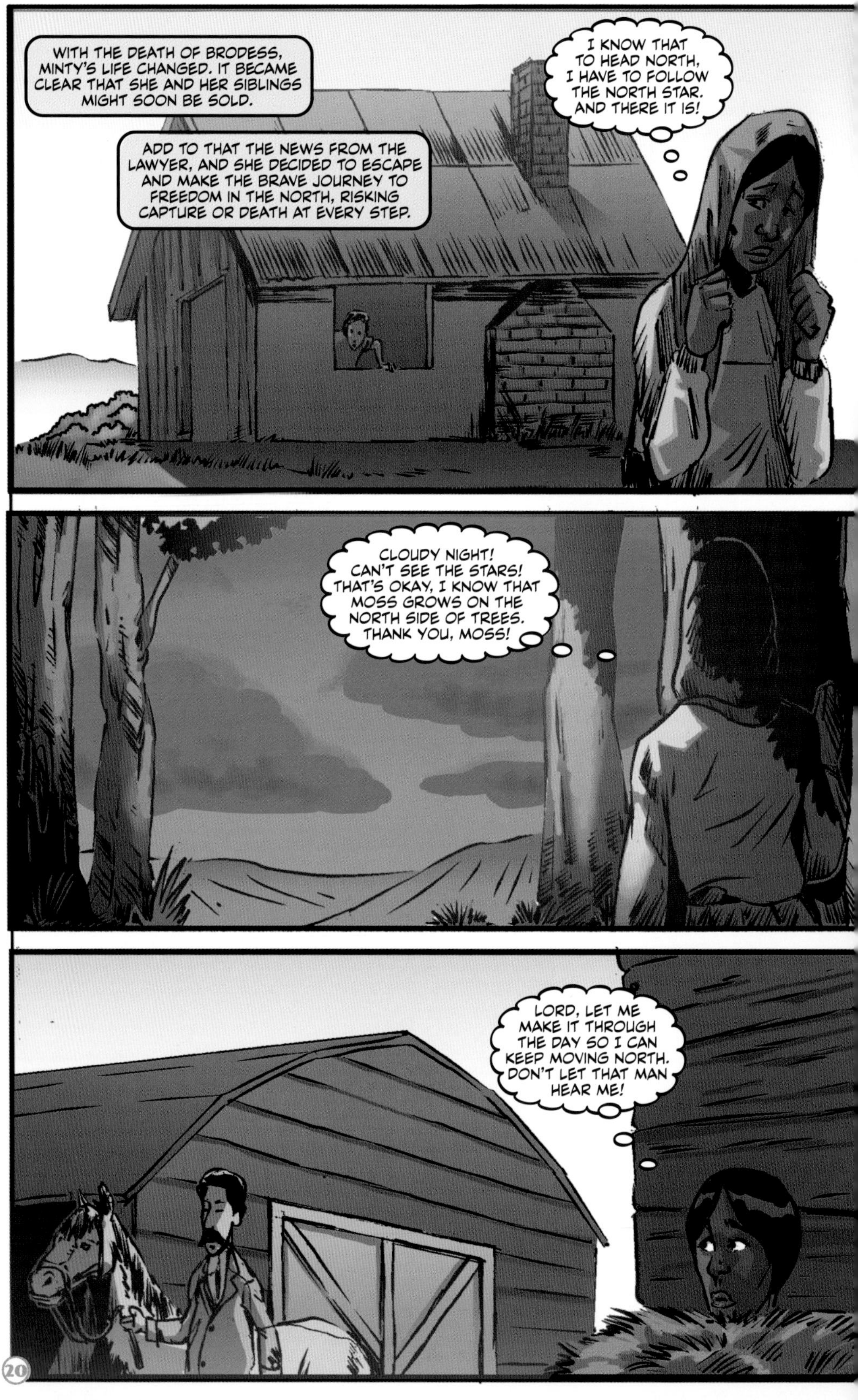

WITH THE DEATH OF BRODESS, MINTY'S LIFE CHANGED. IT BECAME CLEAR THAT SHE AND HER SIBLINGS MIGHT SOON BE SOLD.
ADD TO THAT THE NEWS FROM THE LAWYER, AND SHE DECIDED TO ESCAPE AND MAKE THE BRAVE JOURNEY TO FREEDOM IN THE NORTH, RISKING CAPTURE OR DEATH AT EVERY STEP.
I KNOW THAT TO HEAD NORTH, I HAVE TO FOLLOW THE NORTH STAR. AND THERE IT IS!
CLOUDY NIGHT! CAN'T SEE THE STARS! THAT'S OKAY, I KNOW THAT MOSS GROWS ON THE NORTH SIDE OF TREES. THANK YOU, MOSS!
LORD, LET ME MAKE IT THROUGH THE DAY SO I CAN KEEP MOVING NORTH. DON'T LET THAT MAN HEAR ME!

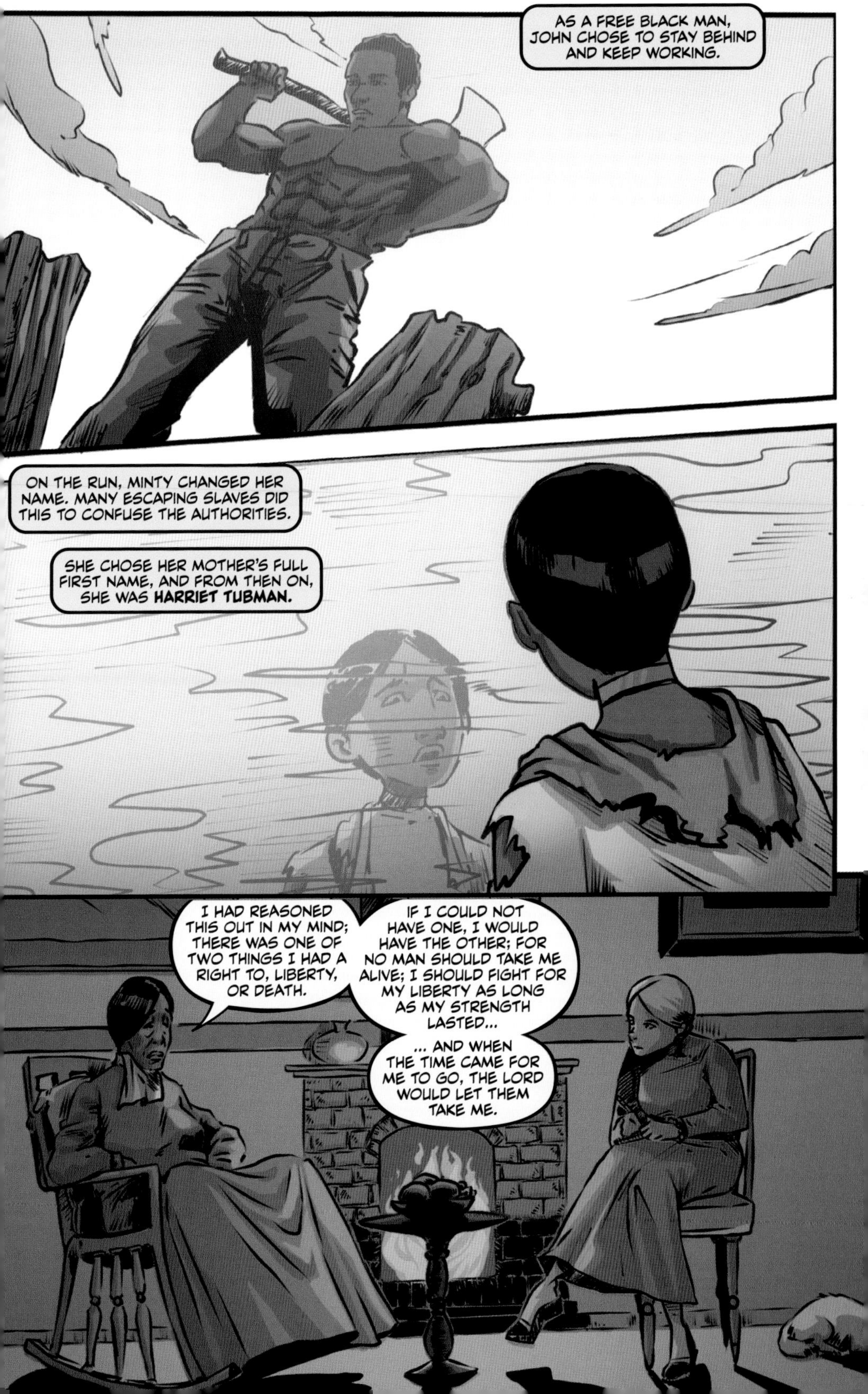
AS A FREE BLACK MAN, JOHN CHOSE TO STAY BEHIND AND KEEP WORKING.
ON THE RUN, MINTY CHANGED HER NAME. MANY ESCAPING SLAVES DID THIS TO CONFUSE THE AUTHORITIES.
SHE CHOSE HER MOTHER'S FULL FIRST NAME, AND FROM THEN ON, SHE WAS **HARRIET TUBMAN.**
I HAD REASONED THIS OUT IN MY MIND; THERE WAS ONE OF TWO THINGS I HAD A RIGHT TO, LIBERTY, OR DEATH.
IF I COULD NOT HAVE ONE, I WOULD HAVE THE OTHER; FOR NO MAN SHOULD TAKE ME ALIVE; I SHOULD FIGHT FOR MY LIBERTY AS LONG AS MY STRENGTH LASTED...
... AND WHEN THE TIME CAME FOR ME TO GO, THE LORD WOULD LET THEM TAKE ME.

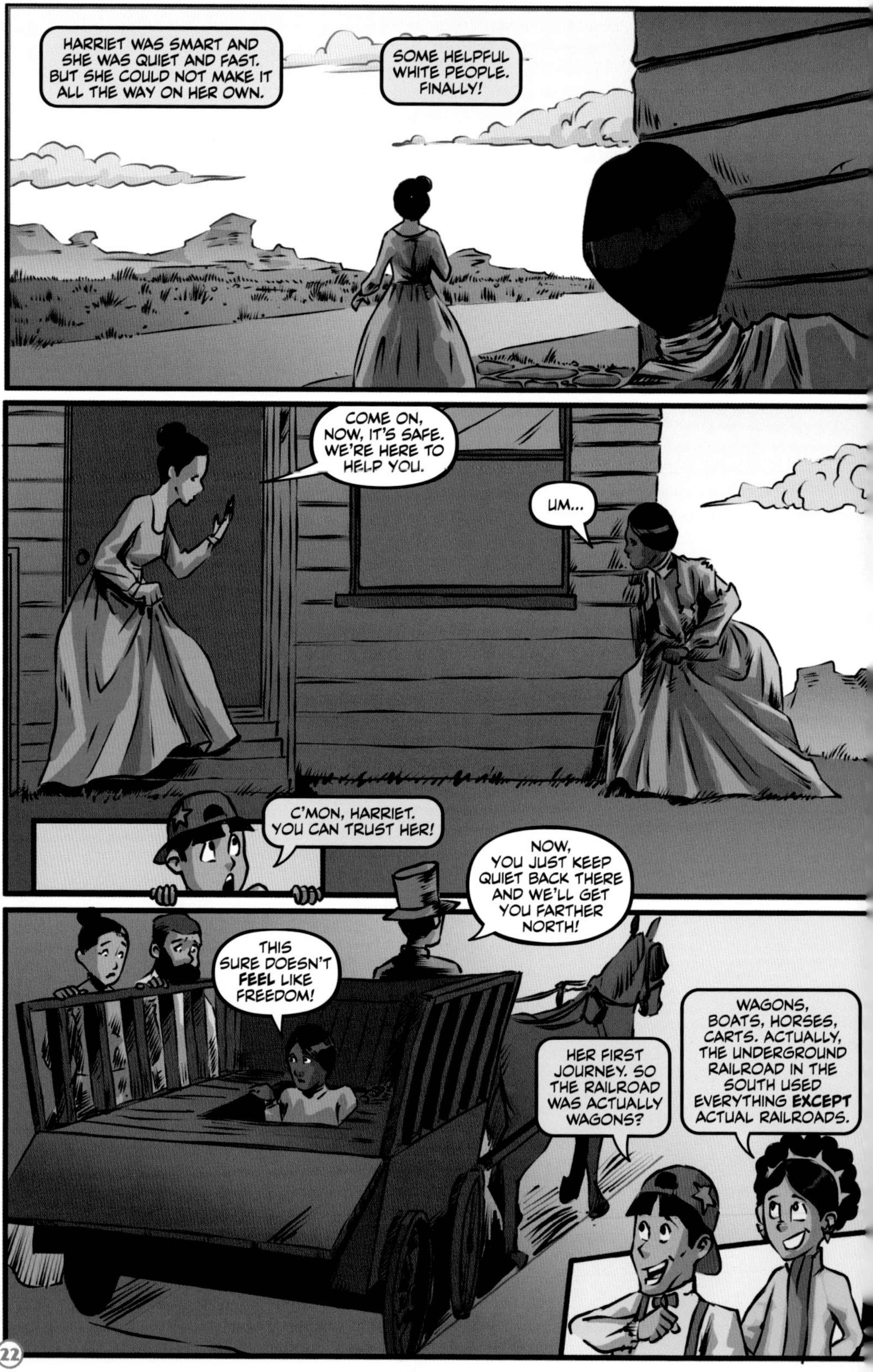

HARRIET WAS SMART AND SHE WAS QUIET AND FAST. BUT SHE COULD NOT MAKE IT ALL THE WAY ON HER OWN.
SOME HELPFUL WHITE PEOPLE. FINALLY!
COME ON, NOW, IT'S SAFE. WE'RE HERE TO HELP YOU.
UM...
C'MON, HARRIET. YOU CAN TRUST HER!
NOW, YOU JUST KEEP QUIET BACK THERE AND WE'LL GET YOU FARTHER NORTH!
THIS SURE DOESN'T **FEEL** LIKE FREEDOM!
HER FIRST JOURNEY. SO THE RAILROAD WAS ACTUALLY WAGONS?
WAGONS, BOATS, HORSES, CARTS. ACTUALLY, THE UNDERGROUND RAILROAD IN THE SOUTH USED EVERYTHING **EXCEPT** ACTUAL RAILROADS.

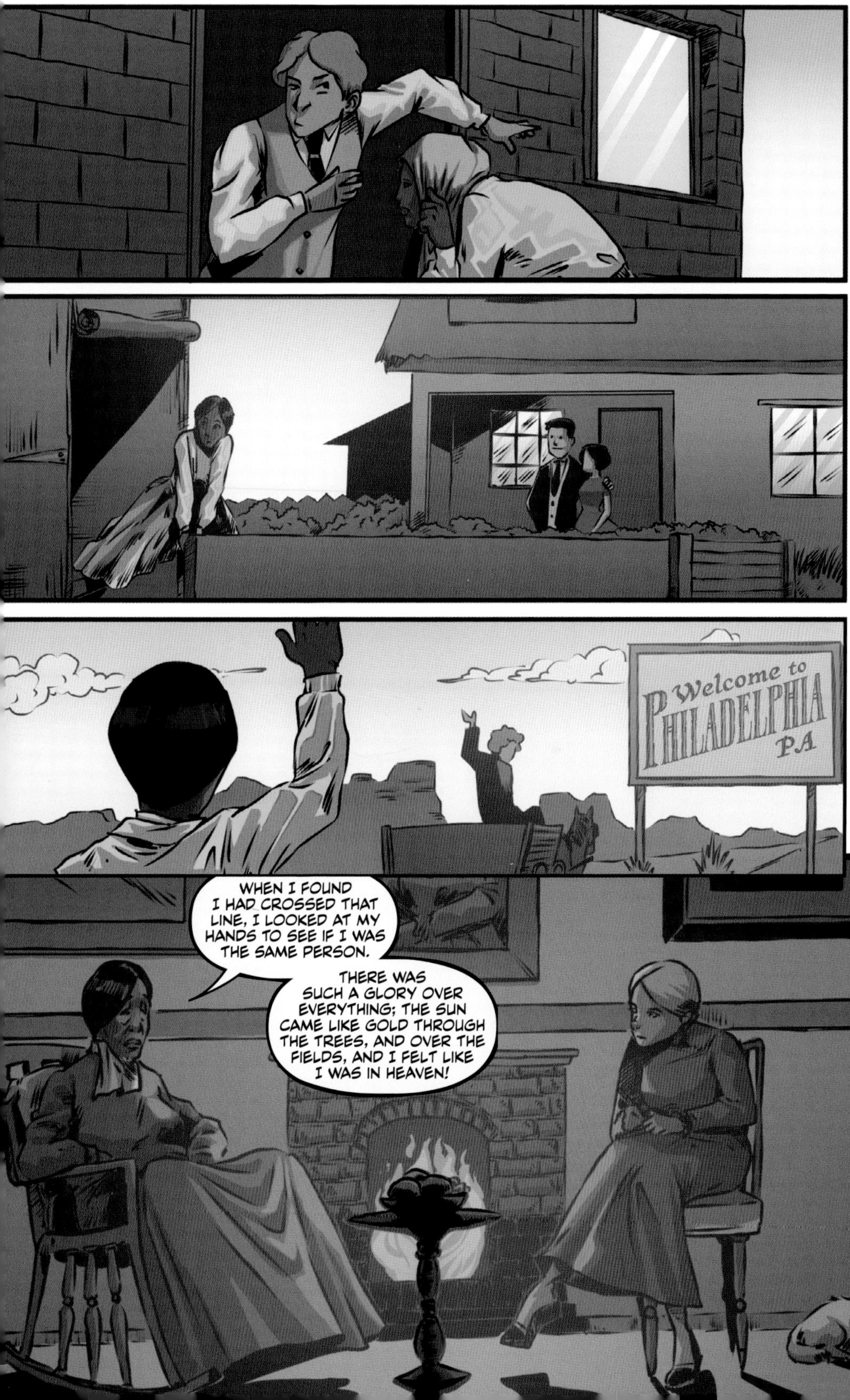
Welcome to
PHILADELPHIA
PA
WHEN I FOUND I HAD CROSSED THAT LINE, I LOOKED AT MY HANDS TO SEE IF I WAS THE SAME PERSON.
THERE WAS SUCH A GLORY OVER EVERYTHING; THE SUN CAME LIKE GOLD THROUGH THE TREES, AND OVER THE FIELDS, AND I FELT LIKE I WAS IN HEAVEN!

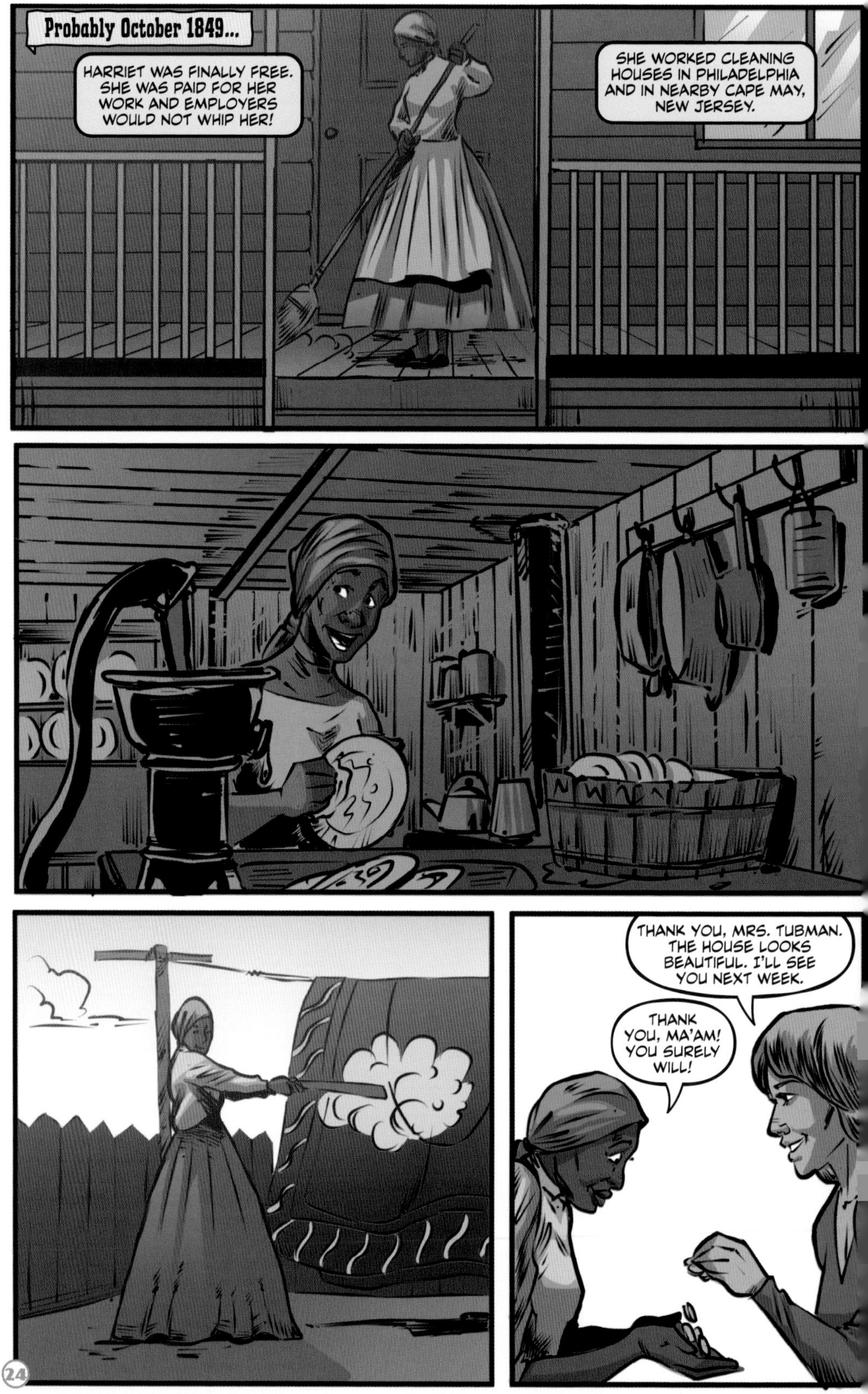

Probably October 1849...
HARRIET WAS FINALLY FREE. SHE WAS PAID FOR HER WORK AND EMPLOYERS WOULD NOT WHIP HER!
SHE WORKED CLEANING HOUSES IN PHILADELPHIA AND IN NEARBY CAPE MAY, NEW JERSEY.
THANK YOU, MRS. TUBMAN. THE HOUSE LOOKS BEAUTIFUL. I'LL SEE YOU NEXT WEEK.
THANK YOU, MA'AM! YOU SURELY WILL!

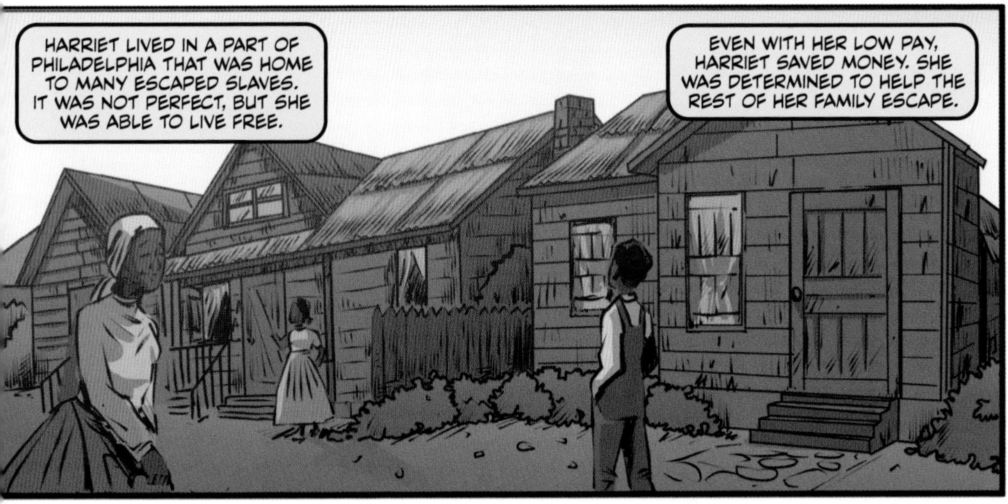
HARRIET LIVED IN A PART OF PHILADELPHIA THAT WAS HOME TO MANY ESCAPED SLAVES. IT WAS NOT PERFECT, BUT SHE WAS ABLE TO LIVE FREE.
EVEN WITH HER LOW PAY, HARRIET SAVED MONEY. SHE WAS DETERMINED TO HELP THE REST OF HER FAMILY ESCAPE.

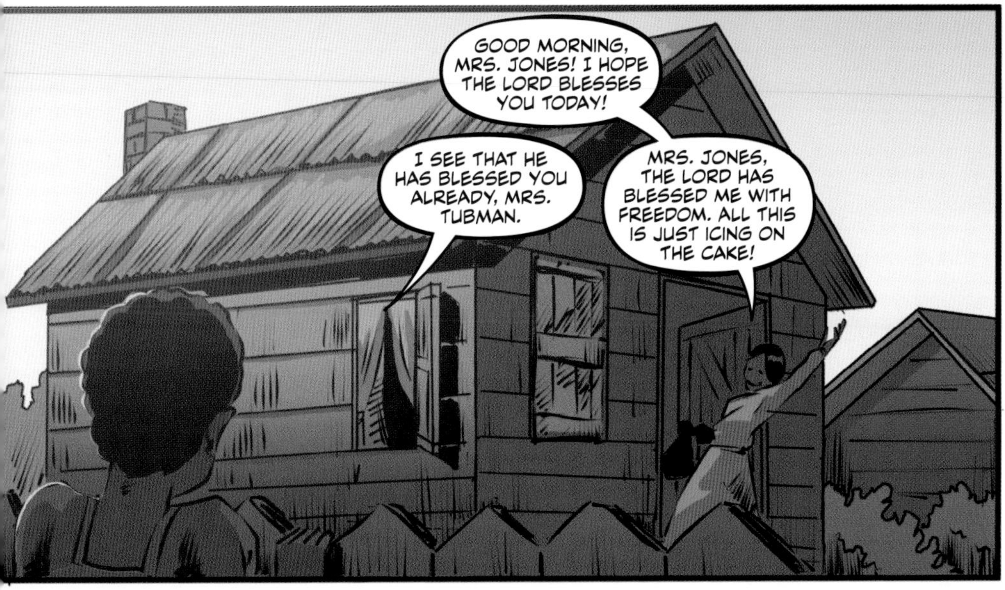
GOOD MORNING, MRS. JONES! I HOPE THE LORD BLESSES YOU TODAY!
I SEE THAT HE HAS BLESSED YOU ALREADY, MRS. TUBMAN.
MRS. JONES, THE LORD HAS BLESSED ME WITH FREEDOM. ALL THIS IS JUST ICING ON THE CAKE!

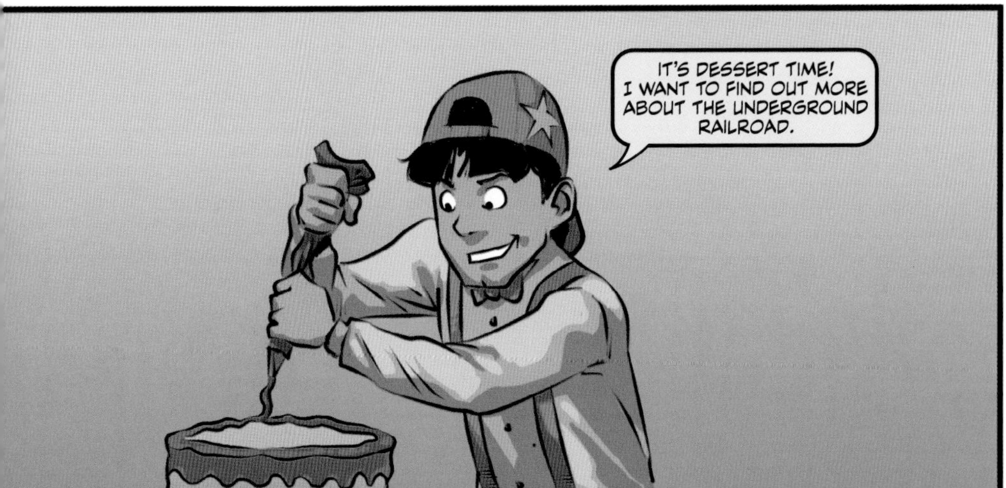
IT'S DESSERT TIME! I WANT TO FIND OUT MORE ABOUT THE UNDERGROUND RAILROAD.

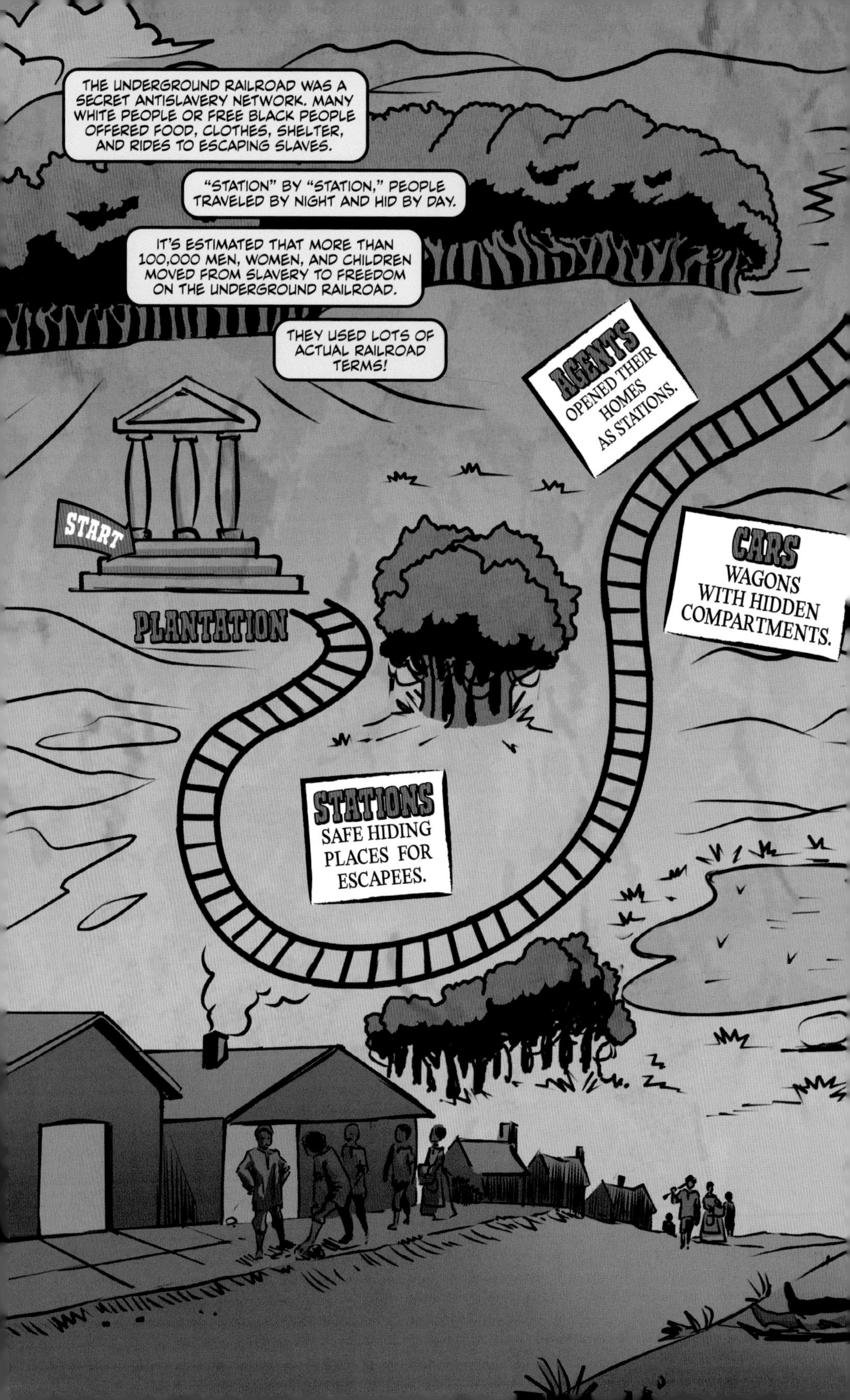
THE UNDERGROUND RAILROAD WAS A SECRET ANTISLAVERY NETWORK. MANY WHITE PEOPLE OR FREE BLACK PEOPLE OFFERED FOOD, CLOTHES, SHELTER, AND RIDES TO ESCAPING SLAVES.
"STATION" BY "STATION," PEOPLE TRAVELED BY NIGHT AND HID BY DAY.
IT'S ESTIMATED THAT MORE THAN 100,000 MEN, WOMEN, AND CHILDREN MOVED FROM SLAVERY TO FREEDOM ON THE UNDERGROUND RAILROAD.
THEY USED LOTS OF ACTUAL RAILROAD TERMS!
AGENTS
OPENED THEIR HOMES AS STATIONS.
START
PLANTATION
CARS
WAGONS WITH HIDDEN COMPARTMENTS.
STATIONS
SAFE HIDING PLACES FOR ESCAPEES.

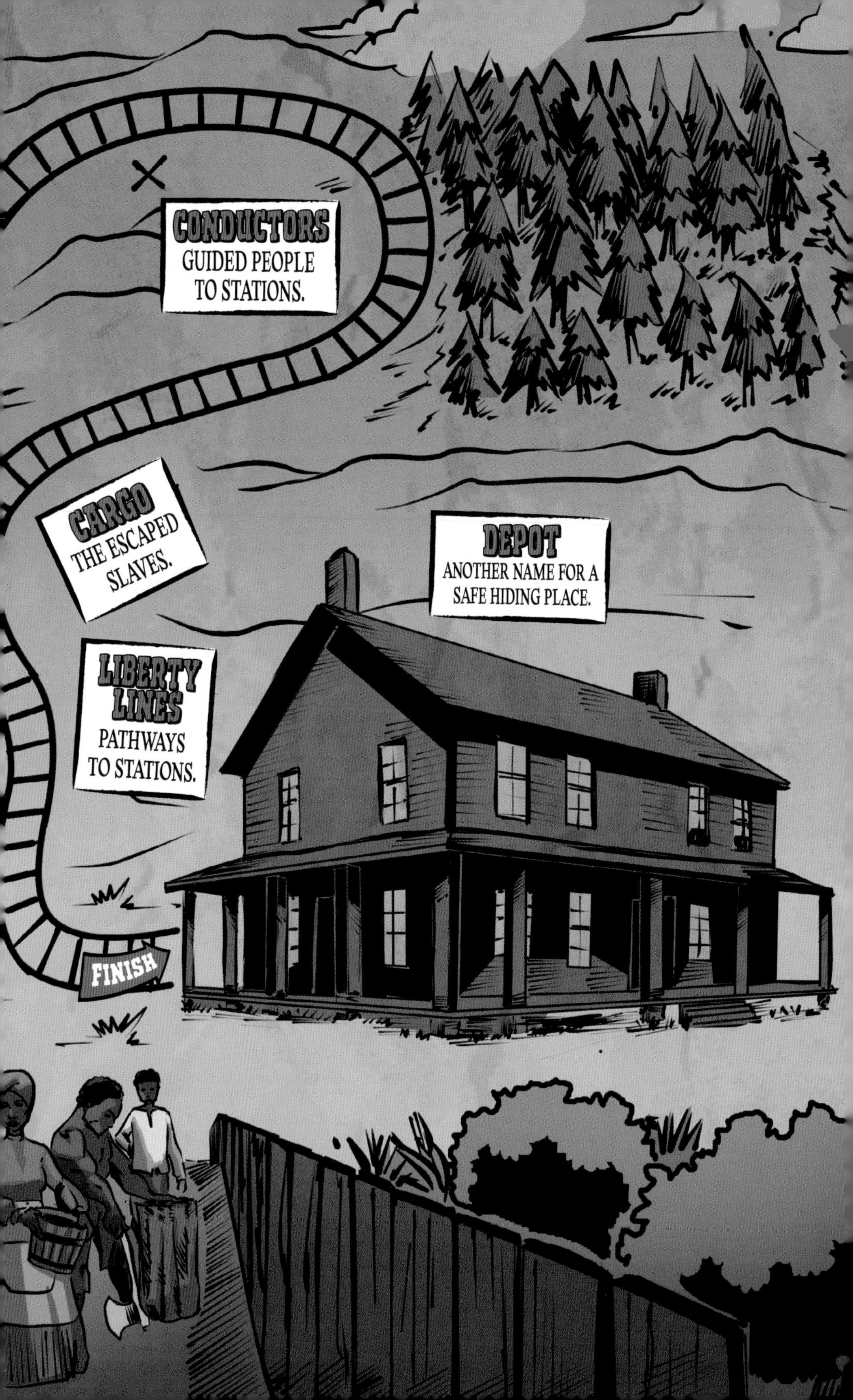
CONDUCTORS
GUIDED PEOPLE TO STATIONS.
CARGO
THE ESCAPED SLAVES.
DEPOT
ANOTHER NAME FOR A SAFE HIDING PLACE.
LIBERTY LINES
PATHWAYS TO STATIONS.
FINISH

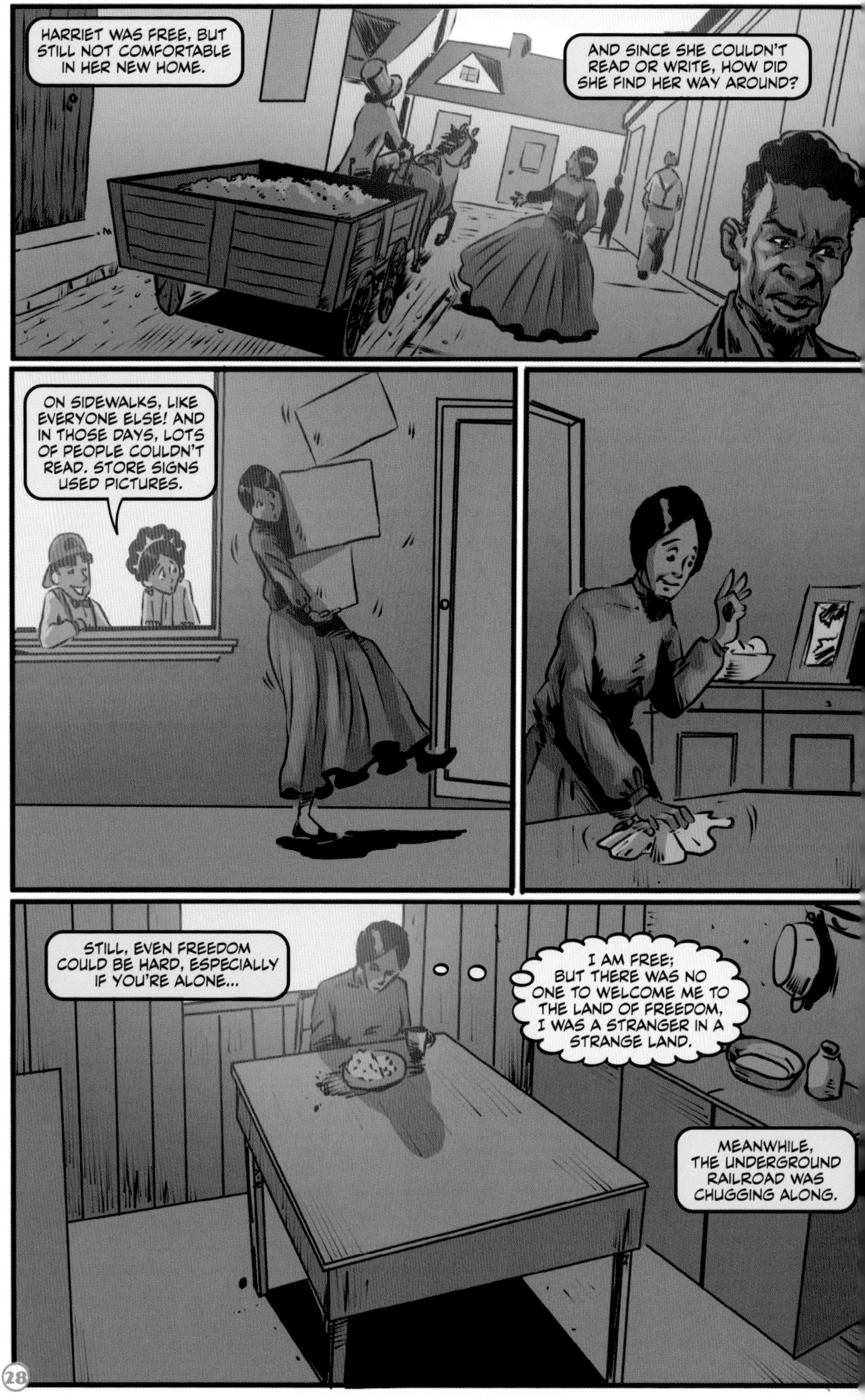
HARRIET WAS FREE, BUT STILL NOT COMFORTABLE IN HER NEW HOME.
AND SINCE SHE COULDN'T READ OR WRITE, HOW DID SHE FIND HER WAY AROUND?
ON SIDEWALKS, LIKE EVERYONE ELSE! AND IN THOSE DAYS, LOTS OF PEOPLE COULDN'T READ. STORE SIGNS USED PICTURES.
STILL, EVEN FREEDOM COULD BE HARD, ESPECIALLY IF YOU'RE ALONE...
I AM FREE; BUT THERE WAS NO ONE TO WELCOME ME TO THE LAND OF FREEDOM, I WAS A STRANGER IN A STRANGE LAND.
MEANWHILE, THE UNDERGROUND RAILROAD WAS CHUGGING ALONG.

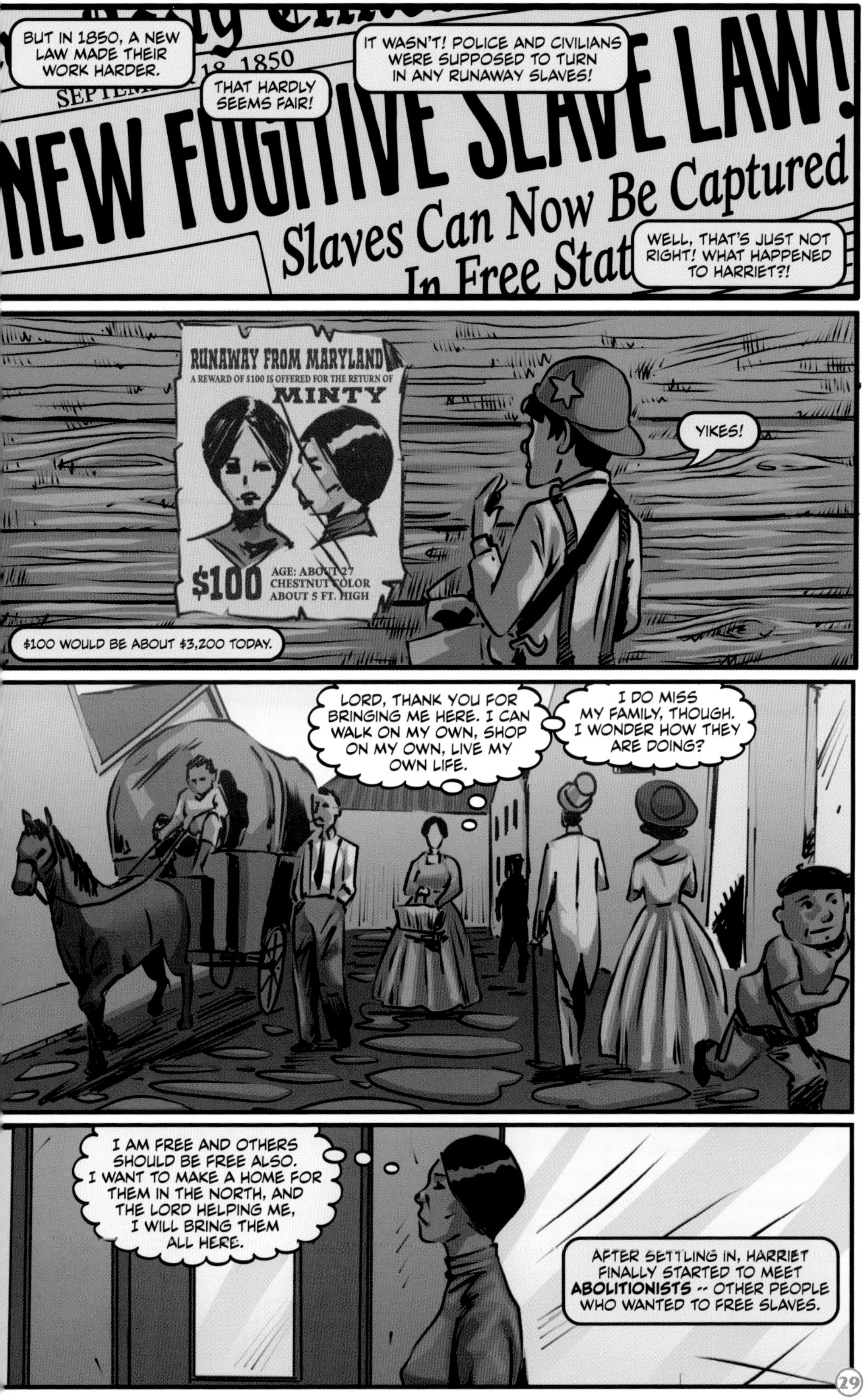

BUT IN 1850, A NEW LAW MADE THEIR WORK HARDER.
THAT HARDLY SEEMS FAIR!
IT WASN'T! POLICE AND CIVILIANS WERE SUPPOSED TO TURN IN ANY RUNAWAY SLAVES!
NEW FUGITIVE SLAVE LAW!
Slaves Can Now Be Captured
WELL, THAT'S JUST NOT RIGHT! WHAT HAPPENED TO HARRIET?!
RUNAWAY FROM MARYLAND
A REWARD OF $100 IS OFFERED FOR THE RETURN OF
MINTY
$100
AGE: ABOUT 27
CHESTNUT COLOR
ABOUT 5 FT. HIGH
YIKES!
$100 WOULD BE ABOUT $3,200 TODAY.
LORD, THANK YOU FOR BRINGING ME HERE. I CAN WALK ON MY OWN, SHOP ON MY OWN, LIVE MY OWN LIFE.
I DO MISS MY FAMILY, THOUGH. I WONDER HOW THEY ARE DOING?
I AM FREE AND OTHERS SHOULD BE FREE ALSO. I WANT TO MAKE A HOME FOR THEM IN THE NORTH, AND THE LORD HELPING ME, I WILL BRING THEM ALL HERE.
AFTER SETTLING IN, HARRIET FINALLY STARTED TO MEET ABOLITIONISTS -- OTHER PEOPLE WHO WANTED TO FREE SLAVES.

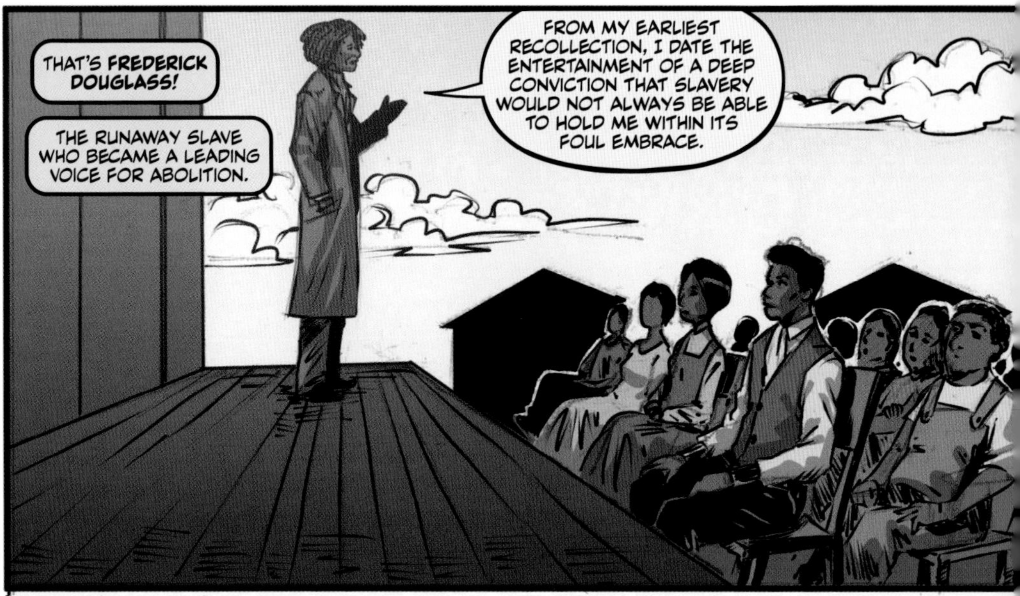
THAT'S FREDERICK DOUGLASS!
THE RUNAWAY SLAVE WHO BECAME A LEADING VOICE FOR ABOLITION.
FROM MY EARLIEST RECOLLECTION, I DATE THE ENTERTAINMENT OF A DEEP CONVICTION THAT SLAVERY WOULD NOT ALWAYS BE ABLE TO HOLD ME WITHIN ITS FOUL EMBRACE.

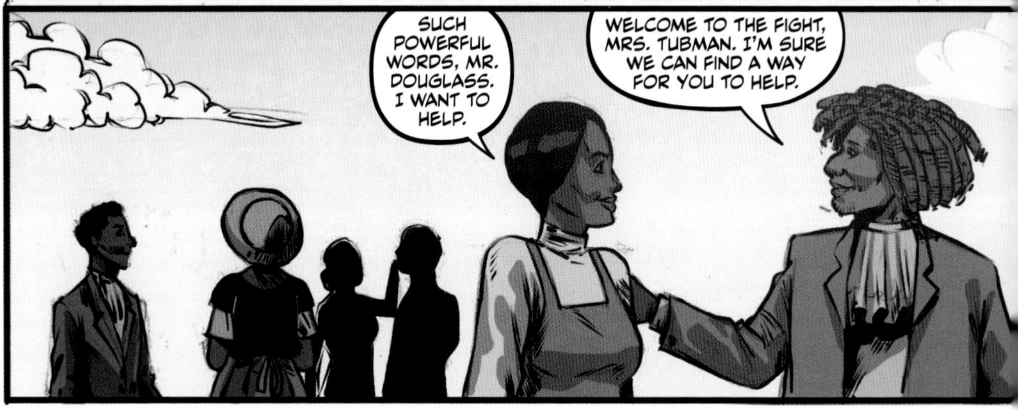
SUCH POWERFUL WORDS, MR. DOUGLASS. I WANT TO HELP.
WELCOME TO THE FIGHT, MRS. TUBMAN. I'M SURE WE CAN FIND A WAY FOR YOU TO HELP.

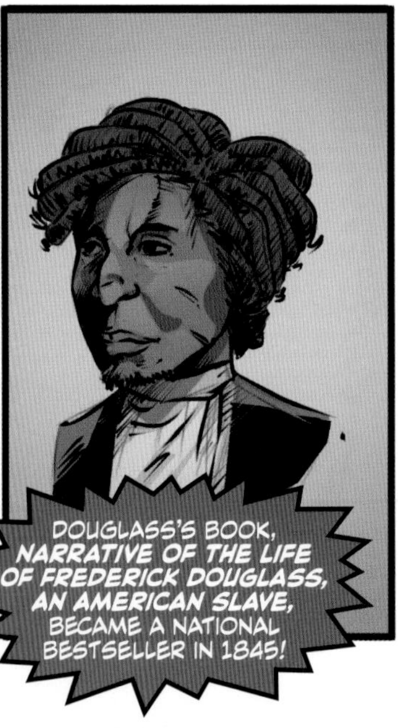
DOUGLASS'S BOOK, NARRATIVE OF THE LIFE OF FREDERICK DOUGLASS, AN AMERICAN SLAVE, BECAME A NATIONAL BESTSELLER IN 1845!

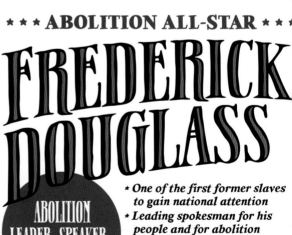

★ ★ ★ **ABOLITION ALL-STAR** ★ ★ ★

FREDERICK DOUGLASS

ABOLITION LEADER, SPEAKER, WRITER

- ***One of the first former slaves to gain national attention***
- ***Leading spokesman for his people and for abolition***
- ***Traveled to Europe to speak against slavery***
- ***Eventually appointed ambassador to the Dominican Republic***

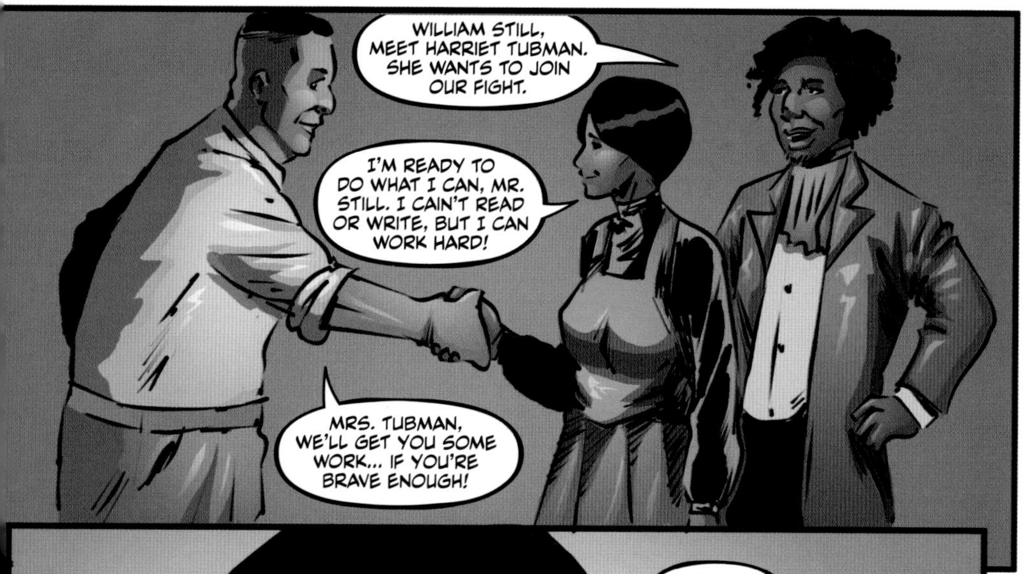
WILLIAM STILL, MEET HARRIET TUBMAN. SHE WANTS TO JOIN OUR FIGHT.
I'M READY TO DO WHAT I CAN, MR. STILL. I CAIN'T READ OR WRITE, BUT I CAN WORK HARD!
MRS. TUBMAN, WE'LL GET YOU SOME WORK... IF YOU'RE BRAVE ENOUGH!

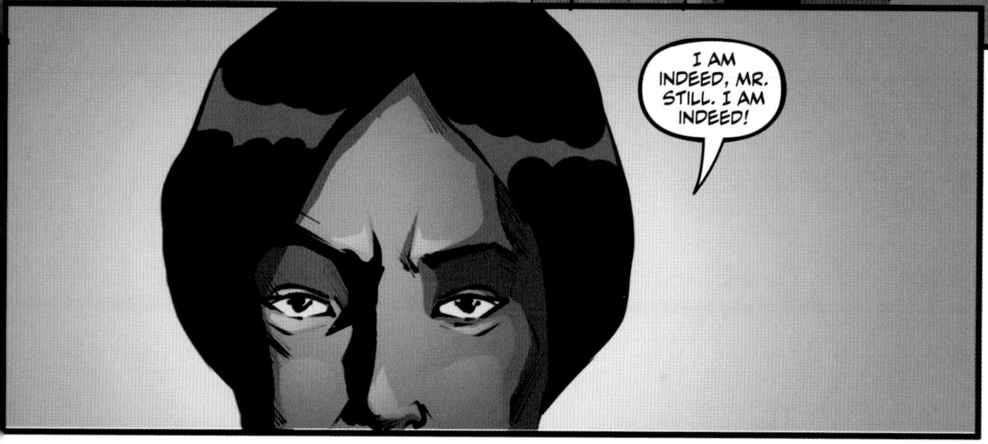
I AM INDEED, MR. STILL. I AM INDEED!

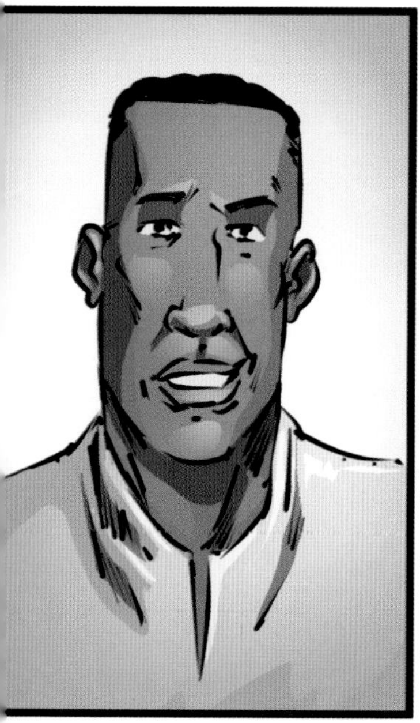

★ ★ ★ **ABOLITION ALL-STAR** ★ ★ ★

WILLIAM STILL

UNDERGROUND RAILROAD CONDUCTOR

* ***Leading black businessman in Philadelphia***
* ***Chairman of committees that aided freed slaves in the North***
* ***Helped black soldiers during the Civil War***

STILL WROTE ***THE UNDERGROUND RAILROAD*** IN 1872, THE FIRST BOOK TO DOCUMENT THE ORGANIZATION'S HEROIC, HIGHLY DANGEROUS, AND ILLEGAL WORK.

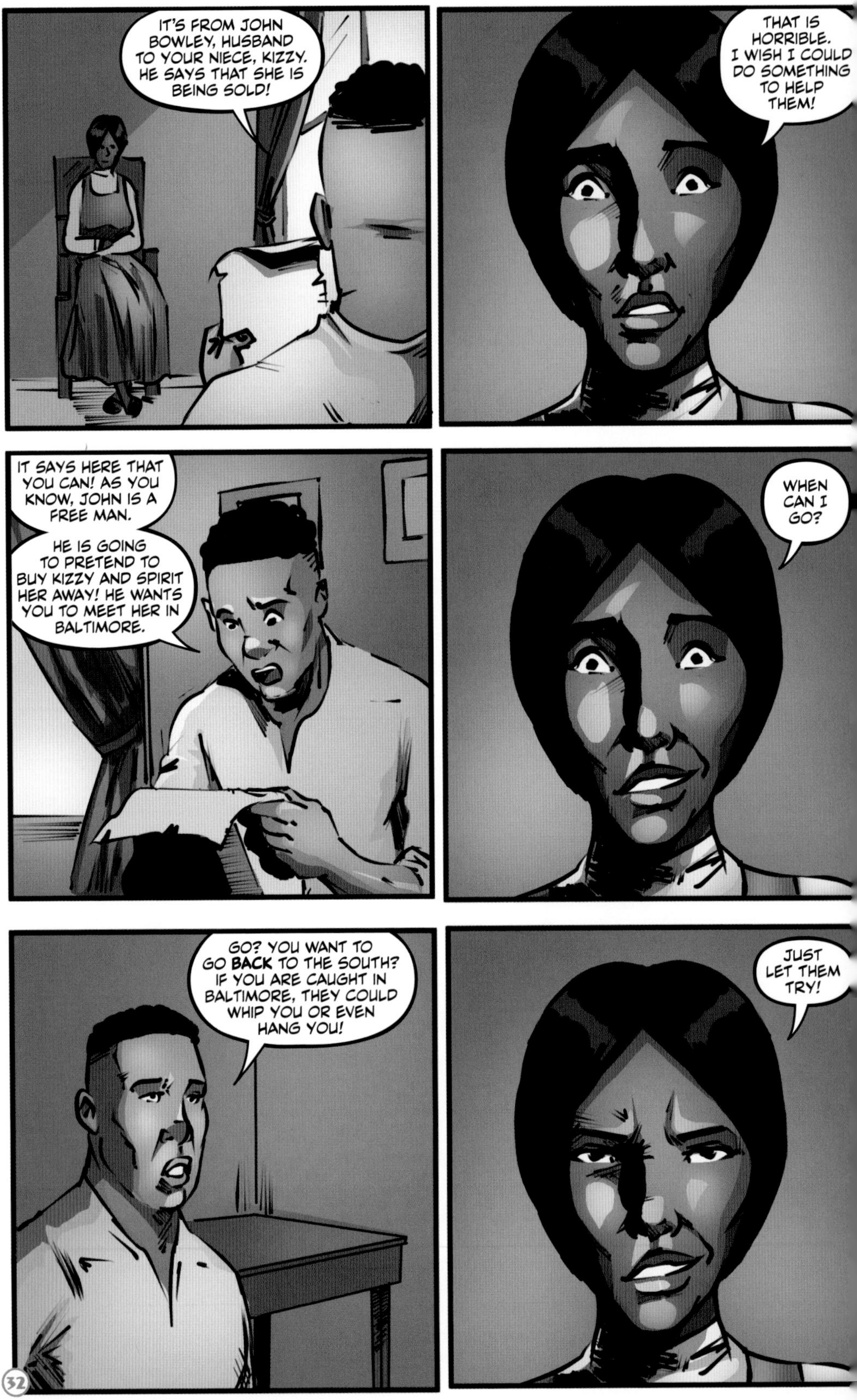
IT'S FROM JOHN BOWLEY, HUSBAND TO YOUR NIECE, KIZZY. HE SAYS THAT SHE IS BEING SOLD!
THAT IS HORRIBLE. I WISH I COULD DO SOMETHING TO HELP THEM!
IT SAYS HERE THAT YOU CAN! AS YOU KNOW, JOHN IS A FREE MAN.
HE IS GOING TO PRETEND TO BUY KIZZY AND SPIRIT HER AWAY! HE WANTS YOU TO MEET HER IN BALTIMORE.
WHEN CAN I GO?
GO? YOU WANT TO GO **BACK** TO THE SOUTH? IF YOU ARE CAUGHT IN BALTIMORE, THEY COULD WHIP YOU OR EVEN HANG YOU!
JUST LET THEM TRY!

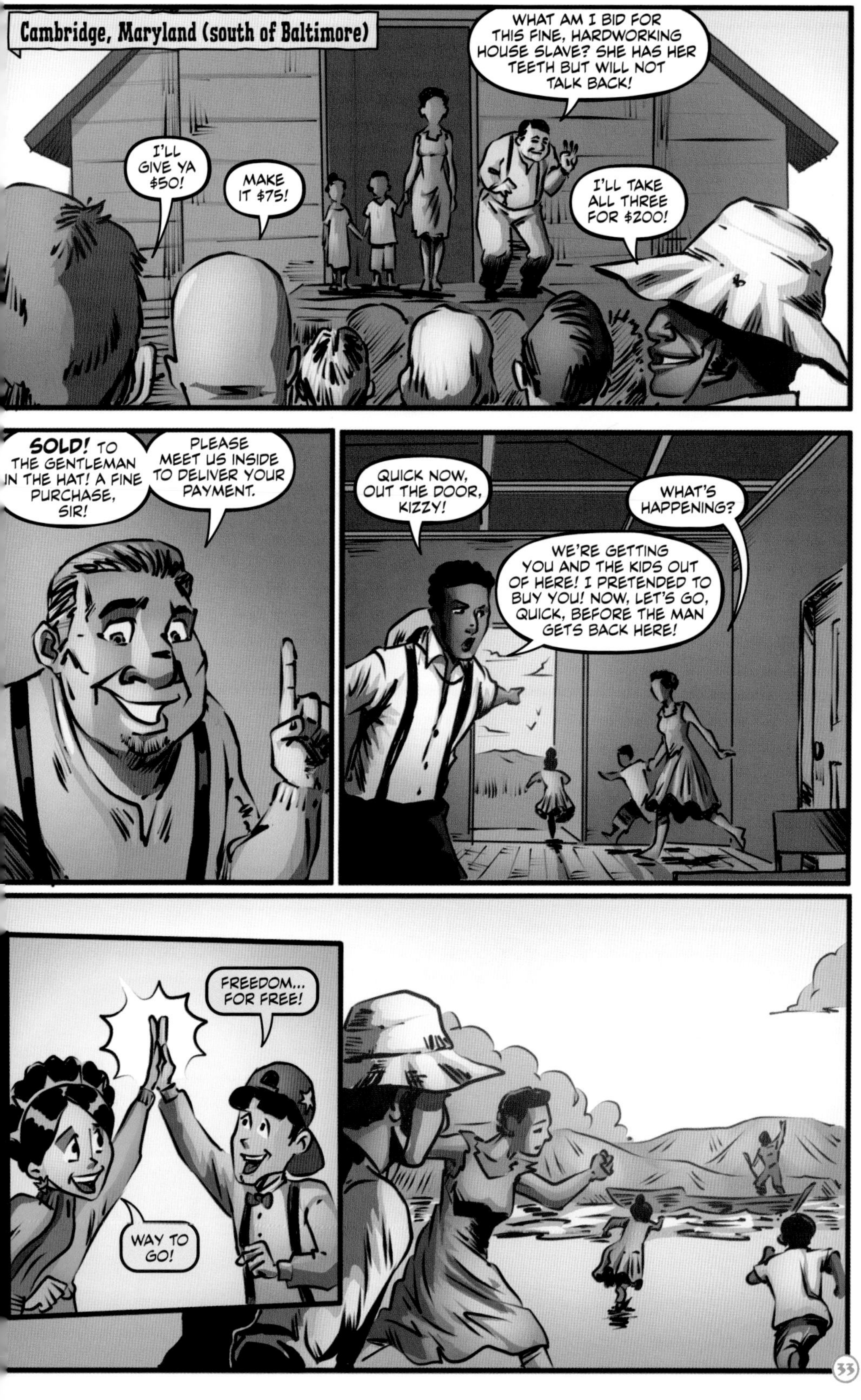
Cambridge, Maryland (south of Baltimore)
WHAT AM I BID FOR THIS FINE, HARDWORKING HOUSE SLAVE? SHE HAS HER TEETH BUT WILL NOT TALK BACK!
I'LL GIVE YA $50!
MAKE IT $75!
I'LL TAKE ALL THREE FOR $200!
SOLD! TO THE GENTLEMAN IN THE HAT! A FINE PURCHASE, SIR!
PLEASE MEET US INSIDE TO DELIVER YOUR PAYMENT.
QUICK NOW, OUT THE DOOR, KIZZY!
WHAT'S HAPPENING?
WE'RE GETTING YOU AND THE KIDS OUT OF HERE! I PRETENDED TO BUY YOU! NOW, LET'S GO, QUICK, BEFORE THE MAN GETS BACK HERE!
FREEDOM... FOR FREE!
WAY TO GO!

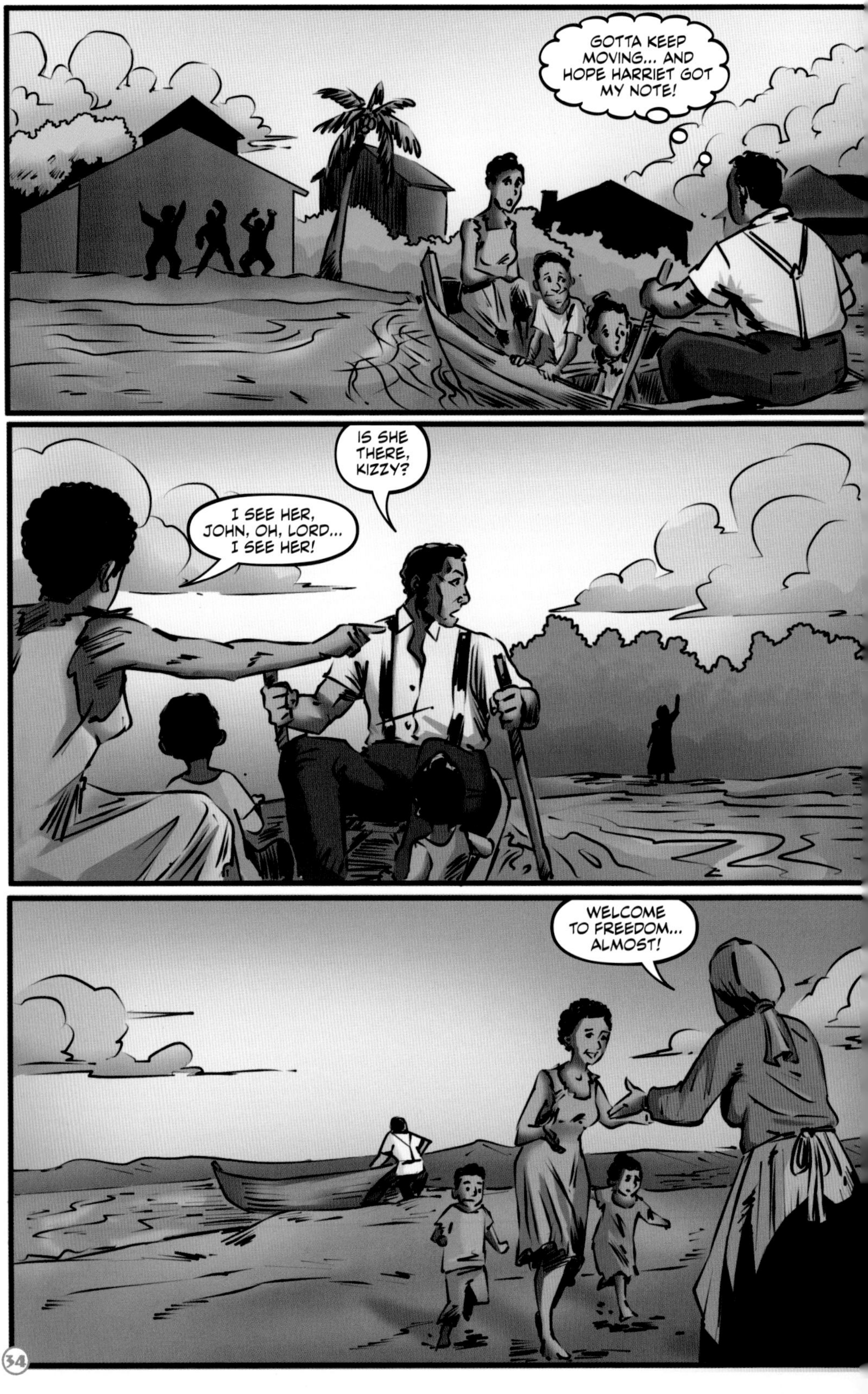
GOTTA KEEP MOVING... AND HOPE HARRIET GOT MY NOTE!
IS SHE THERE, KIZZY?
I SEE HER, JOHN, OH, LORD... I SEE HER!
WELCOME TO FREEDOM... ALMOST!

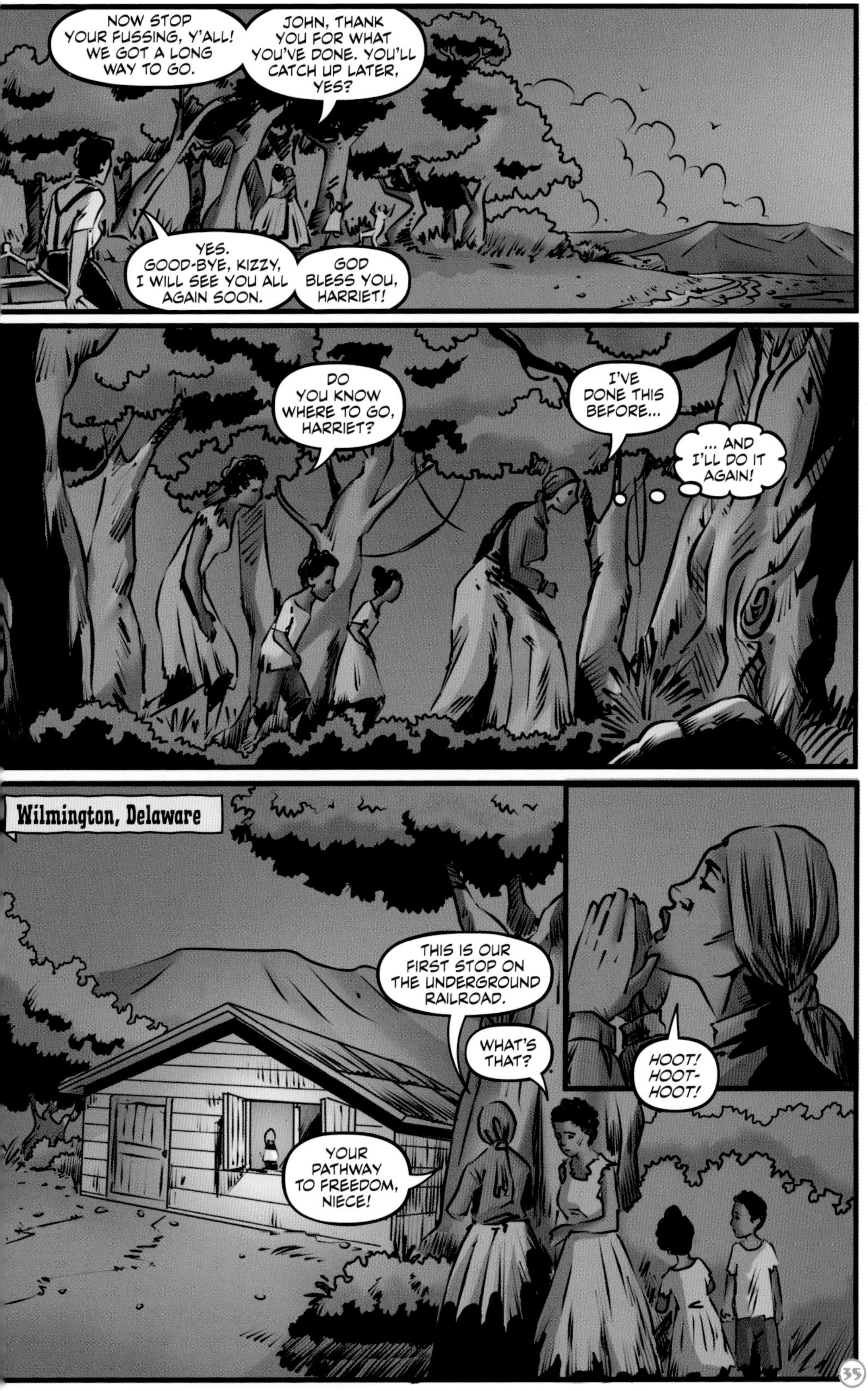
NOW STOP YOUR FUSSING, Y'ALL! WE GOT A LONG WAY TO GO.
JOHN, THANK YOU FOR WHAT YOU'VE DONE. YOU'LL CATCH UP LATER, YES?
YES. GOOD-BYE, KIZZY, I WILL SEE YOU ALL AGAIN SOON.
GOD BLESS YOU, HARRIET!
DO YOU KNOW WHERE TO GO, HARRIET?
I'VE DONE THIS BEFORE...
... AND I'LL DO IT AGAIN!
Wilmington, Delaware
HOOT! HOOT-HOOT!
THIS IS OUR FIRST STOP ON THE UNDERGROUND RAILROAD.
WHAT'S THAT?
YOUR PATHWAY TO FREEDOM, NIECE!

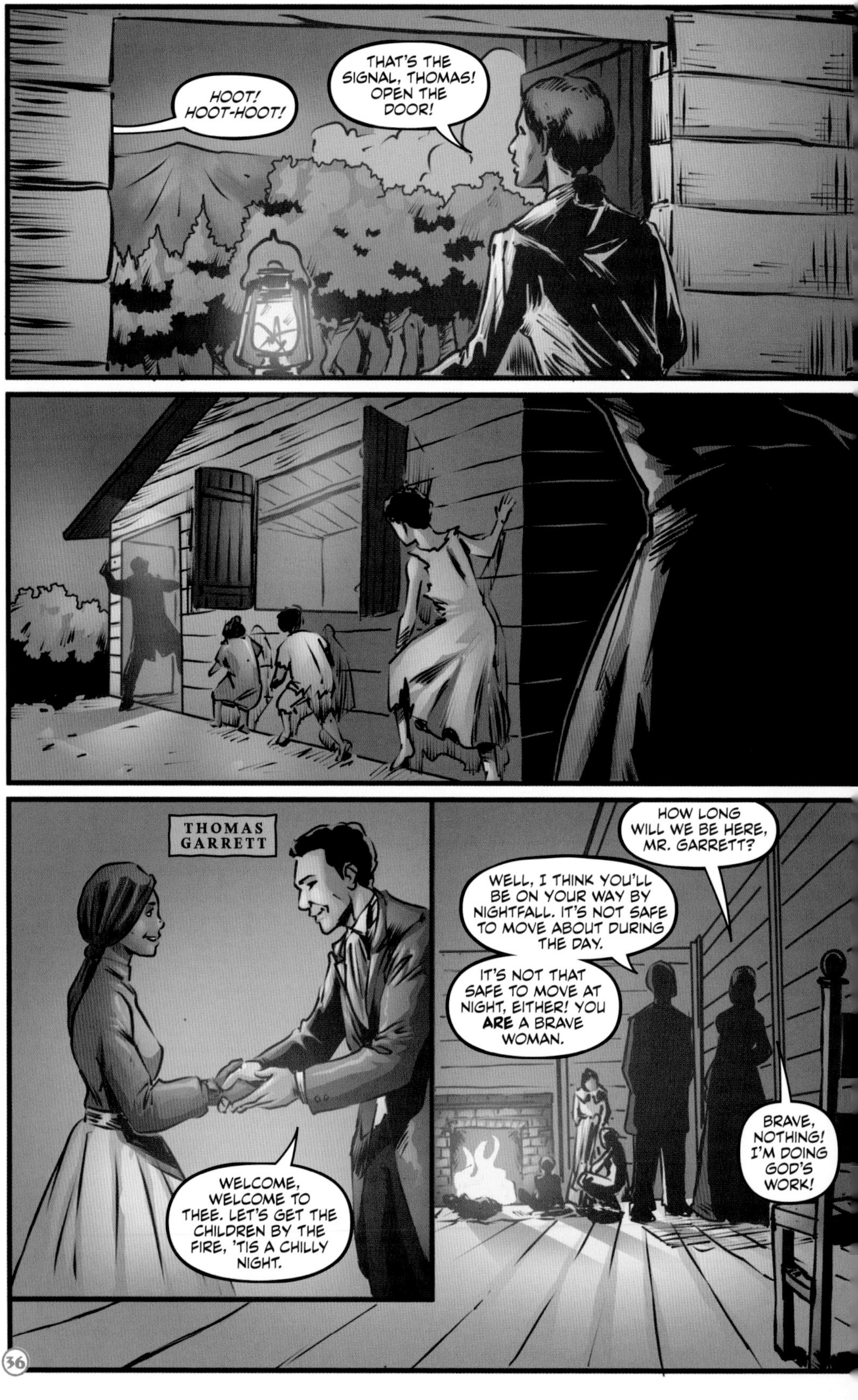
HOOT! HOOT-HOOT!
THAT'S THE SIGNAL, THOMAS! OPEN THE DOOR!
THOMAS GARRETT
WELCOME, WELCOME TO THEE. LET'S GET THE CHILDREN BY THE FIRE, 'TIS A CHILLY NIGHT.
HOW LONG WILL WE BE HERE, MR. GARRETT?
WELL, I THINK YOU'LL BE ON YOUR WAY BY NIGHTFALL. IT'S NOT SAFE TO MOVE ABOUT DURING THE DAY.
IT'S NOT THAT SAFE TO MOVE AT NIGHT, EITHER! YOU **ARE** A BRAVE WOMAN.
BRAVE, NOTHING! I'M DOING GOD'S WORK!

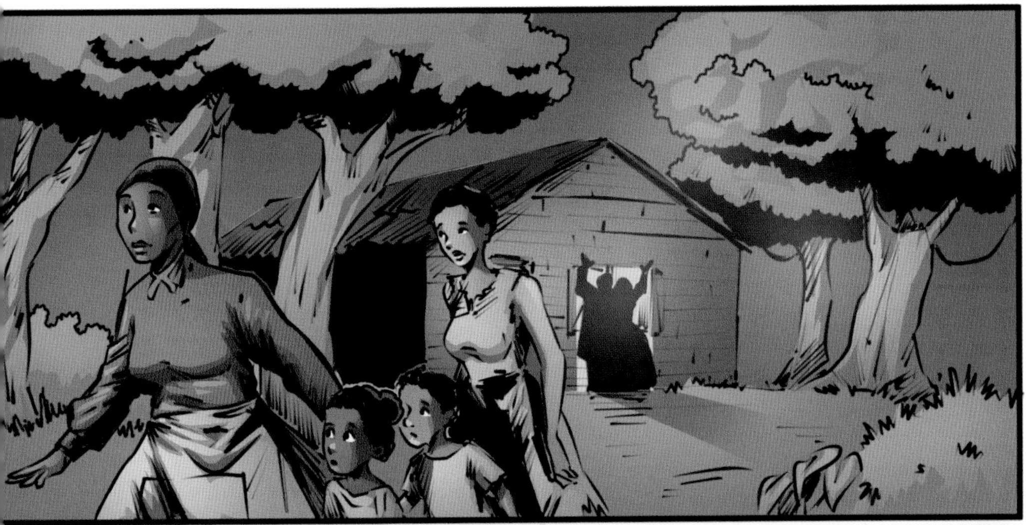

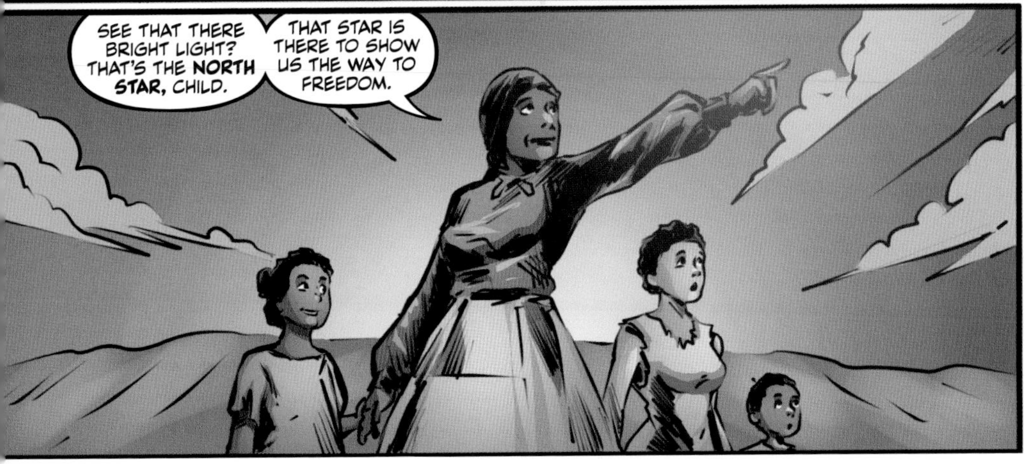

SEE THAT THERE BRIGHT LIGHT? THAT'S THE **NORTH STAR,** CHILD.
THAT STAR IS THERE TO SHOW US THE WAY TO FREEDOM.

★ ★ ★ ABOLITION ALL-STAR ★ ★ ★

THOMAS GARRETT

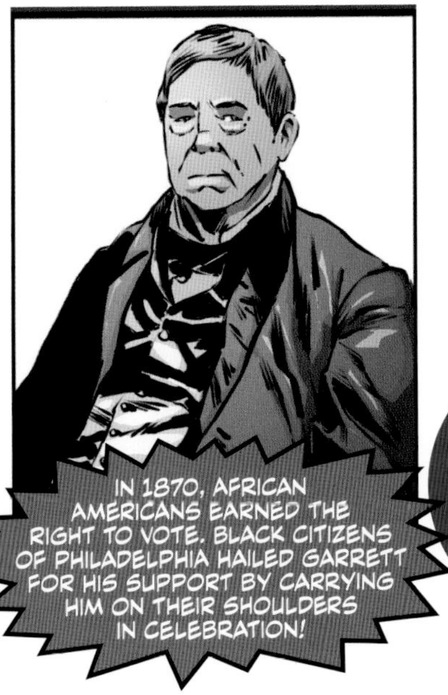

IN 1870, AFRICAN AMERICANS EARNED THE RIGHT TO VOTE. BLACK CITIZENS OF PHILADELPHIA HAILED GARRETT FOR HIS SUPPORT BY CARRYING HIM ON THEIR SHOULDERS IN CELEBRATION!

UNDERGROUND RAILROAD CONDUCTOR

- *Quaker: inspired by his faith to help*
- *Assisted over 2,000 escaped slaves*
- *Organized funds to help other Underground stations*
- *Member of Philadelphia Vigilance Committee that helped escaped slaves*
- *Helped African Americans get the right to vote in 1870*

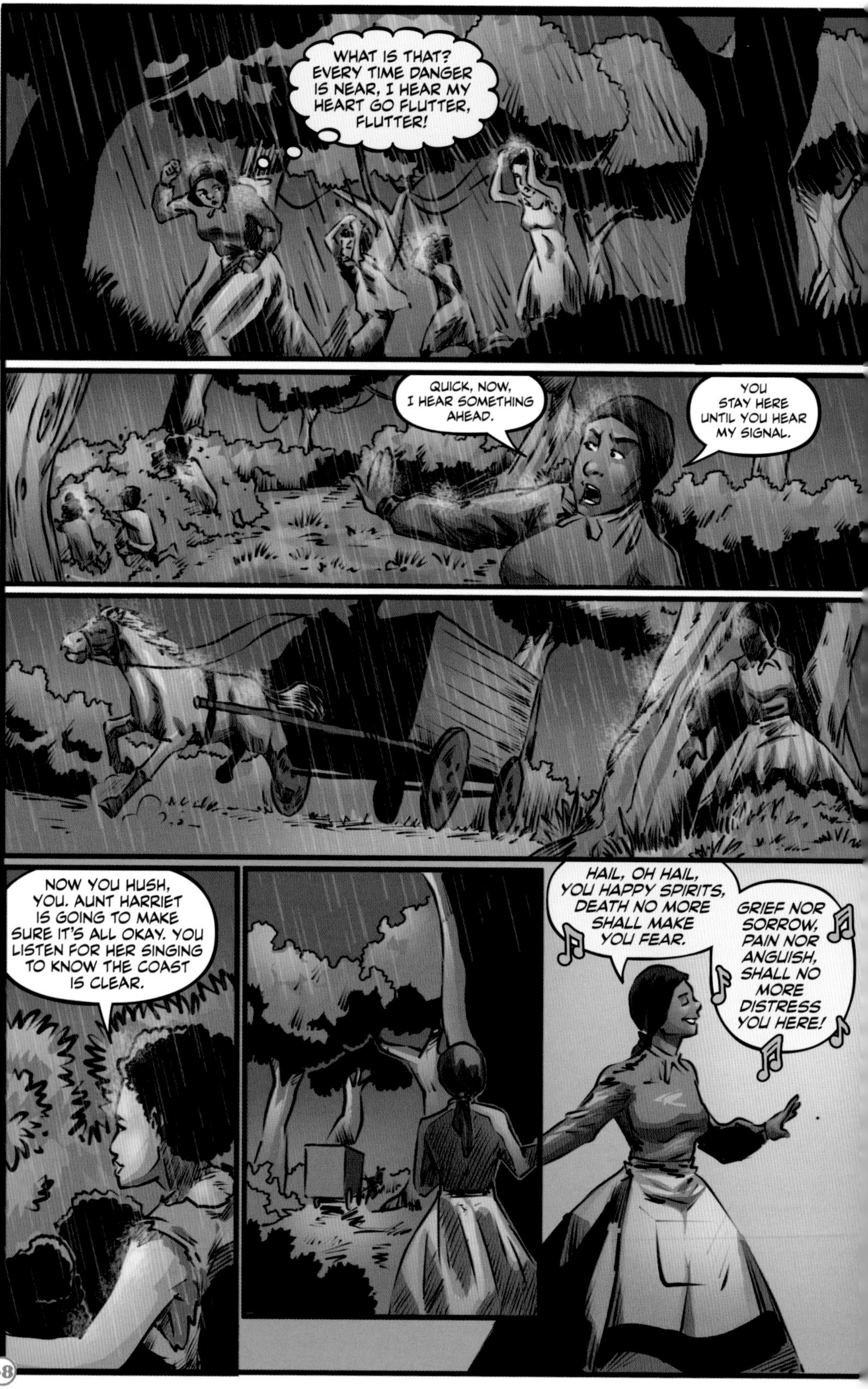
WHAT IS THAT? EVERY TIME DANGER IS NEAR, I HEAR MY HEART GO FLUTTER, FLUTTER!
QUICK, NOW, I HEAR SOMETHING AHEAD.
YOU STAY HERE UNTIL YOU HEAR MY SIGNAL.
NOW YOU HUSH, YOU. AUNT HARRIET IS GOING TO MAKE SURE IT'S ALL OKAY. YOU LISTEN FOR HER SINGING TO KNOW THE COAST IS CLEAR.
HAIL, OH HAIL, YOU HAPPY SPIRITS, DEATH NO MORE SHALL MAKE YOU FEAR.
GRIEF NOR SORROW, PAIN NOR ANGUISH, SHALL NO MORE DISTRESS YOU HERE!

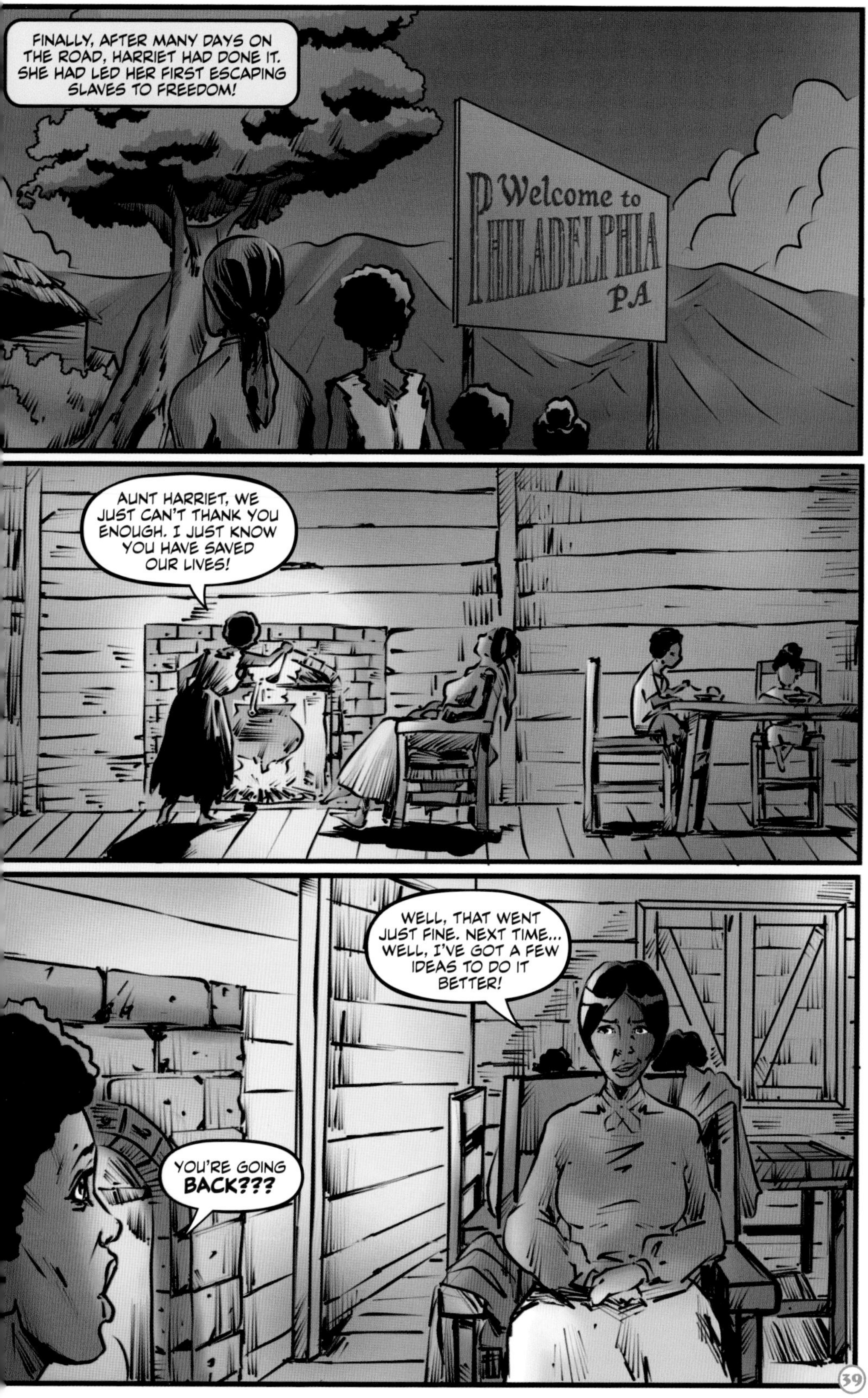
FINALLY, AFTER MANY DAYS ON THE ROAD, HARRIET HAD DONE IT. SHE HAD LED HER FIRST ESCAPING SLAVES TO FREEDOM!
Welcome to PHILADELPHIA PA
AUNT HARRIET, WE JUST CAN'T THANK YOU ENOUGH. I JUST KNOW YOU HAVE SAVED OUR LIVES!
WELL, THAT WENT JUST FINE. NEXT TIME... WELL, I'VE GOT A FEW IDEAS TO DO IT BETTER!
YOU'RE GOING **BACK???**

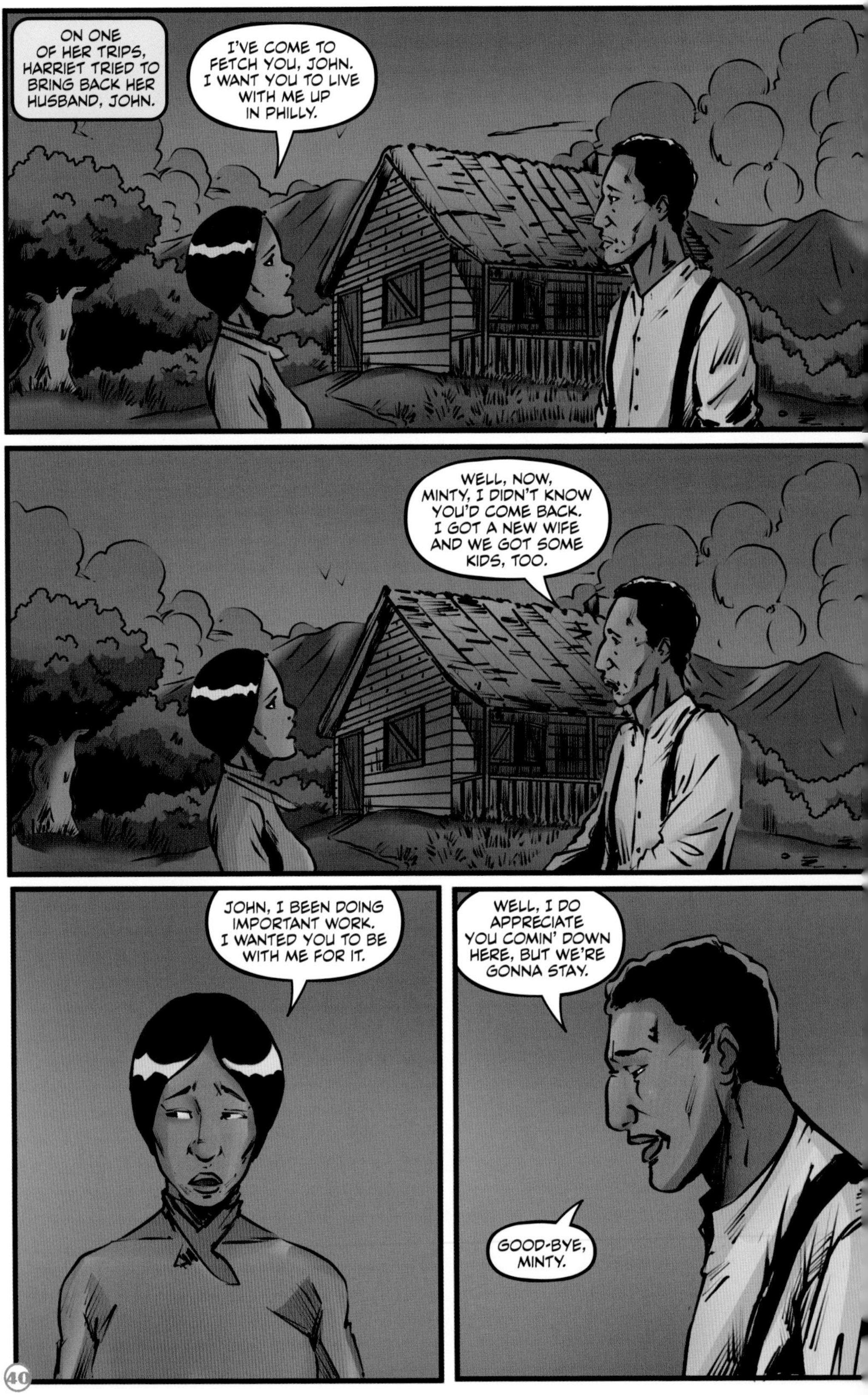
ON ONE OF HER TRIPS, HARRIET TRIED TO BRING BACK HER HUSBAND, JOHN.
I'VE COME TO FETCH YOU, JOHN. I WANT YOU TO LIVE WITH ME UP IN PHILLY.
WELL, NOW, MINTY, I DIDN'T KNOW YOU'D COME BACK. I GOT A NEW WIFE AND WE GOT SOME KIDS, TOO.
JOHN, I BEEN DOING IMPORTANT WORK. I WANTED YOU TO BE WITH ME FOR IT.
WELL, I DO APPRECIATE YOU COMIN' DOWN HERE, BUT WE'RE GONNA STAY.
GOOD-BYE, MINTY.

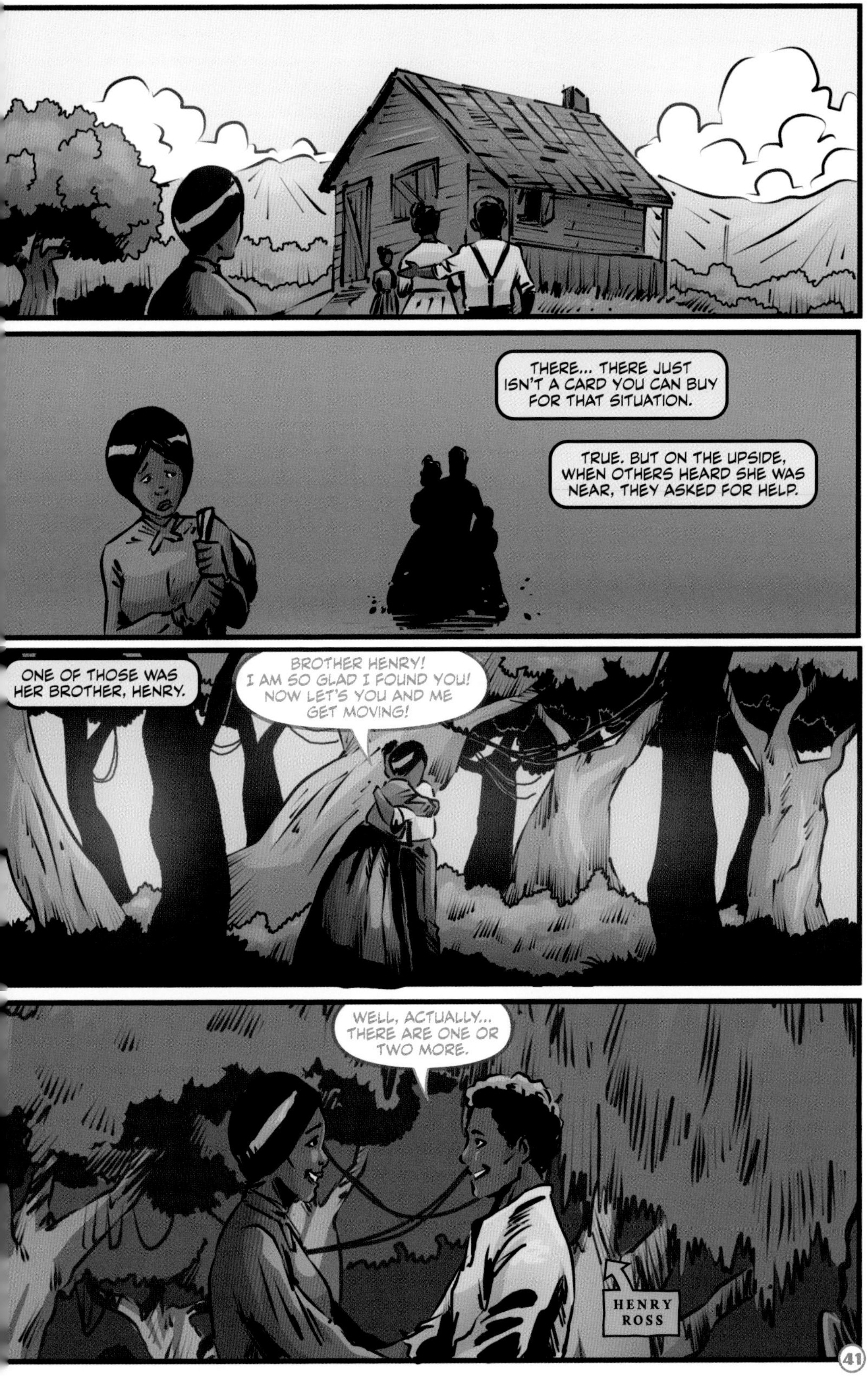
THERE... THERE JUST ISN'T A CARD YOU CAN BUY FOR THAT SITUATION.
TRUE. BUT ON THE UPSIDE, WHEN OTHERS HEARD SHE WAS NEAR, THEY ASKED FOR HELP.
ONE OF THOSE WAS HER BROTHER, HENRY.
BROTHER HENRY! I AM SO GLAD I FOUND YOU! NOW LET'S YOU AND ME GET MOVING!
WELL, ACTUALLY... THERE ARE ONE OR TWO MORE.
HENRY ROSS

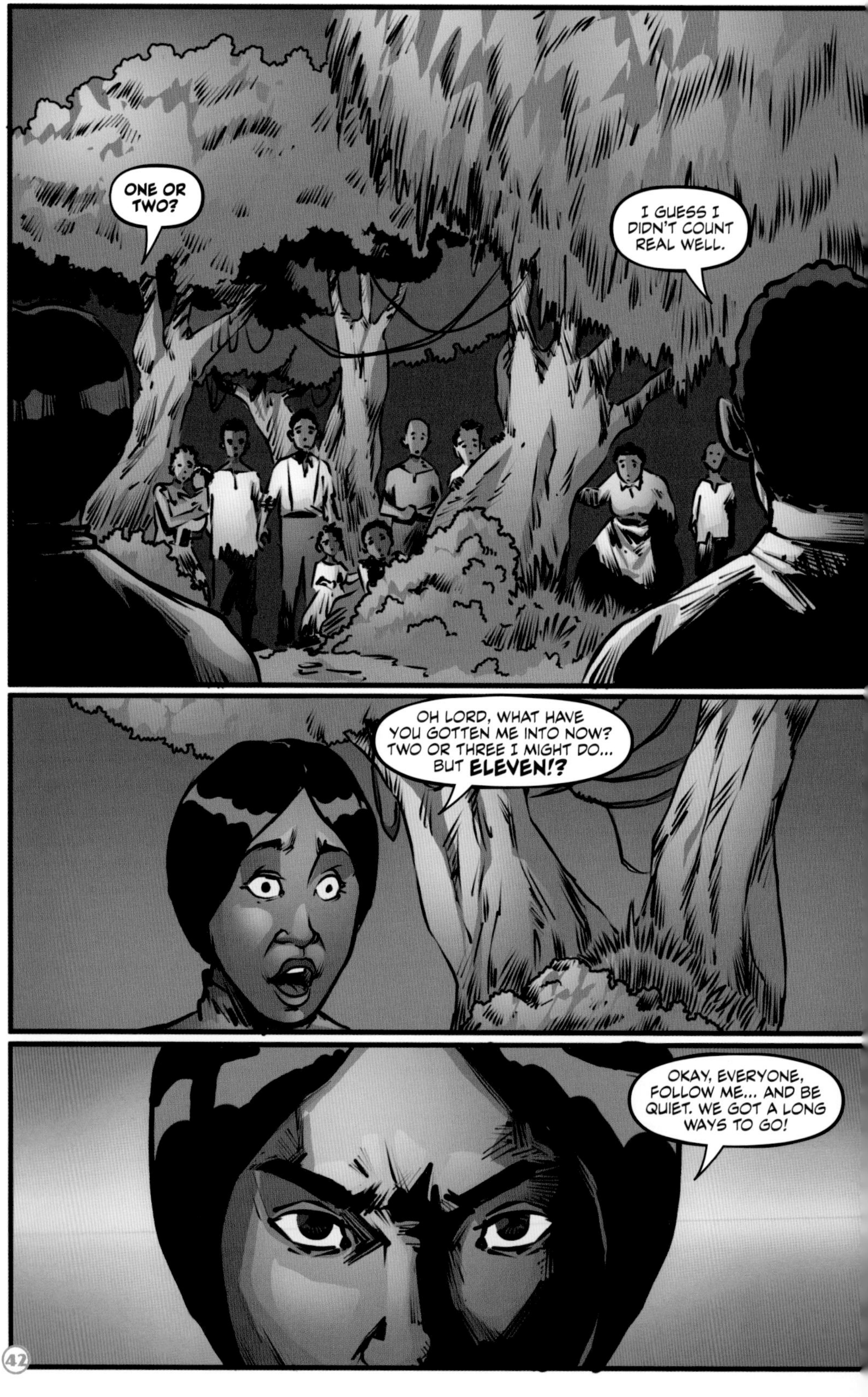
ONE OR TWO?
I GUESS I DIDN'T COUNT REAL WELL.
OH LORD, WHAT HAVE YOU GOTTEN ME INTO NOW? TWO OR THREE I MIGHT DO... BUT **ELEVEN!?**
OKAY, EVERYONE, FOLLOW ME... AND BE QUIET. WE GOT A LONG WAYS TO GO!

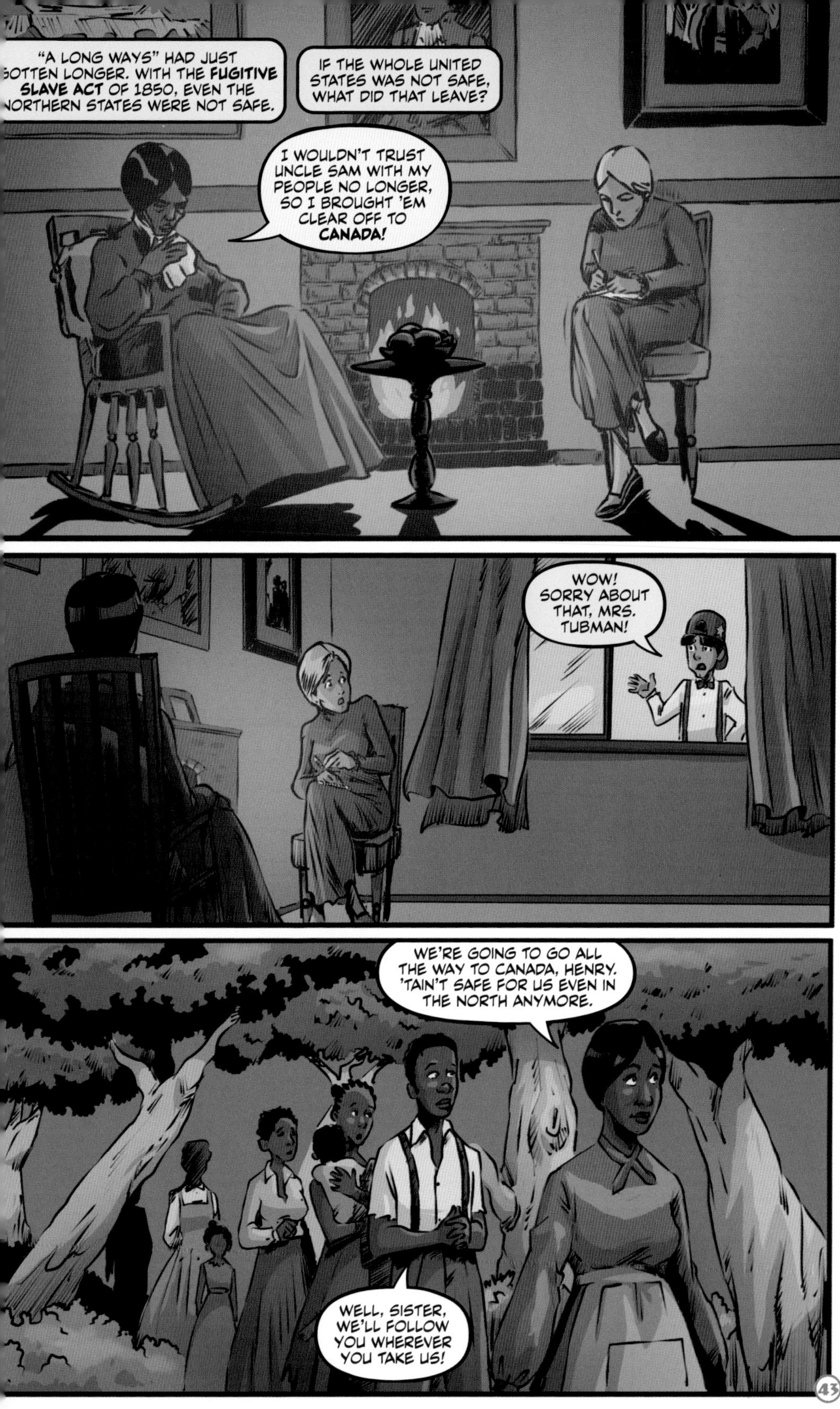
"A LONG WAYS" HAD JUST GOTTEN LONGER. WITH THE FUGITIVE SLAVE ACT OF 1850, EVEN THE NORTHERN STATES WERE NOT SAFE.
IF THE WHOLE UNITED STATES WAS NOT SAFE, WHAT DID THAT LEAVE?
I WOULDN'T TRUST UNCLE SAM WITH MY PEOPLE NO LONGER, SO I BROUGHT 'EM CLEAR OFF TO CANADA!
WOW! SORRY ABOUT THAT, MRS. TUBMAN!
WE'RE GOING TO GO ALL THE WAY TO CANADA, HENRY. 'TAIN'T SAFE FOR US EVEN IN THE NORTH ANYMORE.
WELL, SISTER, WE'LL FOLLOW YOU WHEREVER YOU TAKE US!

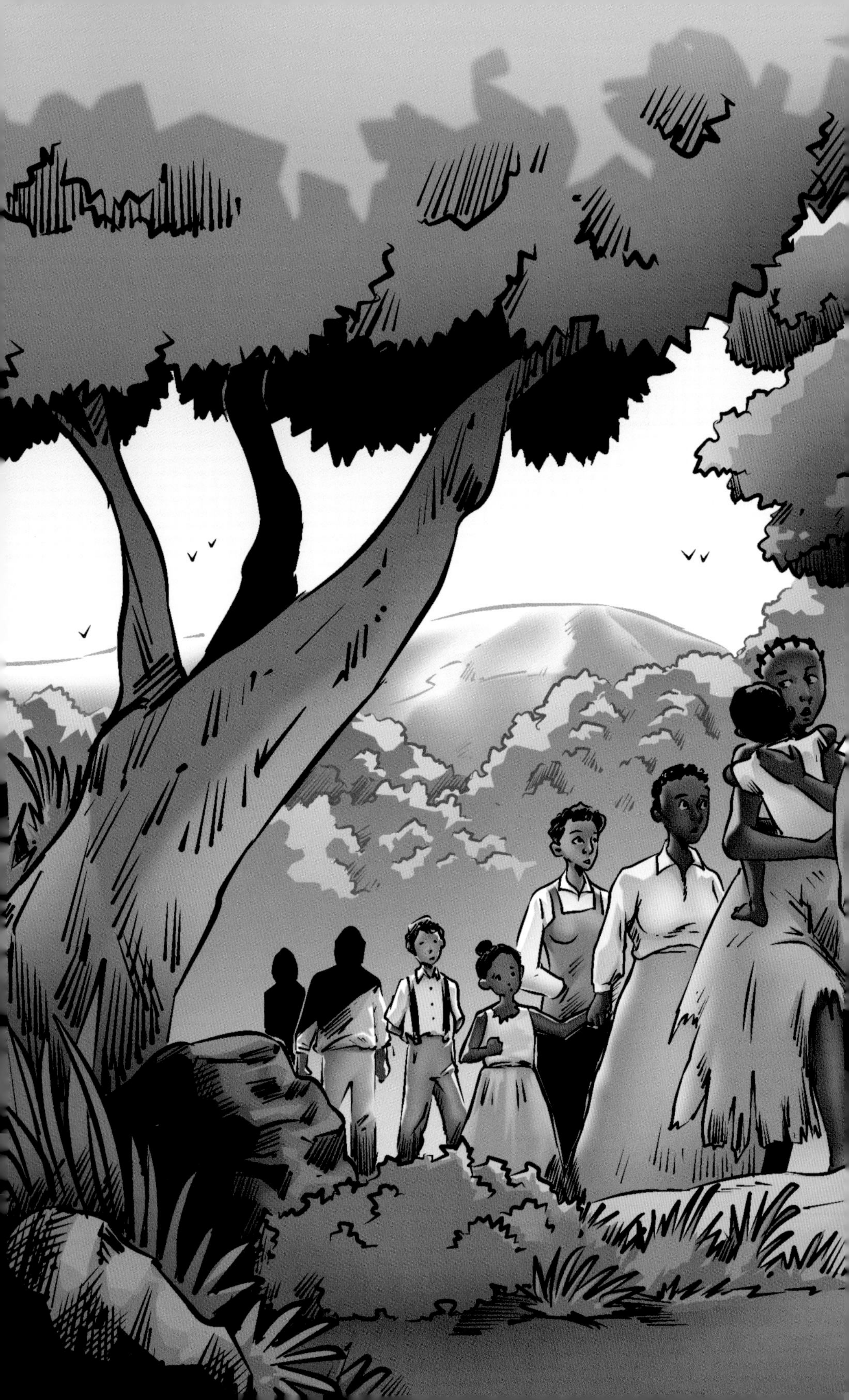

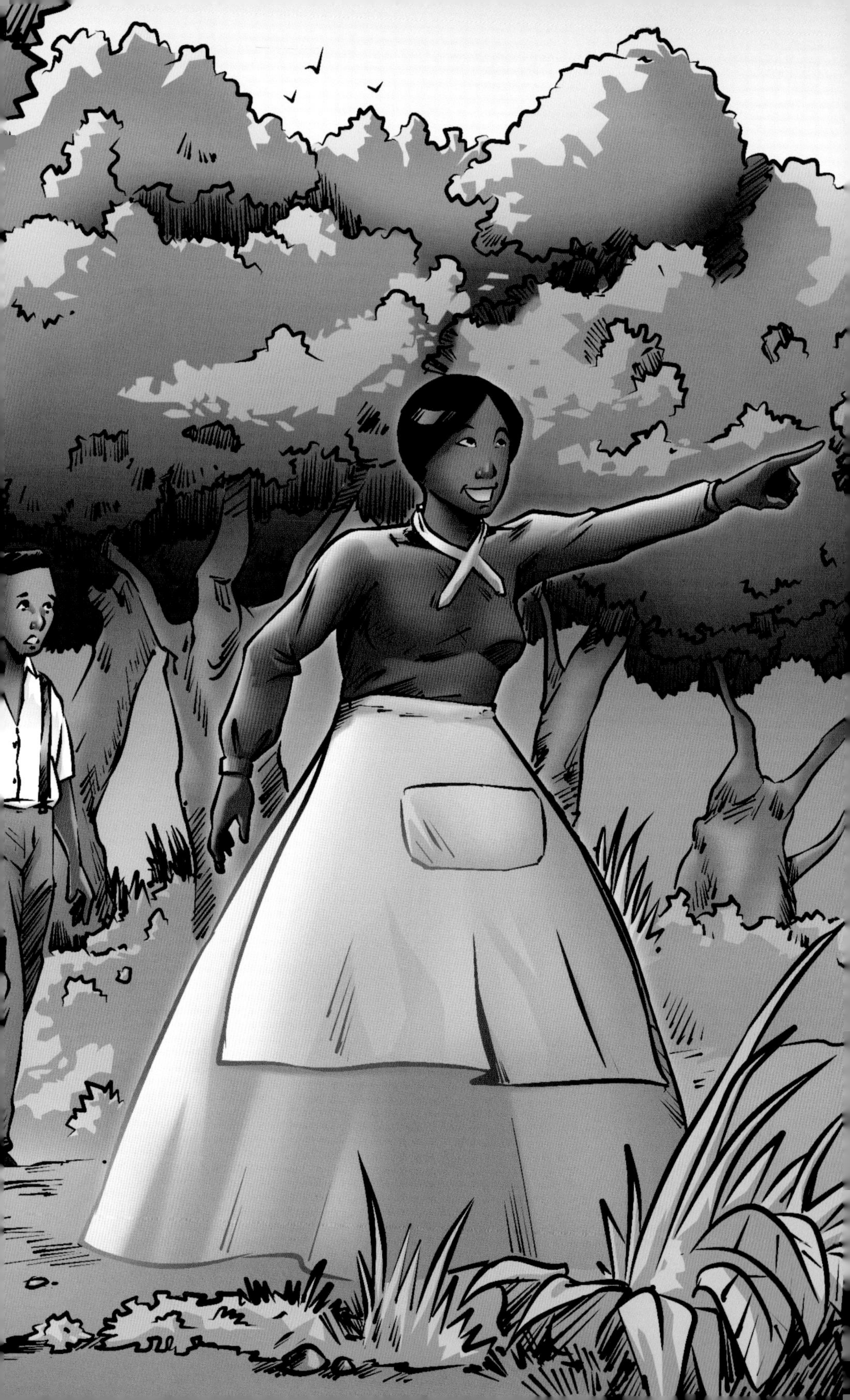

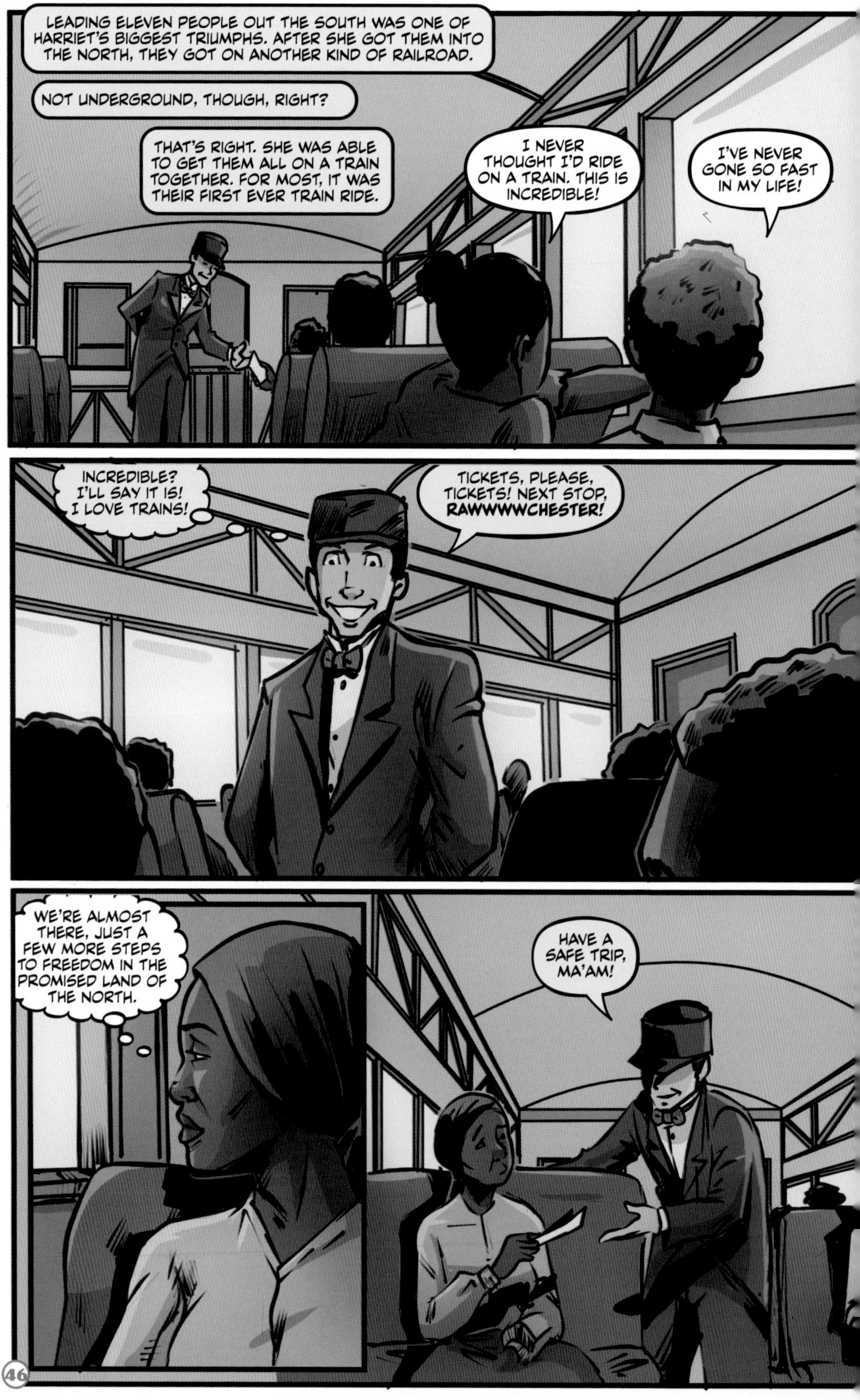
LEADING ELEVEN PEOPLE OUT THE SOUTH WAS ONE OF HARRIET'S BIGGEST TRIUMPHS. AFTER SHE GOT THEM INTO THE NORTH, THEY GOT ON ANOTHER KIND OF RAILROAD.
NOT UNDERGROUND, THOUGH, RIGHT?
THAT'S RIGHT. SHE WAS ABLE TO GET THEM ALL ON A TRAIN TOGETHER. FOR MOST, IT WAS THEIR FIRST EVER TRAIN RIDE.
I NEVER THOUGHT I'D RIDE ON A TRAIN. THIS IS INCREDIBLE!
I'VE NEVER GONE SO FAST IN MY LIFE!
INCREDIBLE? I'LL SAY IT IS! I LOVE TRAINS!
TICKETS, PLEASE, TICKETS! NEXT STOP, RAWWWWCHESTER!
WE'RE ALMOST THERE, JUST A FEW MORE STEPS TO FREEDOM IN THE PROMISED LAND OF THE NORTH.
HAVE A SAFE TRIP, MA'AM!

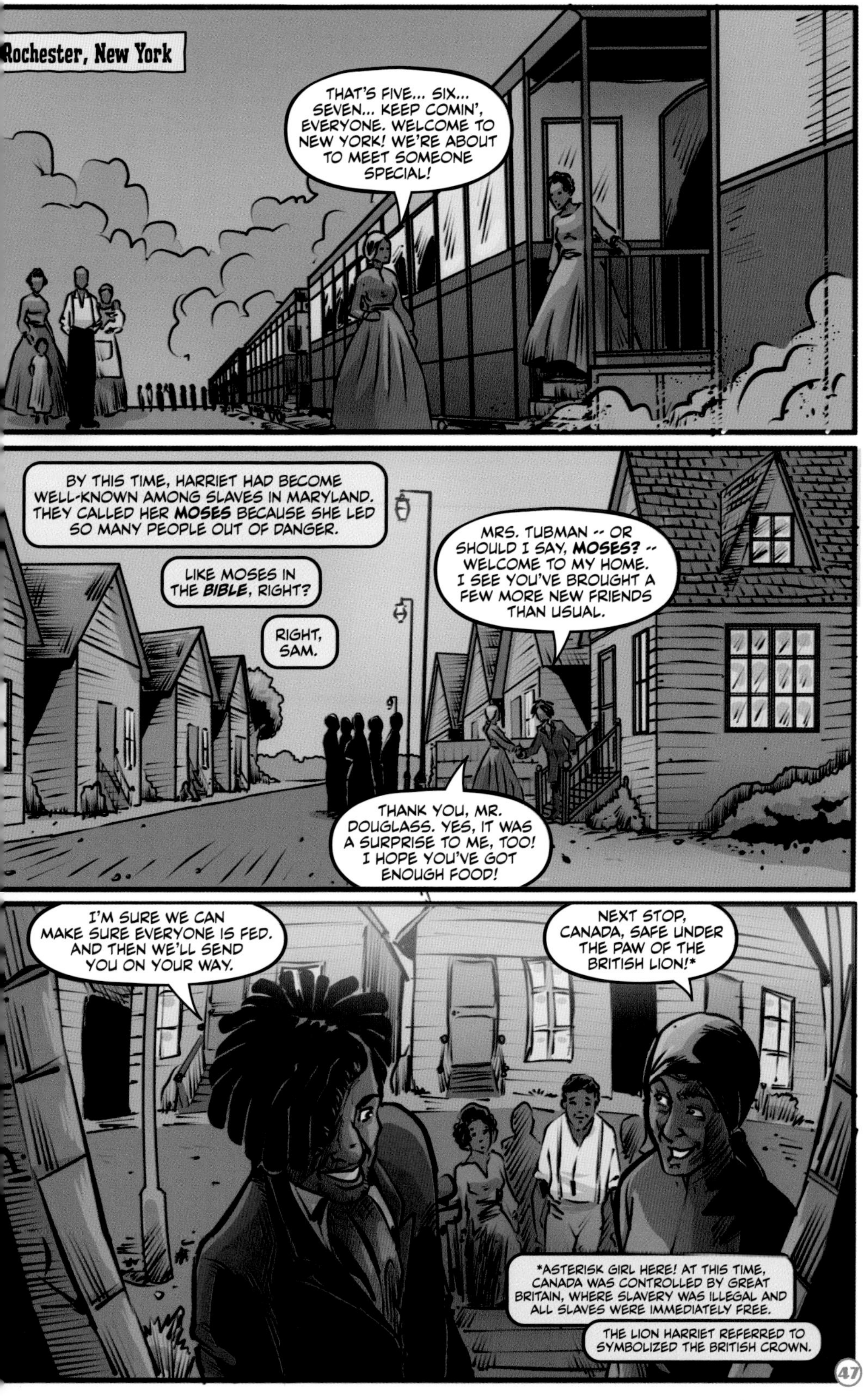
Rochester, New York
THAT'S FIVE... SIX... SEVEN... KEEP COMIN', EVERYONE. WELCOME TO NEW YORK! WE'RE ABOUT TO MEET SOMEONE SPECIAL!
BY THIS TIME, HARRIET HAD BECOME WELL-KNOWN AMONG SLAVES IN MARYLAND. THEY CALLED HER **MOSES** BECAUSE SHE LED SO MANY PEOPLE OUT OF DANGER.
LIKE MOSES IN THE ***BIBLE***, RIGHT?
RIGHT, SAM.
MRS. TUBMAN -- OR SHOULD I SAY, **MOSES?** -- WELCOME TO MY HOME. I SEE YOU'VE BROUGHT A FEW MORE NEW FRIENDS THAN USUAL.
THANK YOU, MR. DOUGLASS. YES, IT WAS A SURPRISE TO ME, TOO! I HOPE YOU'VE GOT ENOUGH FOOD!
I'M SURE WE CAN MAKE SURE EVERYONE IS FED. AND THEN WE'LL SEND YOU ON YOUR WAY.
NEXT STOP, CANADA, SAFE UNDER THE PAW OF THE BRITISH LION!*
*ASTERISK GIRL HERE! AT THIS TIME, CANADA WAS CONTROLLED BY GREAT BRITAIN, WHERE SLAVERY WAS ILLEGAL AND ALL SLAVES WERE IMMEDIATELY FREE.
THE LION HARRIET REFERRED TO SYMBOLIZED THE BRITISH CROWN.

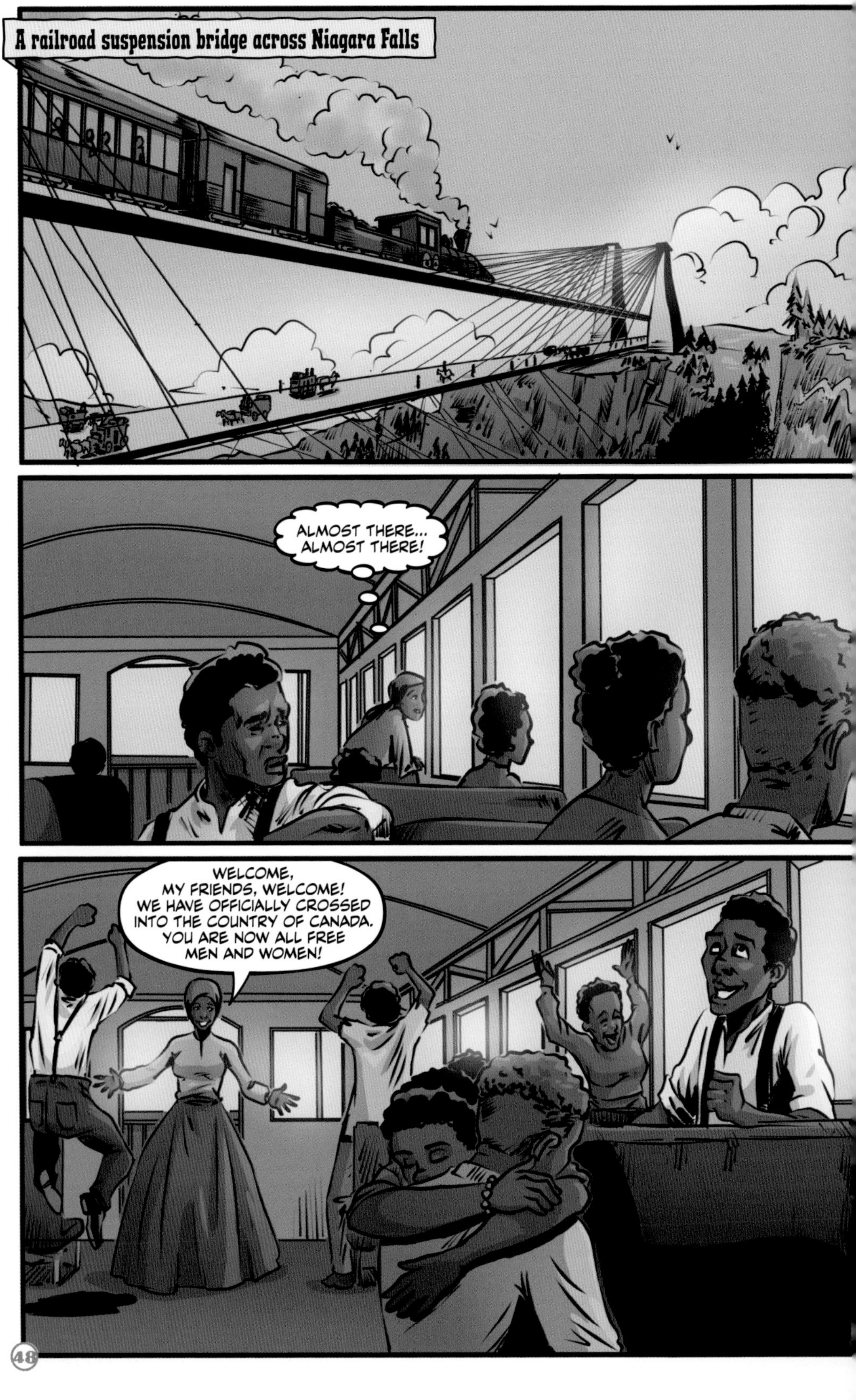
A railroad suspension bridge across Niagara Falls
ALMOST THERE... ALMOST THERE!
WELCOME, MY FRIENDS, WELCOME! WE HAVE OFFICIALLY CROSSED INTO THE COUNTRY OF CANADA. YOU ARE NOW ALL FREE MEN AND WOMEN!

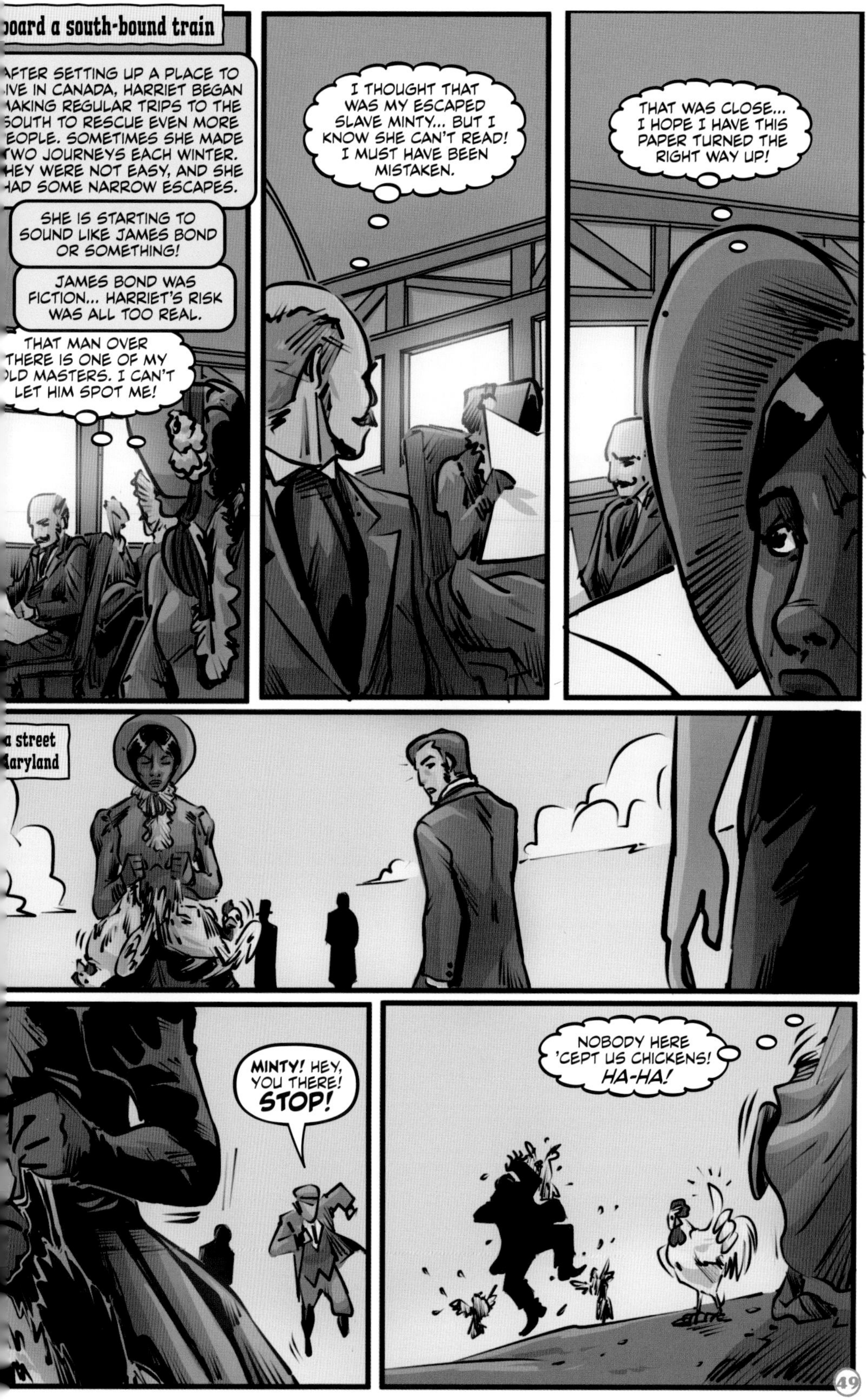

board a south-bound train
AFTER SETTING UP A PLACE TO LIVE IN CANADA, HARRIET BEGAN MAKING REGULAR TRIPS TO THE SOUTH TO RESCUE EVEN MORE PEOPLE. SOMETIMES SHE MADE TWO JOURNEYS EACH WINTER. THEY WERE NOT EASY, AND SHE HAD SOME NARROW ESCAPES.
SHE IS STARTING TO SOUND LIKE JAMES BOND OR SOMETHING!
JAMES BOND WAS FICTION... HARRIET'S RISK WAS ALL TOO REAL.
THAT MAN OVER THERE IS ONE OF MY OLD MASTERS. I CAN'T LET HIM SPOT ME!
I THOUGHT THAT WAS MY ESCAPED SLAVE MINTY... BUT I KNOW SHE CAN'T READ! I MUST HAVE BEEN MISTAKEN.
THAT WAS CLOSE... I HOPE I HAVE THIS PAPER TURNED THE RIGHT WAY UP!
a street
Maryland
MINTY! HEY, YOU THERE! STOP!
NOBODY HERE 'CEPT US CHICKENS! HA-HA!

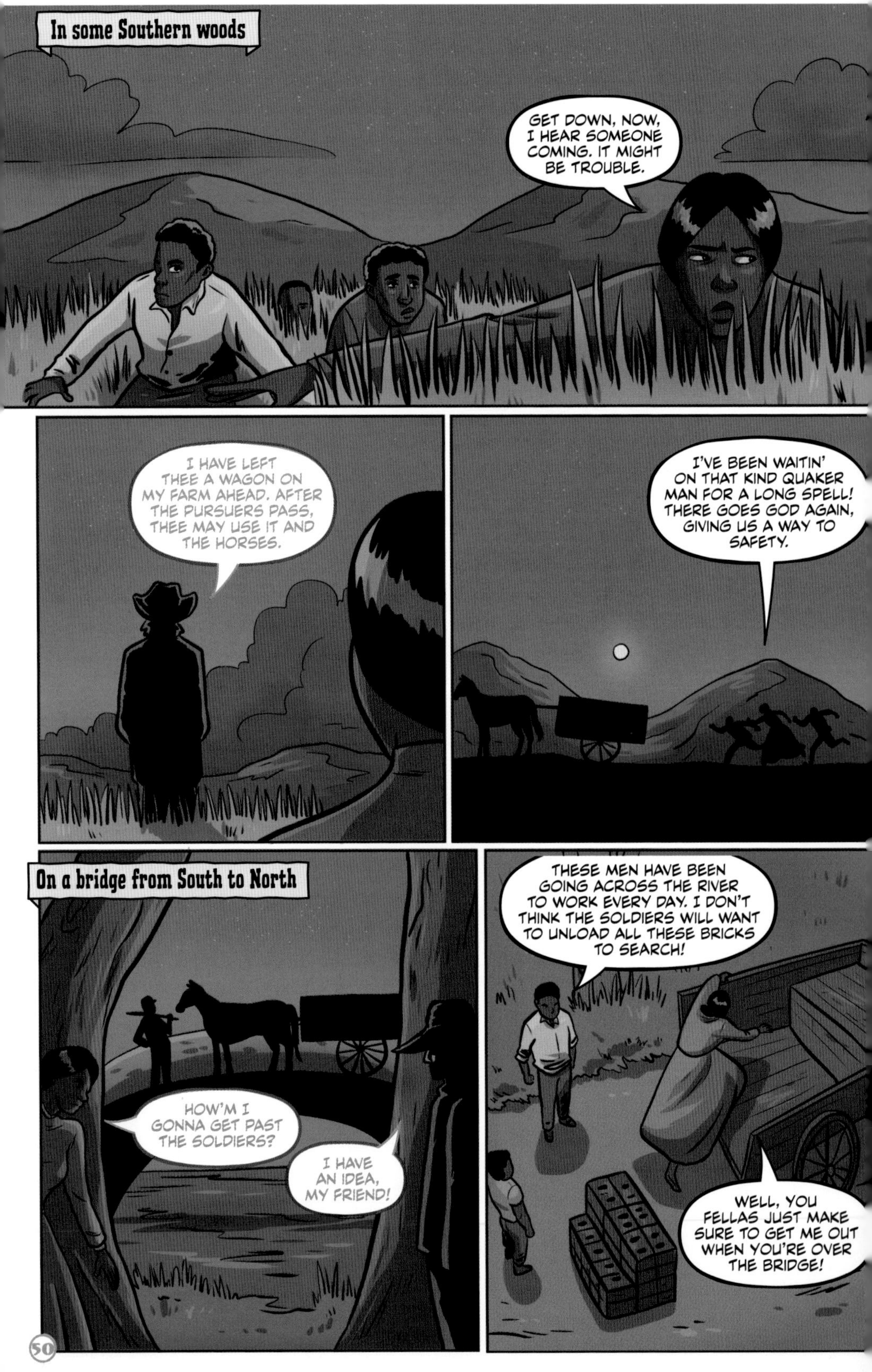
In some Southern woods
GET DOWN, NOW, I HEAR SOMEONE COMING. IT MIGHT BE TROUBLE.
I HAVE LEFT THEE A WAGON ON MY FARM AHEAD. AFTER THE PURSUERS PASS, THEE MAY USE IT AND THE HORSES.
I'VE BEEN WAITIN' ON THAT KIND QUAKER MAN FOR A LONG SPELL! THERE GOES GOD AGAIN, GIVING US A WAY TO SAFETY.
On a bridge from South to North
HOW'M I GONNA GET PAST THE SOLDIERS?
I HAVE AN IDEA, MY FRIEND!
THESE MEN HAVE BEEN GOING ACROSS THE RIVER TO WORK EVERY DAY. I DON'T THINK THE SOLDIERS WILL WANT TO UNLOAD ALL THESE BRICKS TO SEARCH!
WELL, YOU FELLAS JUST MAKE SURE TO GET ME OUT WHEN YOU'RE OVER THE BRIDGE!

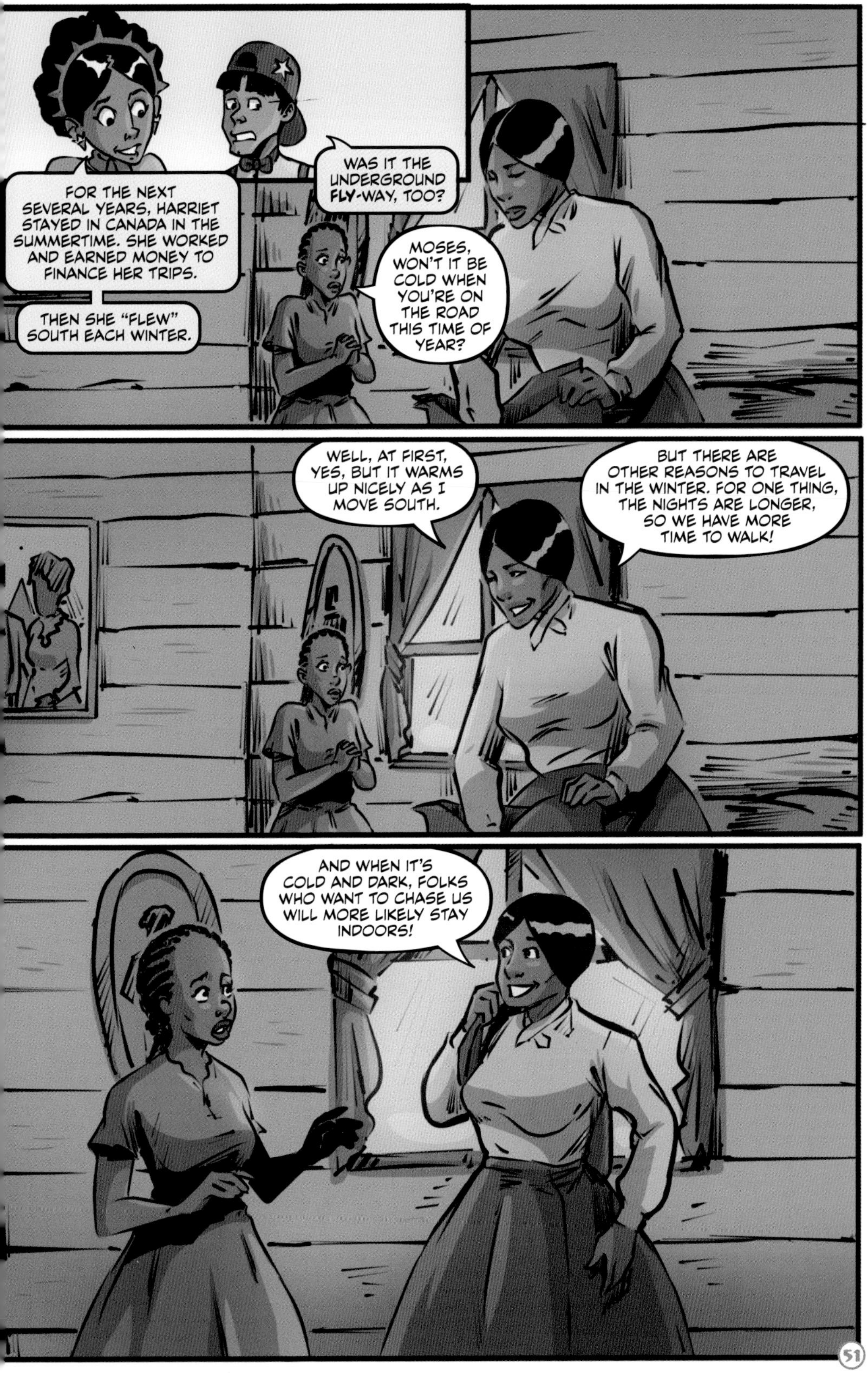
FOR THE NEXT SEVERAL YEARS, HARRIET STAYED IN CANADA IN THE SUMMERTIME. SHE WORKED AND EARNED MONEY TO FINANCE HER TRIPS.
THEN SHE "FLEW" SOUTH EACH WINTER.
WAS IT THE UNDERGROUND **FLY**-WAY, TOO?
MOSES, WON'T IT BE COLD WHEN YOU'RE ON THE ROAD THIS TIME OF YEAR?
WELL, AT FIRST, YES, BUT IT WARMS UP NICELY AS I MOVE SOUTH.
BUT THERE ARE OTHER REASONS TO TRAVEL IN THE WINTER. FOR ONE THING, THE NIGHTS ARE LONGER, SO WE HAVE MORE TIME TO WALK!
AND WHEN IT'S COLD AND DARK, FOLKS WHO WANT TO CHASE US WILL MORE LIKELY STAY INDOORS!

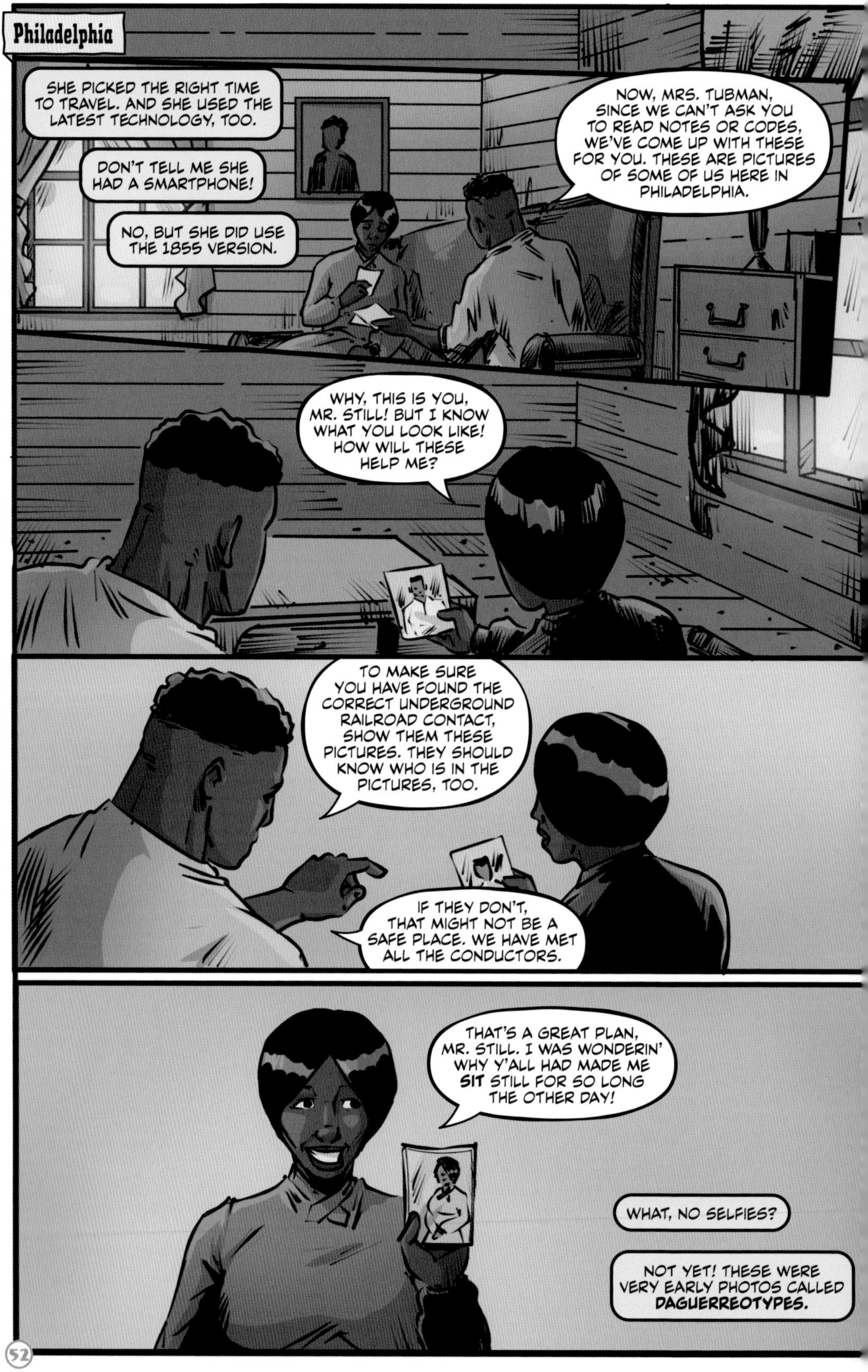
Philadelphia
SHE PICKED THE RIGHT TIME TO TRAVEL. AND SHE USED THE LATEST TECHNOLOGY, TOO.
DON'T TELL ME SHE HAD A SMARTPHONE!
NO, BUT SHE DID USE THE 1855 VERSION.
NOW, MRS. TUBMAN, SINCE WE CAN'T ASK YOU TO READ NOTES OR CODES, WE'VE COME UP WITH THESE FOR YOU. THESE ARE PICTURES OF SOME OF US HERE IN PHILADELPHIA.
WHY, THIS IS YOU, MR. STILL! BUT I KNOW WHAT YOU LOOK LIKE! HOW WILL THESE HELP ME?
TO MAKE SURE YOU HAVE FOUND THE CORRECT UNDERGROUND RAILROAD CONTACT, SHOW THEM THESE PICTURES. THEY SHOULD KNOW WHO IS IN THE PICTURES, TOO.
IF THEY DON'T, THAT MIGHT NOT BE A SAFE PLACE. WE HAVE MET ALL THE CONDUCTORS.
THAT'S A GREAT PLAN, MR. STILL. I WAS WONDERIN' WHY Y'ALL HAD MADE ME **SIT** STILL FOR SO LONG THE OTHER DAY!
WHAT, NO SELFIES?
NOT YET! THESE WERE VERY EARLY PHOTOS CALLED **DAGUERREOTYPES.**

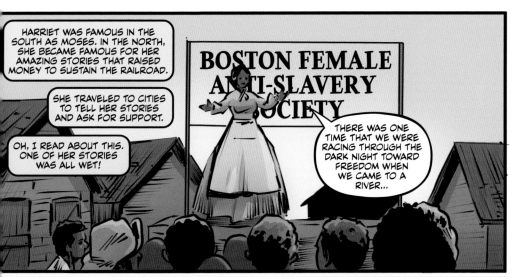

HARRIET WAS FAMOUS IN THE SOUTH AS MOSES. IN THE NORTH, SHE BECAME FAMOUS FOR HER AMAZING STORIES THAT RAISED MONEY TO SUSTAIN THE RAILROAD.

SHE TRAVELED TO CITIES TO TELL HER STORIES AND ASK FOR SUPPORT.

OH, I READ ABOUT THIS. ONE OF HER STORIES WAS ALL WET!

BOSTON FEMALE ANTI-SLAVERY SOCIETY

THERE WAS ONE TIME THAT WE WERE RACING THROUGH THE DARK NIGHT TOWARD FREEDOM WHEN WE CAME TO A RIVER...

THIS RIVER IS THE END!

I CAN'T SWIM, MOSES. WE HAVE TO GO BACK.

NO! THIS CAN'T BE THE END. WELL, LORD, I'M GONNA LEAVE IT UP TO YOU.

I'M GOIN' ACROSS. IF YOU WANT TO BE FREE, YOU'LL FOLLOW ME.

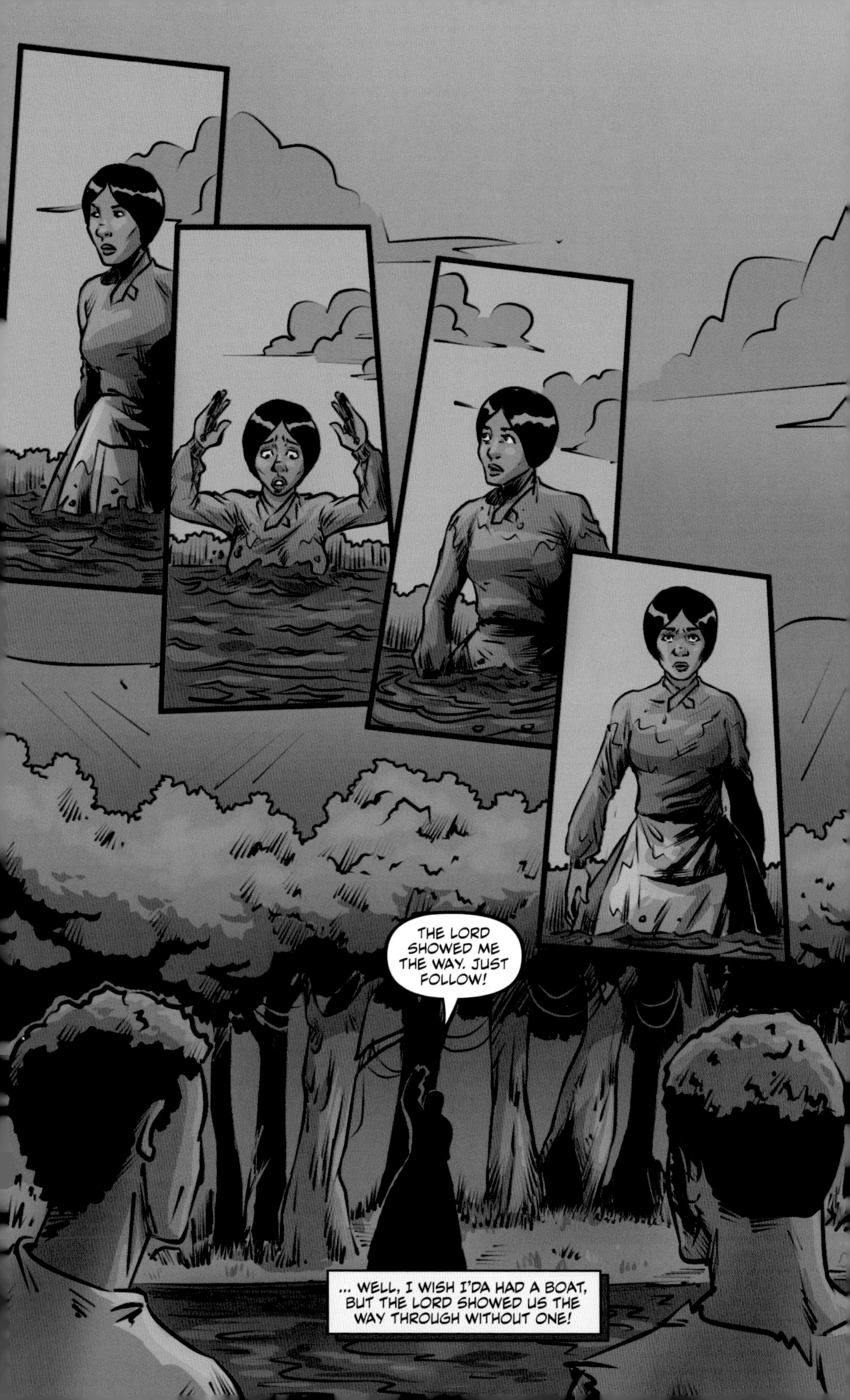
THE LORD SHOWED ME THE WAY. JUST FOLLOW!
... WELL, I WISH I'DA HAD A BOAT, BUT THE LORD SHOWED US THE WAY THROUGH WITHOUT ONE!

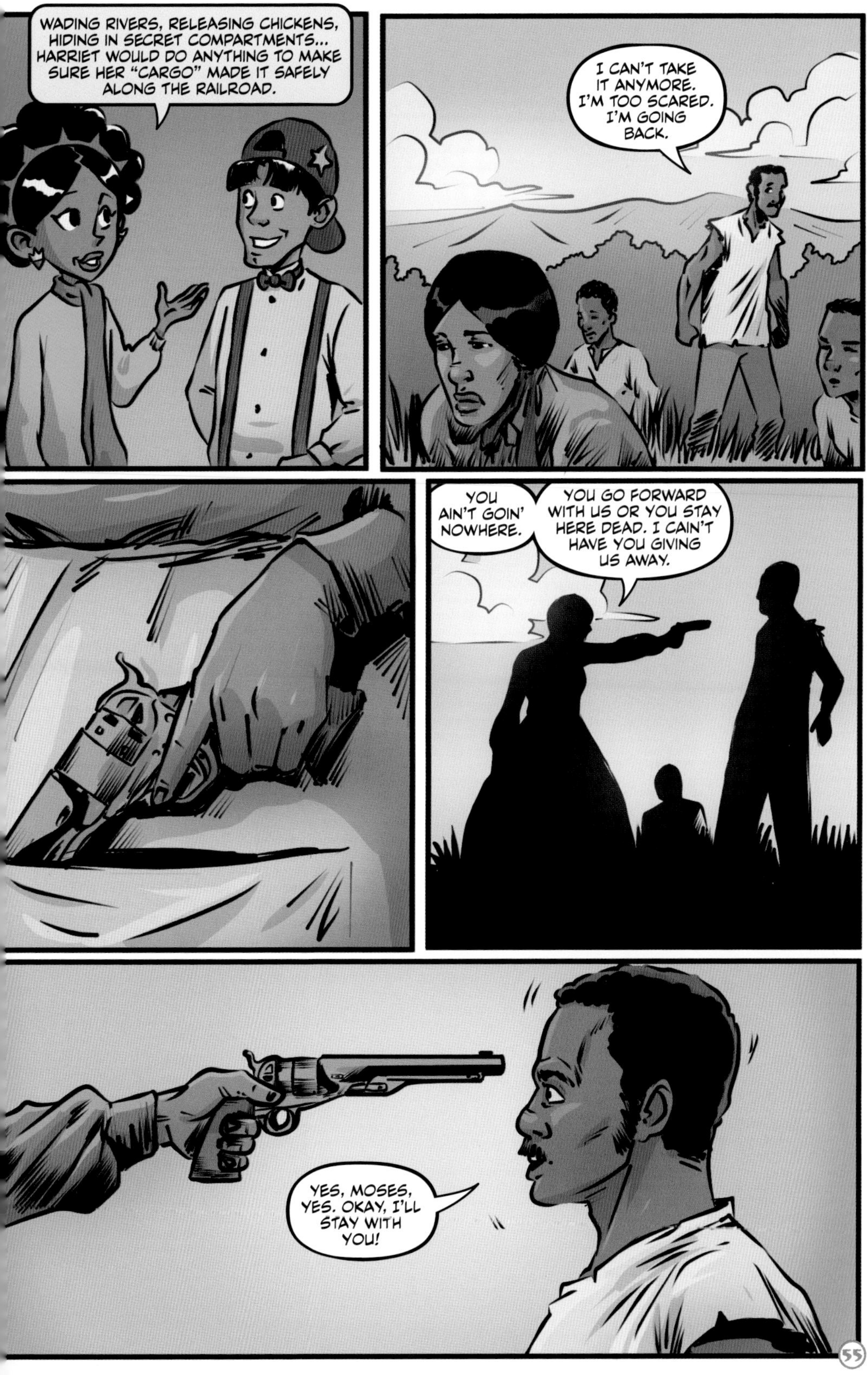
WADING RIVERS, RELEASING CHICKENS, HIDING IN SECRET COMPARTMENTS... HARRIET WOULD DO ANYTHING TO MAKE SURE HER "CARGO" MADE IT SAFELY ALONG THE RAILROAD.
I CAN'T TAKE IT ANYMORE. I'M TOO SCARED. I'M GOING BACK.
YOU AIN'T GOIN' NOWHERE.
YOU GO FORWARD WITH US OR YOU STAY HERE DEAD. I CAIN'T HAVE YOU GIVING US AWAY.
YES, MOSES, YES. OKAY, I'LL STAY WITH YOU!

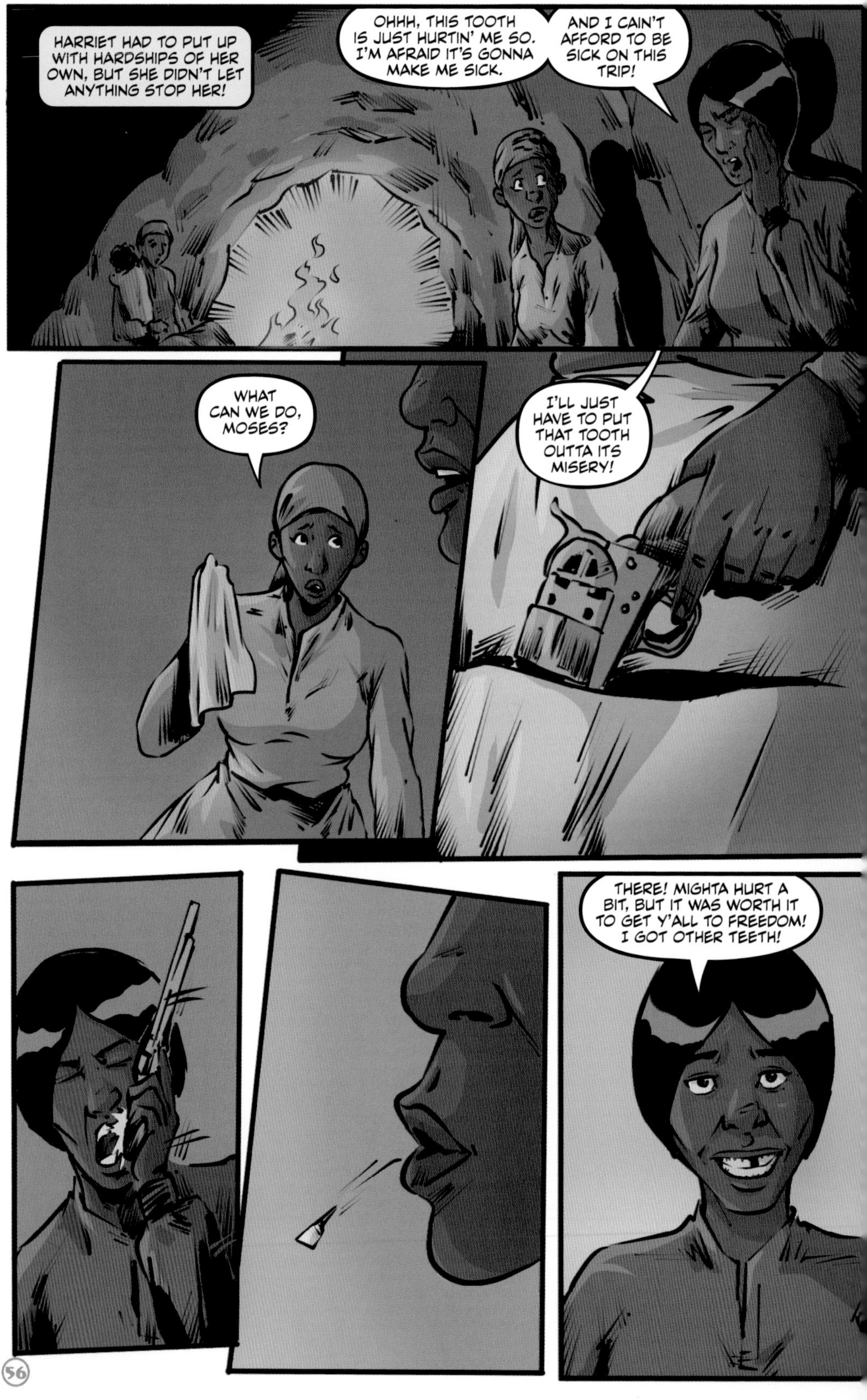
HARRIET HAD TO PUT UP WITH HARDSHIPS OF HER OWN, BUT SHE DIDN'T LET ANYTHING STOP HER!
OHHH, THIS TOOTH IS JUST HURTIN' ME SO. I'M AFRAID IT'S GONNA MAKE ME SICK.
AND I CAIN'T AFFORD TO BE SICK ON THIS TRIP!
WHAT CAN WE DO, MOSES?
I'LL JUST HAVE TO PUT THAT TOOTH OUTTA ITS MISERY!
THERE! MIGHTA HURT A BIT, BUT IT WAS WORTH IT TO GET Y'ALL TO FREEDOM! I GOT OTHER TEETH!

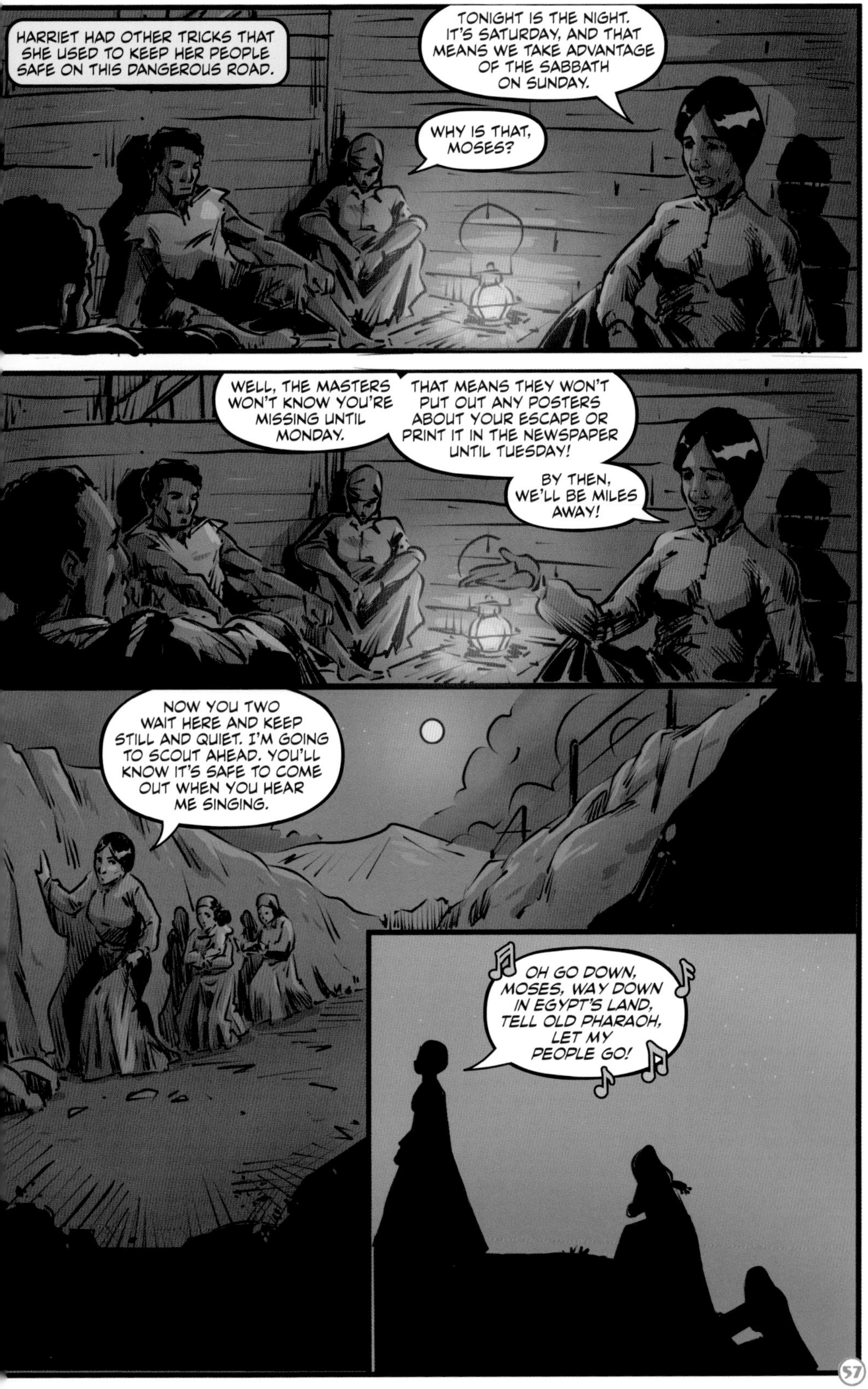
HARRIET HAD OTHER TRICKS THAT SHE USED TO KEEP HER PEOPLE SAFE ON THIS DANGEROUS ROAD.
TONIGHT IS THE NIGHT. IT'S SATURDAY, AND THAT MEANS WE TAKE ADVANTAGE OF THE SABBATH ON SUNDAY.
WHY IS THAT, MOSES?
WELL, THE MASTERS WON'T KNOW YOU'RE MISSING UNTIL MONDAY.
THAT MEANS THEY WON'T PUT OUT ANY POSTERS ABOUT YOUR ESCAPE OR PRINT IT IN THE NEWSPAPER UNTIL TUESDAY!
BY THEN, WE'LL BE MILES AWAY!
NOW YOU TWO WAIT HERE AND KEEP STILL AND QUIET. I'M GOING TO SCOUT AHEAD. YOU'LL KNOW IT'S SAFE TO COME OUT WHEN YOU HEAR ME SINGING.
OH GO DOWN, MOSES, WAY DOWN IN EGYPT'S LAND, TELL OLD PHARAOH, LET MY PEOPLE GO!

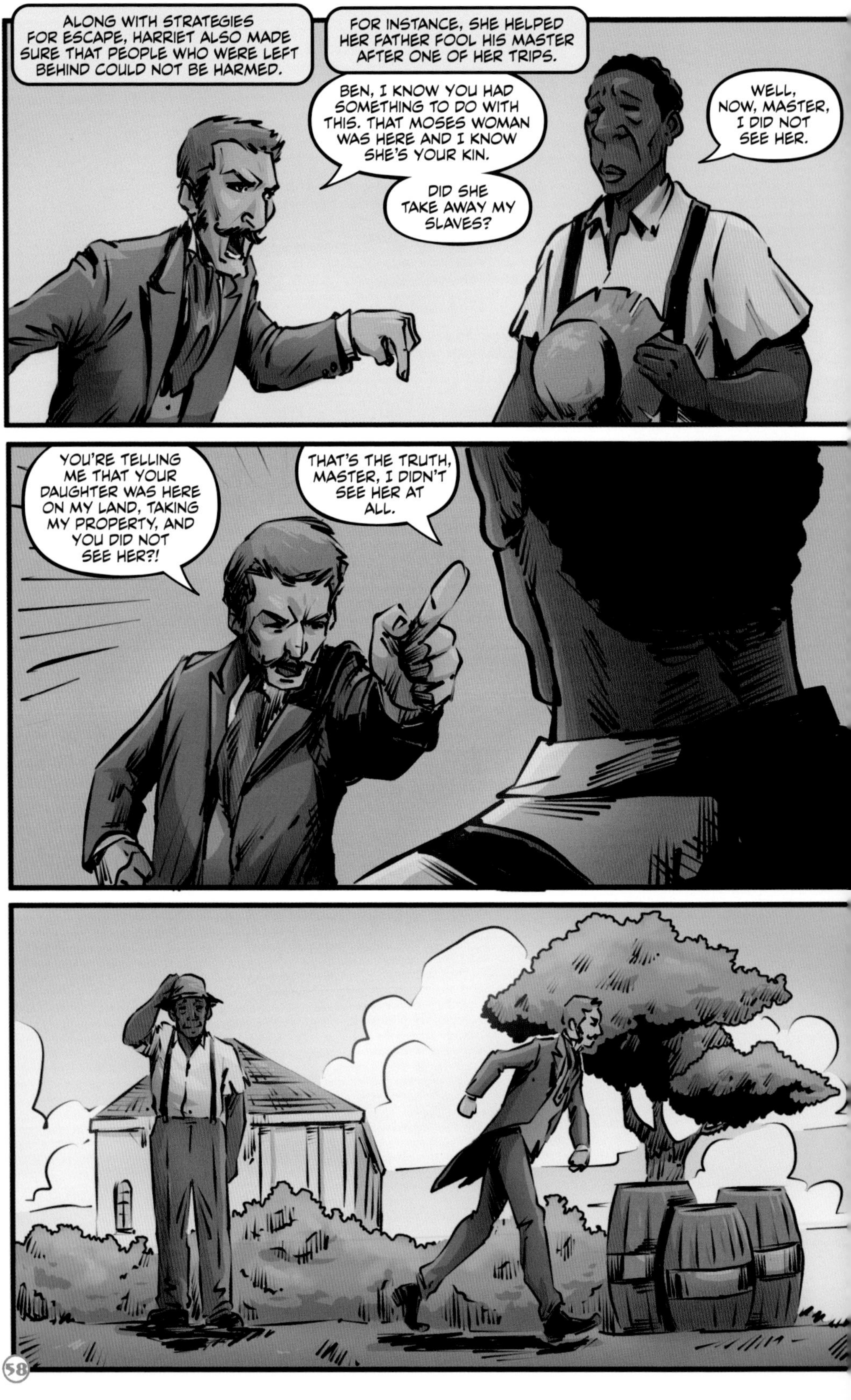
ALONG WITH STRATEGIES FOR ESCAPE, HARRIET ALSO MADE SURE THAT PEOPLE WHO WERE LEFT BEHIND COULD NOT BE HARMED.
FOR INSTANCE, SHE HELPED HER FATHER FOOL HIS MASTER AFTER ONE OF HER TRIPS.
BEN, I KNOW YOU HAD SOMETHING TO DO WITH THIS. THAT MOSES WOMAN WAS HERE AND I KNOW SHE'S YOUR KIN.
DID SHE TAKE AWAY MY SLAVES?
WELL, NOW, MASTER, I DID NOT SEE HER.
YOU'RE TELLING ME THAT YOUR DAUGHTER WAS HERE ON MY LAND, TAKING MY PROPERTY, AND YOU DID NOT SEE HER?!
THAT'S THE TRUTH, MASTER, I DIDN'T SEE HER AT ALL.

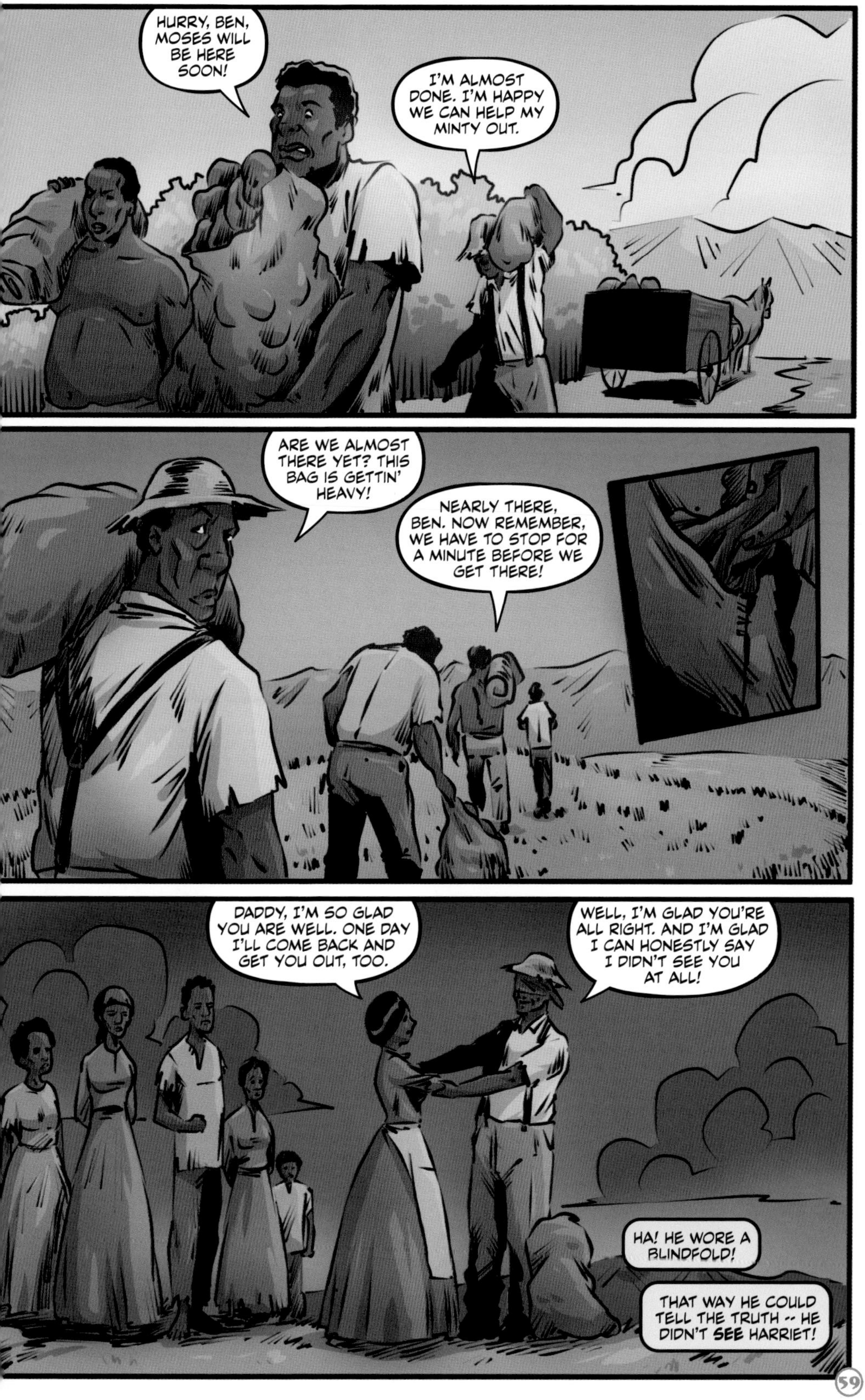
HURRY, BEN, MOSES WILL BE HERE SOON!
I'M ALMOST DONE. I'M HAPPY WE CAN HELP MY MINTY OUT.
ARE WE ALMOST THERE YET? THIS BAG IS GETTIN' HEAVY!
NEARLY THERE, BEN. NOW REMEMBER, WE HAVE TO STOP FOR A MINUTE BEFORE WE GET THERE!
DADDY, I'M SO GLAD YOU ARE WELL. ONE DAY I'LL COME BACK AND GET YOU OUT, TOO.
WELL, I'M GLAD YOU'RE ALL RIGHT. AND I'M GLAD I CAN HONESTLY SAY I DIDN'T SEE YOU AT ALL!
HA! HE WORE A BLINDFOLD!
THAT WAY HE COULD TELL THE TRUTH -- HE DIDN'T **SEE** HARRIET!

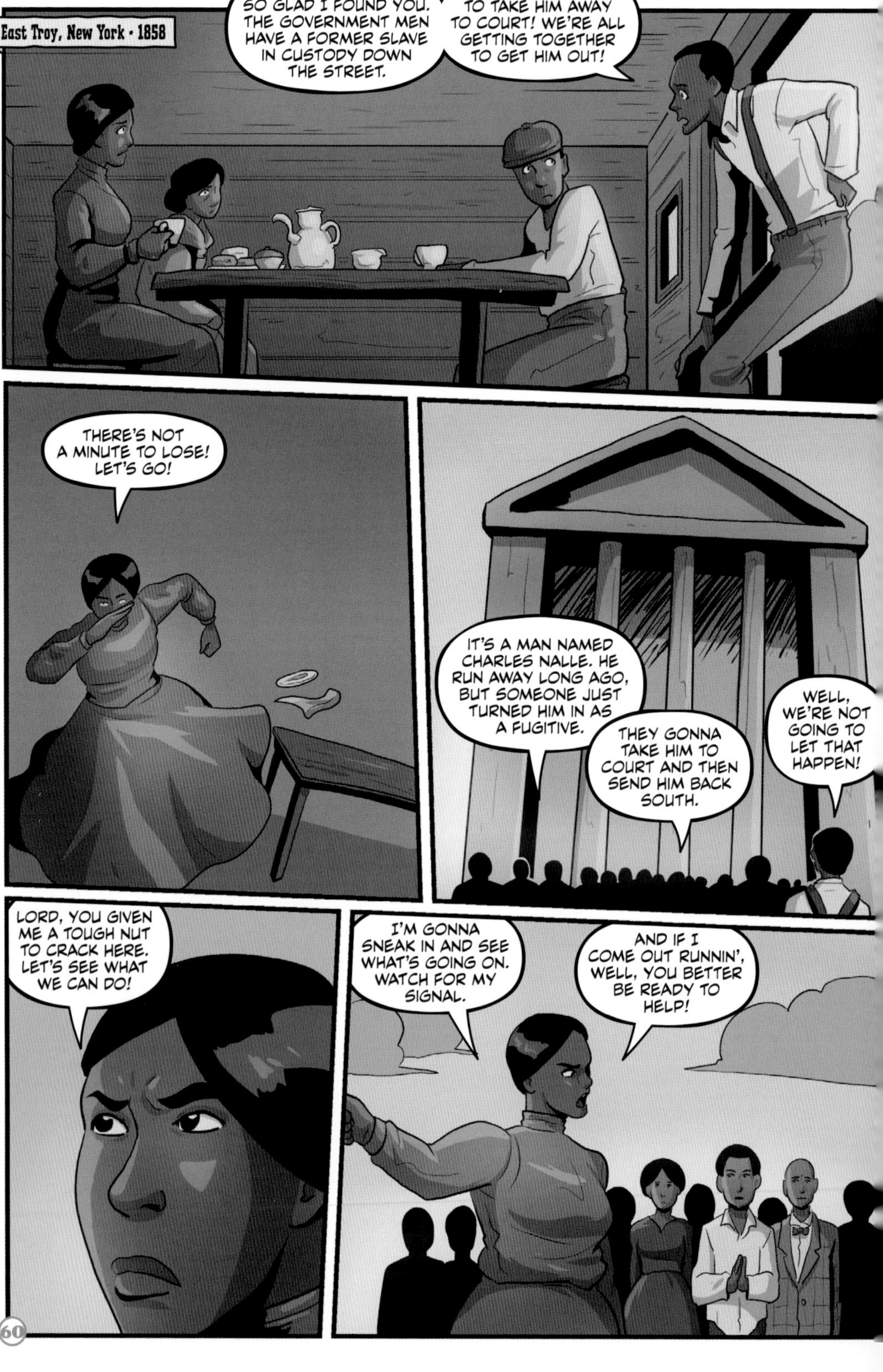
East Troy, New York • 1858
MRS. TUBMAN, I'M SO GLAD I FOUND YOU. THE GOVERNMENT MEN HAVE A FORMER SLAVE IN CUSTODY DOWN THE STREET.
THEY'RE ABOUT TO TAKE HIM AWAY TO COURT! WE'RE ALL GETTING TOGETHER TO GET HIM OUT!
THERE'S NOT A MINUTE TO LOSE! LET'S GO!
IT'S A MAN NAMED CHARLES NALLE. HE RUN AWAY LONG AGO, BUT SOMEONE JUST TURNED HIM IN AS A FUGITIVE.
THEY GONNA TAKE HIM TO COURT AND THEN SEND HIM BACK SOUTH.
WELL, WE'RE NOT GOING TO LET THAT HAPPEN!
LORD, YOU GIVEN ME A TOUGH NUT TO CRACK HERE. LET'S SEE WHAT WE CAN DO!
I'M GONNA SNEAK IN AND SEE WHAT'S GOING ON. WATCH FOR MY SIGNAL.
AND IF I COME OUT RUNNIN', WELL, YOU BETTER BE READY TO HELP!

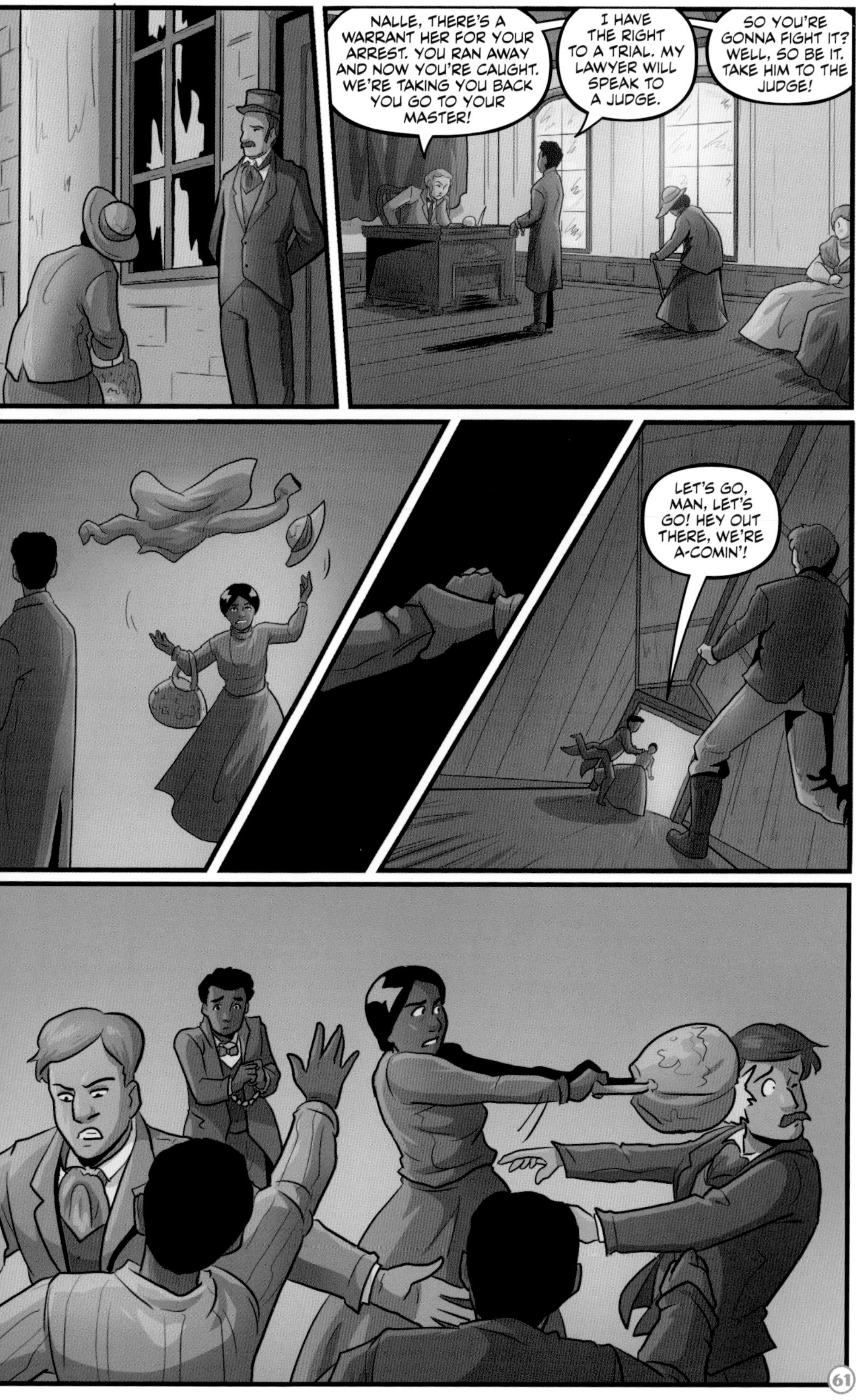
NALLE, THERE'S A WARRANT HER FOR YOUR ARREST. YOU RAN AWAY AND NOW YOU'RE CAUGHT. WE'RE TAKING YOU BACK YOU GO TO YOUR MASTER!
I HAVE THE RIGHT TO A TRIAL. MY LAWYER WILL SPEAK TO A JUDGE.
SO YOU'RE GONNA FIGHT IT? WELL, SO BE IT. TAKE HIM TO THE JUDGE!
LET'S GO, MAN, LET'S GO! HEY OUT THERE, WE'RE A-COMIN'!

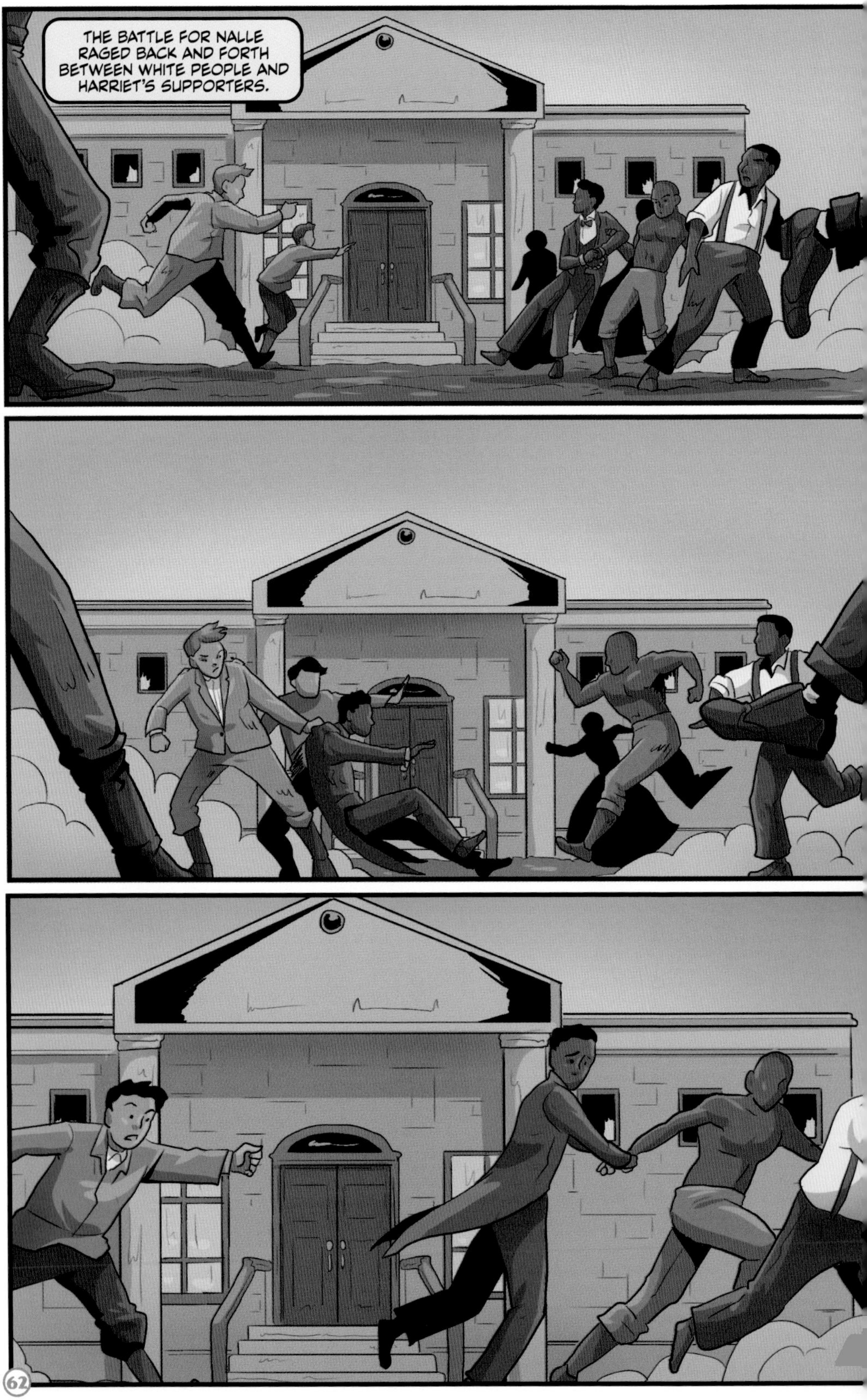
THE BATTLE FOR NALLE RAGED BACK AND FORTH BETWEEN WHITE PEOPLE AND HARRIET'S SUPPORTERS.

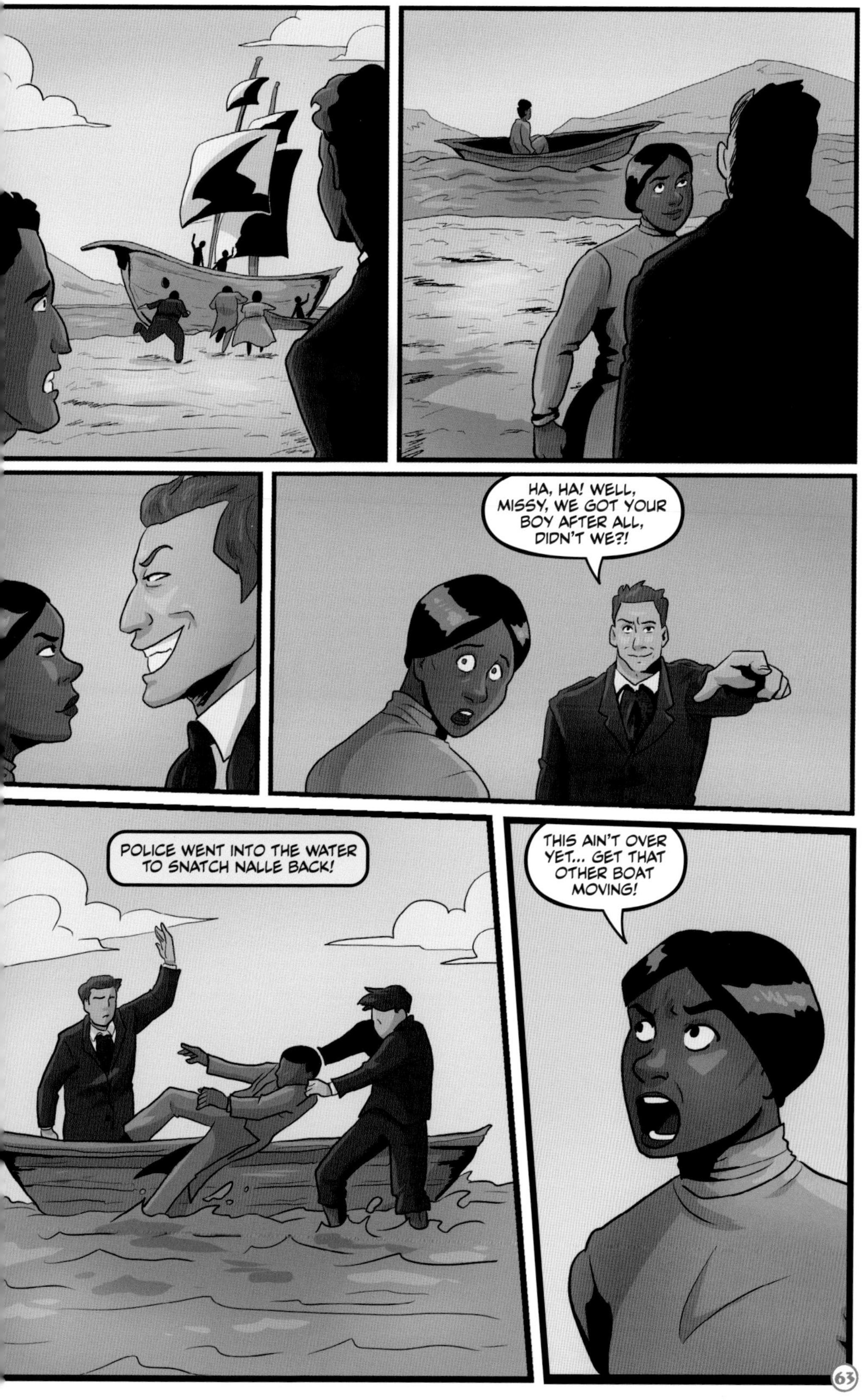
HA, HA! WELL, MISSY, WE GOT YOUR BOY AFTER ALL, DIDN'T WE?!
POLICE WENT INTO THE WATER TO SNATCH NALLE BACK!
THIS AIN'T OVER YET... GET THAT OTHER BOAT MOVING!

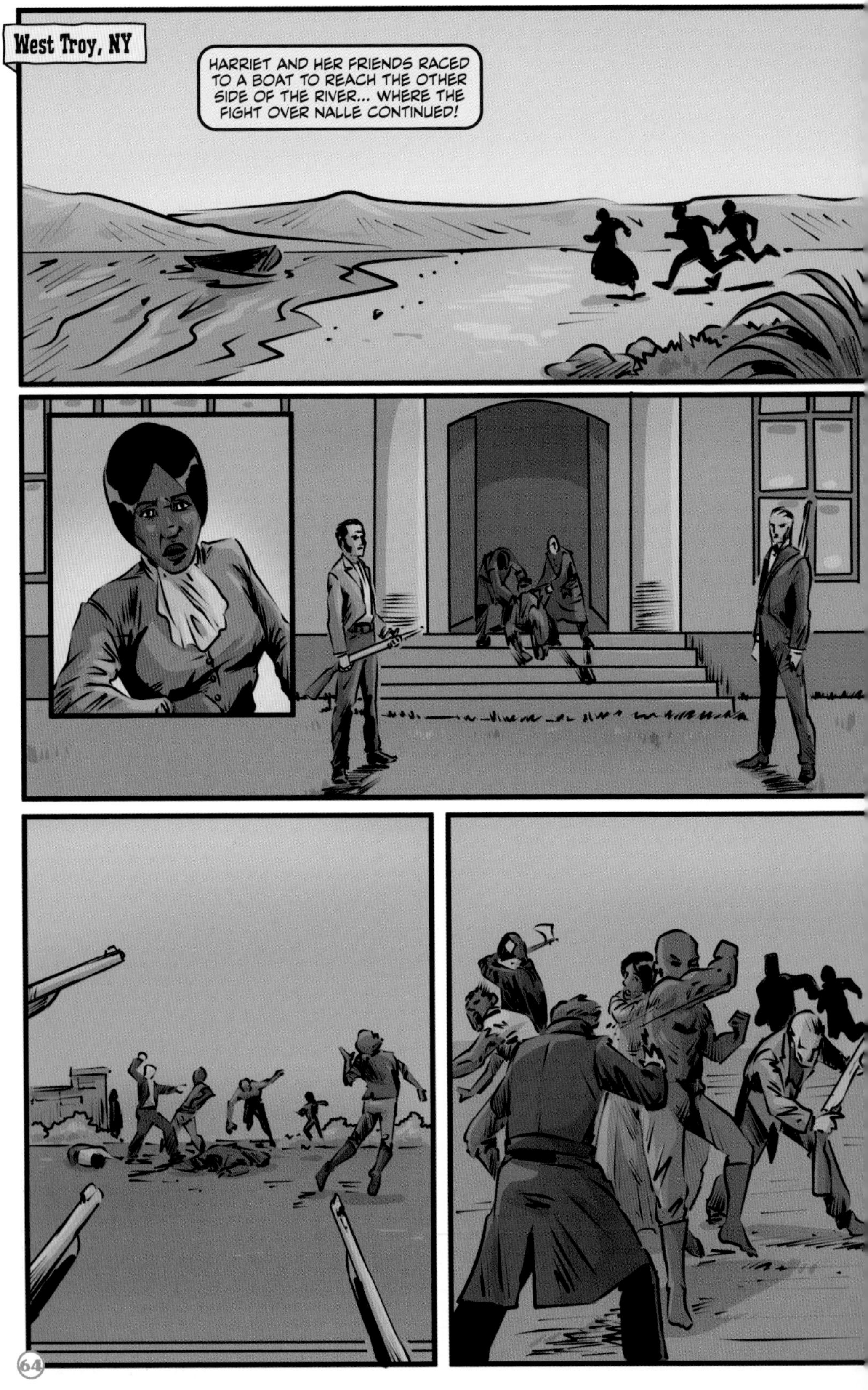
West Troy, NY
HARRIET AND HER FRIENDS RACED TO A BOAT TO REACH THE OTHER SIDE OF THE RIVER... WHERE THE FIGHT OVER NALLE CONTINUED!

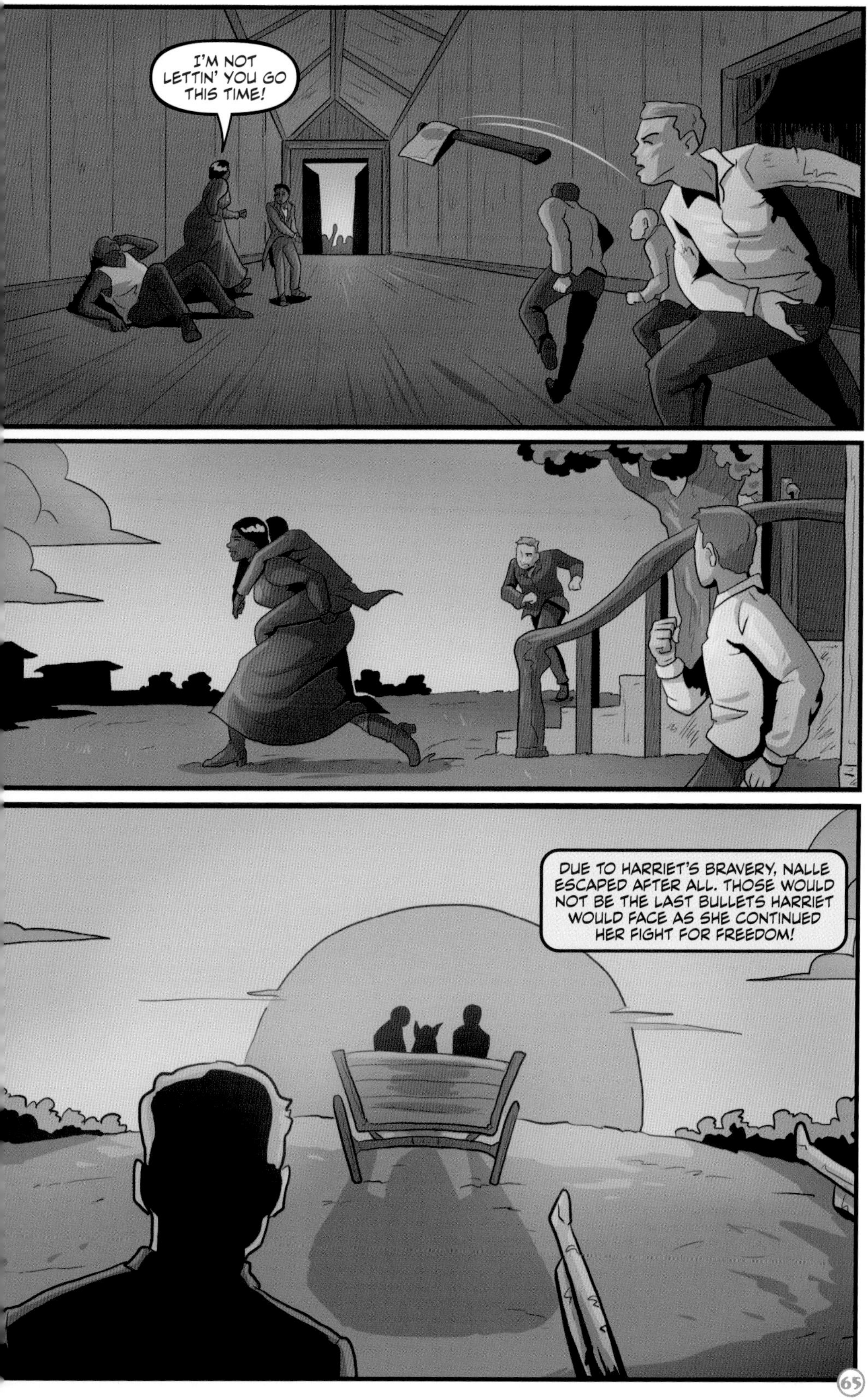
I'M NOT LETTIN' YOU GO THIS TIME!
DUE TO HARRIET'S BRAVERY, NALLE ESCAPED AFTER ALL. THOSE WOULD NOT BE THE LAST BULLETS HARRIET WOULD FACE AS SHE CONTINUED HER FIGHT FOR FREEDOM!

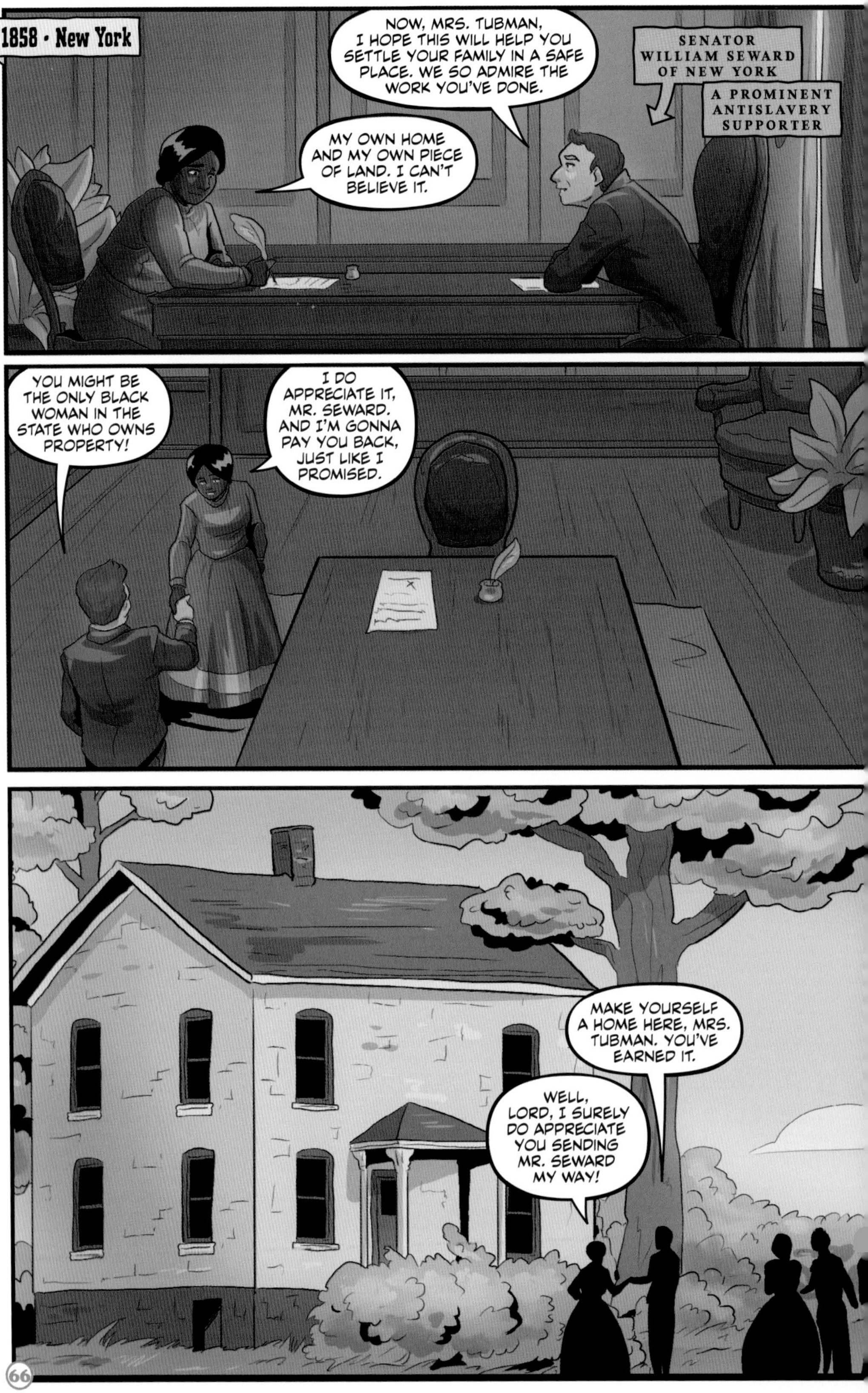
1858 • New York
NOW, MRS. TUBMAN, I HOPE THIS WILL HELP YOU SETTLE YOUR FAMILY IN A SAFE PLACE. WE SO ADMIRE THE WORK YOU'VE DONE.
SENATOR WILLIAM SEWARD OF NEW YORK
A PROMINENT ANTISLAVERY SUPPORTER
MY OWN HOME AND MY OWN PIECE OF LAND. I CAN'T BELIEVE IT.
YOU MIGHT BE THE ONLY BLACK WOMAN IN THE STATE WHO OWNS PROPERTY!
I DO APPRECIATE IT, MR. SEWARD. AND I'M GONNA PAY YOU BACK, JUST LIKE I PROMISED.
MAKE YOURSELF A HOME HERE, MRS. TUBMAN. YOU'VE EARNED IT.
WELL, LORD, I SURELY DO APPRECIATE YOU SENDING MR. SEWARD MY WAY!

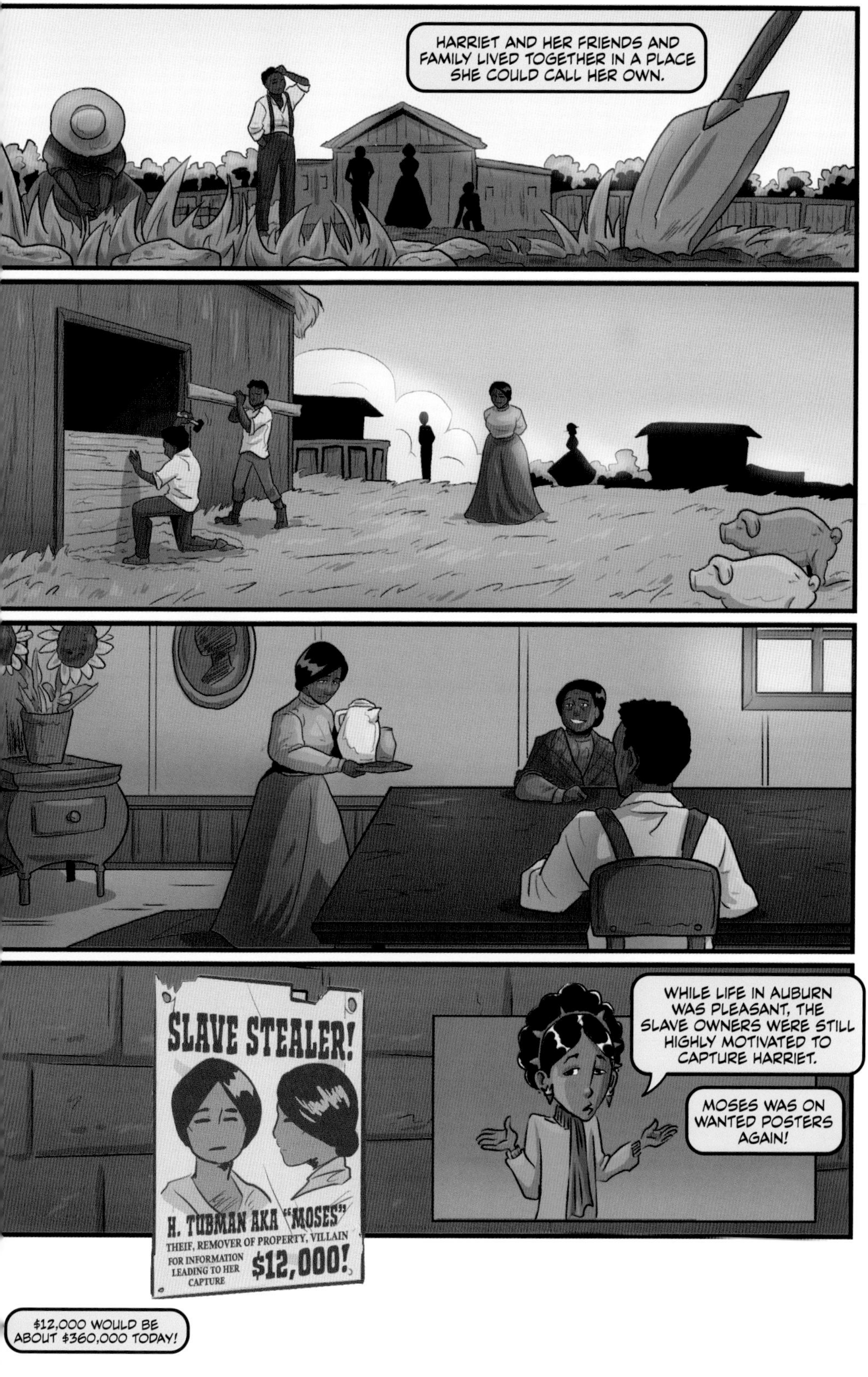
HARRIET AND HER FRIENDS AND FAMILY LIVED TOGETHER IN A PLACE SHE COULD CALL HER OWN.
SLAVE STEALER!
H. TUBMAN AKA "MOSES"
THEIF, REMOVER OF PROPERTY, VILLAIN
FOR INFORMATION LEADING TO HER CAPTURE
$12,000!
WHILE LIFE IN AUBURN WAS PLEASANT, THE SLAVE OWNERS WERE STILL HIGHLY MOTIVATED TO CAPTURE HARRIET.
MOSES WAS ON WANTED POSTERS AGAIN!
$12,000 WOULD BE ABOUT $360,000 TODAY!

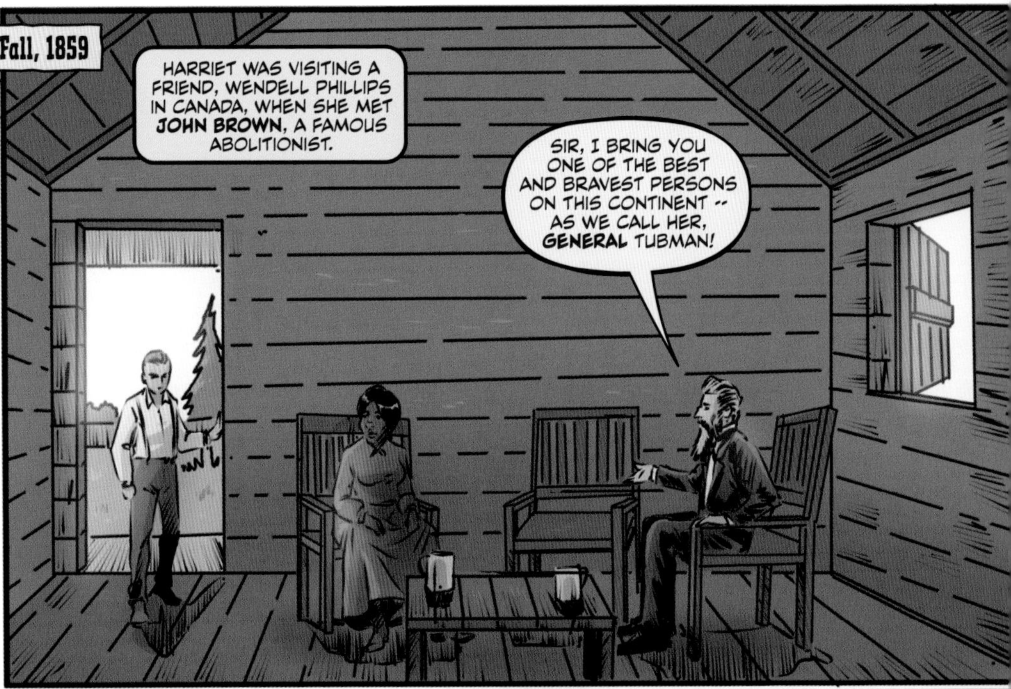
Fall, 1859
HARRIET WAS VISITING A FRIEND, WENDELL PHILLIPS IN CANADA, WHEN SHE MET **JOHN BROWN**, A FAMOUS ABOLITIONIST.
SIR, I BRING YOU ONE OF THE BEST AND BRAVEST PERSONS ON THIS CONTINENT -- AS WE CALL HER, **GENERAL** TUBMAN!

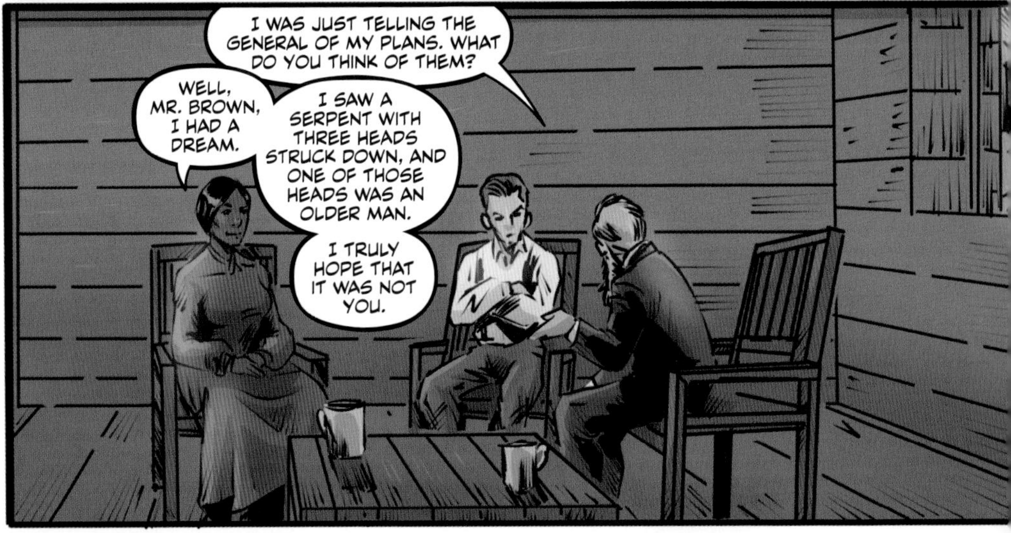
I WAS JUST TELLING THE GENERAL OF MY PLANS. WHAT DO YOU THINK OF THEM?
WELL, MR. BROWN, I HAD A DREAM.
I SAW A SERPENT WITH THREE HEADS STRUCK DOWN, AND ONE OF THOSE HEADS WAS AN OLDER MAN.
I TRULY HOPE THAT IT WAS NOT YOU.

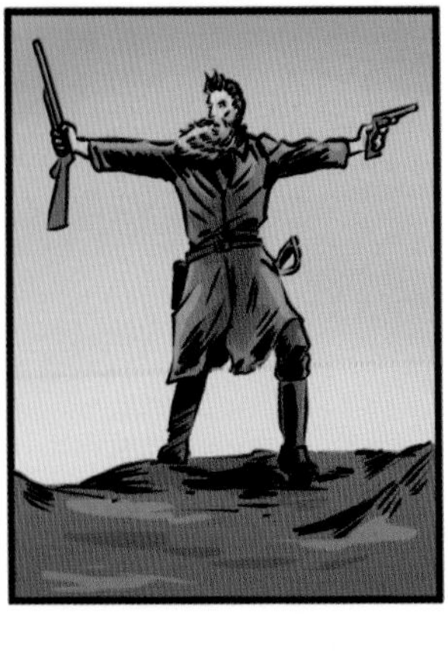

* * * ABOLITION ALL-STAR * * *

JOHN BROWN

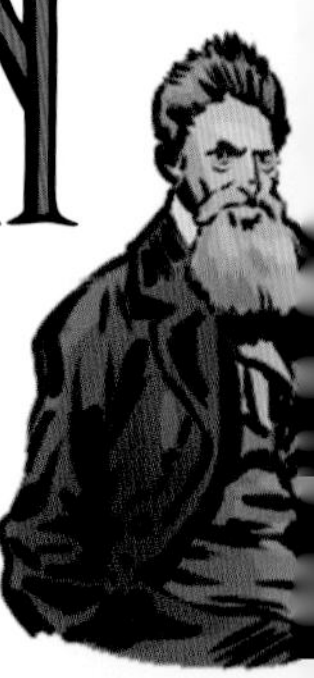

RADICAL ABOLITIONIST

- *Former soldier turned intense abolitionist*
- *Believed slavery could only be ended through violent means*
- *Attacked slave owners in Kansas*
- *Recruited group for government storehouse takedown*

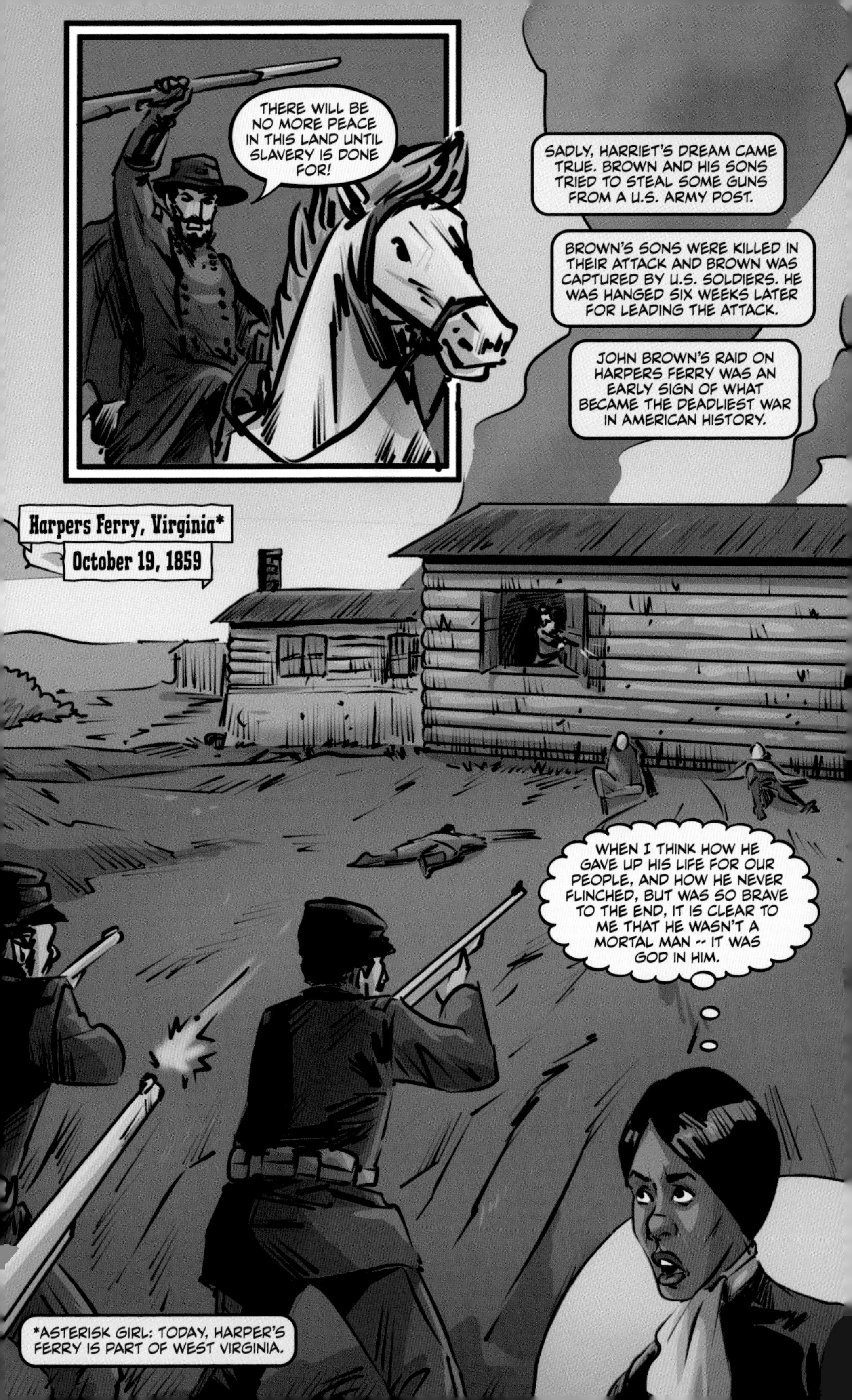
THERE WILL BE NO MORE PEACE IN THIS LAND UNTIL SLAVERY IS DONE FOR!
SADLY, HARRIET'S DREAM CAME TRUE. BROWN AND HIS SONS TRIED TO STEAL SOME GUNS FROM A U.S. ARMY POST.
BROWN'S SONS WERE KILLED IN THEIR ATTACK AND BROWN WAS CAPTURED BY U.S. SOLDIERS. HE WAS HANGED SIX WEEKS LATER FOR LEADING THE ATTACK.
JOHN BROWN'S RAID ON HARPERS FERRY WAS AN EARLY SIGN OF WHAT BECAME THE DEADLIEST WAR IN AMERICAN HISTORY.
Harpers Ferry, Virginia*
October 19, 1859
WHEN I THINK HOW HE GAVE UP HIS LIFE FOR OUR PEOPLE, AND HOW HE NEVER FLINCHED, BUT WAS SO BRAVE TO THE END, IT IS CLEAR TO ME THAT HE WASN'T A MORTAL MAN -- IT WAS GOD IN HIM.
*ASTERISK GIRL: TODAY, HARPER'S FERRY IS PART OF WEST VIRGINIA.

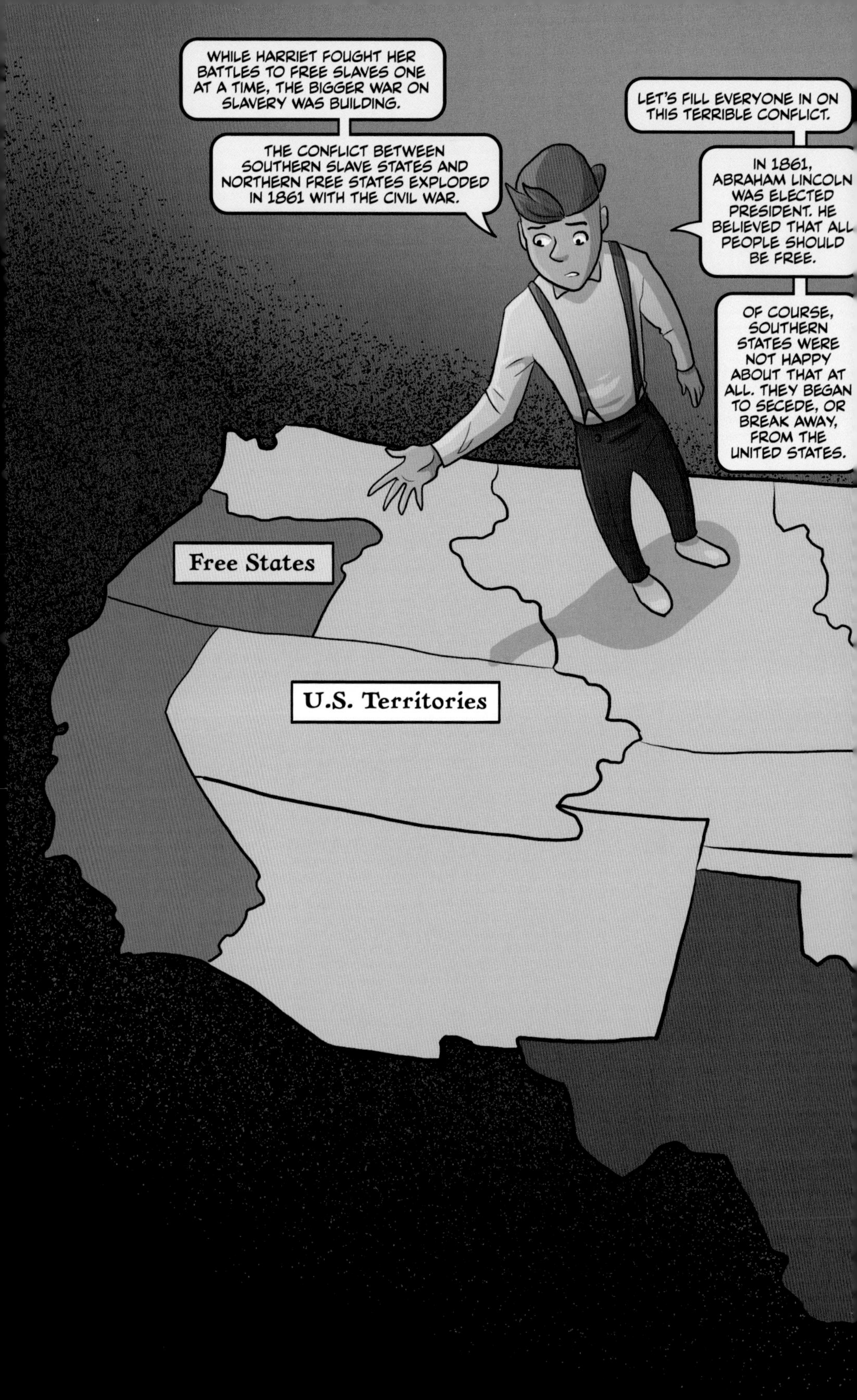
WHILE HARRIET FOUGHT HER BATTLES TO FREE SLAVES ONE AT A TIME, THE BIGGER WAR ON SLAVERY WAS BUILDING.
THE CONFLICT BETWEEN SOUTHERN SLAVE STATES AND NORTHERN FREE STATES EXPLODED IN 1861 WITH THE CIVIL WAR.
LET'S FILL EVERYONE IN ON THIS TERRIBLE CONFLICT.
IN 1861, ABRAHAM LINCOLN WAS ELECTED PRESIDENT. HE BELIEVED THAT ALL PEOPLE SHOULD BE FREE.
OF COURSE, SOUTHERN STATES WERE NOT HAPPY ABOUT THAT AT ALL. THEY BEGAN TO SECEDE, OR BREAK AWAY, FROM THE UNITED STATES.
Free States
U.S. Territories

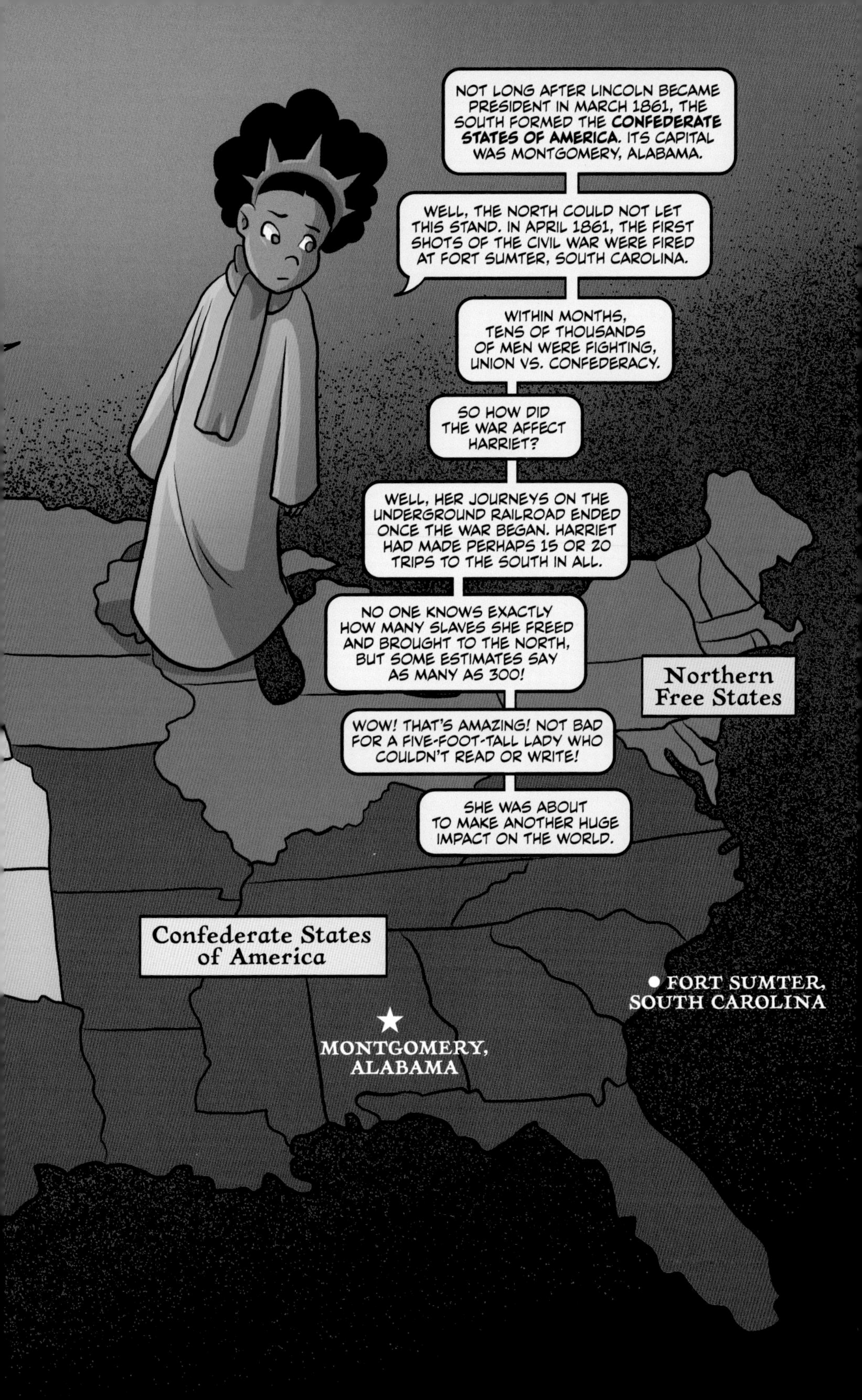
NOT LONG AFTER LINCOLN BECAME PRESIDENT IN MARCH 1861, THE SOUTH FORMED THE **CONFEDERATE STATES OF AMERICA**. ITS CAPITAL WAS MONTGOMERY, ALABAMA.
WELL, THE NORTH COULD NOT LET THIS STAND. IN APRIL 1861, THE FIRST SHOTS OF THE CIVIL WAR WERE FIRED AT FORT SUMTER, SOUTH CAROLINA.
WITHIN MONTHS, TENS OF THOUSANDS OF MEN WERE FIGHTING, UNION VS. CONFEDERACY.
SO HOW DID THE WAR AFFECT HARRIET?
WELL, HER JOURNEYS ON THE UNDERGROUND RAILROAD ENDED ONCE THE WAR BEGAN. HARRIET HAD MADE PERHAPS 15 OR 20 TRIPS TO THE SOUTH IN ALL.
NO ONE KNOWS EXACTLY HOW MANY SLAVES SHE FREED AND BROUGHT TO THE NORTH, BUT SOME ESTIMATES SAY AS MANY AS 300!
WOW! THAT'S AMAZING! NOT BAD FOR A FIVE-FOOT-TALL LADY WHO COULDN'T READ OR WRITE!
SHE WAS ABOUT TO MAKE ANOTHER HUGE IMPACT ON THE WORLD.
Northern Free States
Confederate States of America
FORT SUMTER, SOUTH CAROLINA
MONTGOMERY, ALABAMA

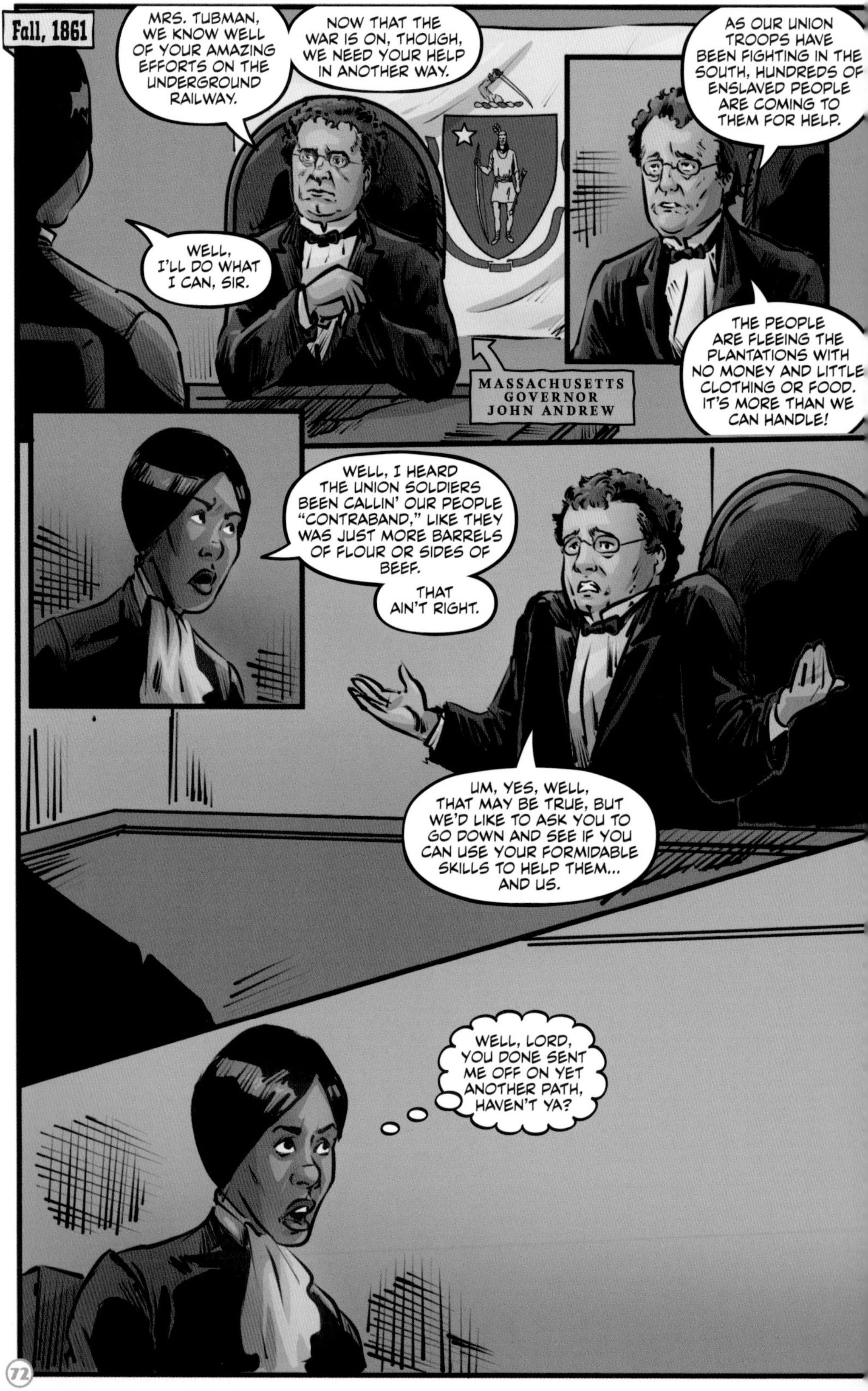
Fall, 1861
MRS. TUBMAN, WE KNOW WELL OF YOUR AMAZING EFFORTS ON THE UNDERGROUND RAILWAY.
NOW THAT THE WAR IS ON, THOUGH, WE NEED YOUR HELP IN ANOTHER WAY.
WELL, I'LL DO WHAT I CAN, SIR.
MASSACHUSETTS GOVERNOR JOHN ANDREW
AS OUR UNION TROOPS HAVE BEEN FIGHTING IN THE SOUTH, HUNDREDS OF ENSLAVED PEOPLE ARE COMING TO THEM FOR HELP.
THE PEOPLE ARE FLEEING THE PLANTATIONS WITH NO MONEY AND LITTLE CLOTHING OR FOOD. IT'S MORE THAN WE CAN HANDLE!
WELL, I HEARD THE UNION SOLDIERS BEEN CALLIN' OUR PEOPLE "CONTRABAND," LIKE THEY WAS JUST MORE BARRELS OF FLOUR OR SIDES OF BEEF.
THAT AIN'T RIGHT.
UM, YES, WELL, THAT MAY BE TRUE, BUT WE'D LIKE TO ASK YOU TO GO DOWN AND SEE IF YOU CAN USE YOUR FORMIDABLE SKILLS TO HELP THEM... AND US.
WELL, LORD, YOU DONE SENT ME OFF ON YET ANOTHER PATH, HAVEN'T YA?

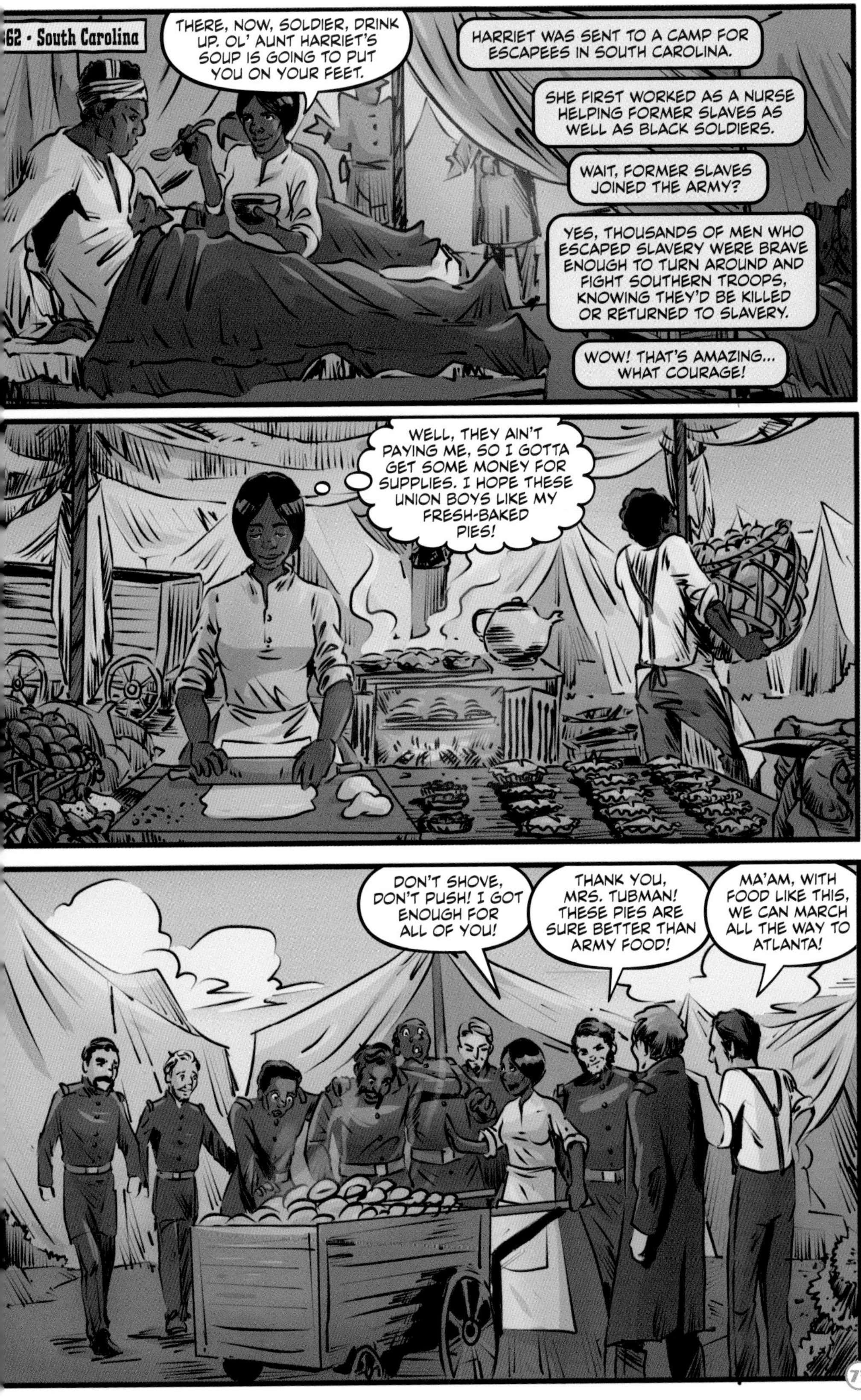
62 - South Carolina
THERE, NOW, SOLDIER, DRINK UP. OL' AUNT HARRIET'S SOUP IS GOING TO PUT YOU ON YOUR FEET.
HARRIET WAS SENT TO A CAMP FOR ESCAPEES IN SOUTH CAROLINA.
SHE FIRST WORKED AS A NURSE HELPING FORMER SLAVES AS WELL AS BLACK SOLDIERS.
WAIT, FORMER SLAVES JOINED THE ARMY?
YES, THOUSANDS OF MEN WHO ESCAPED SLAVERY WERE BRAVE ENOUGH TO TURN AROUND AND FIGHT SOUTHERN TROOPS, KNOWING THEY'D BE KILLED OR RETURNED TO SLAVERY.
WOW! THAT'S AMAZING... WHAT COURAGE!
WELL, THEY AIN'T PAYING ME, SO I GOTTA GET SOME MONEY FOR SUPPLIES. I HOPE THESE UNION BOYS LIKE MY FRESH-BAKED PIES!
DON'T SHOVE, DON'T PUSH! I GOT ENOUGH FOR ALL OF YOU!
THANK YOU, MRS. TUBMAN! THESE PIES ARE SURE BETTER THAN ARMY FOOD!
MA'AM, WITH FOOD LIKE THIS, WE CAN MARCH ALL THE WAY TO ATLANTA!

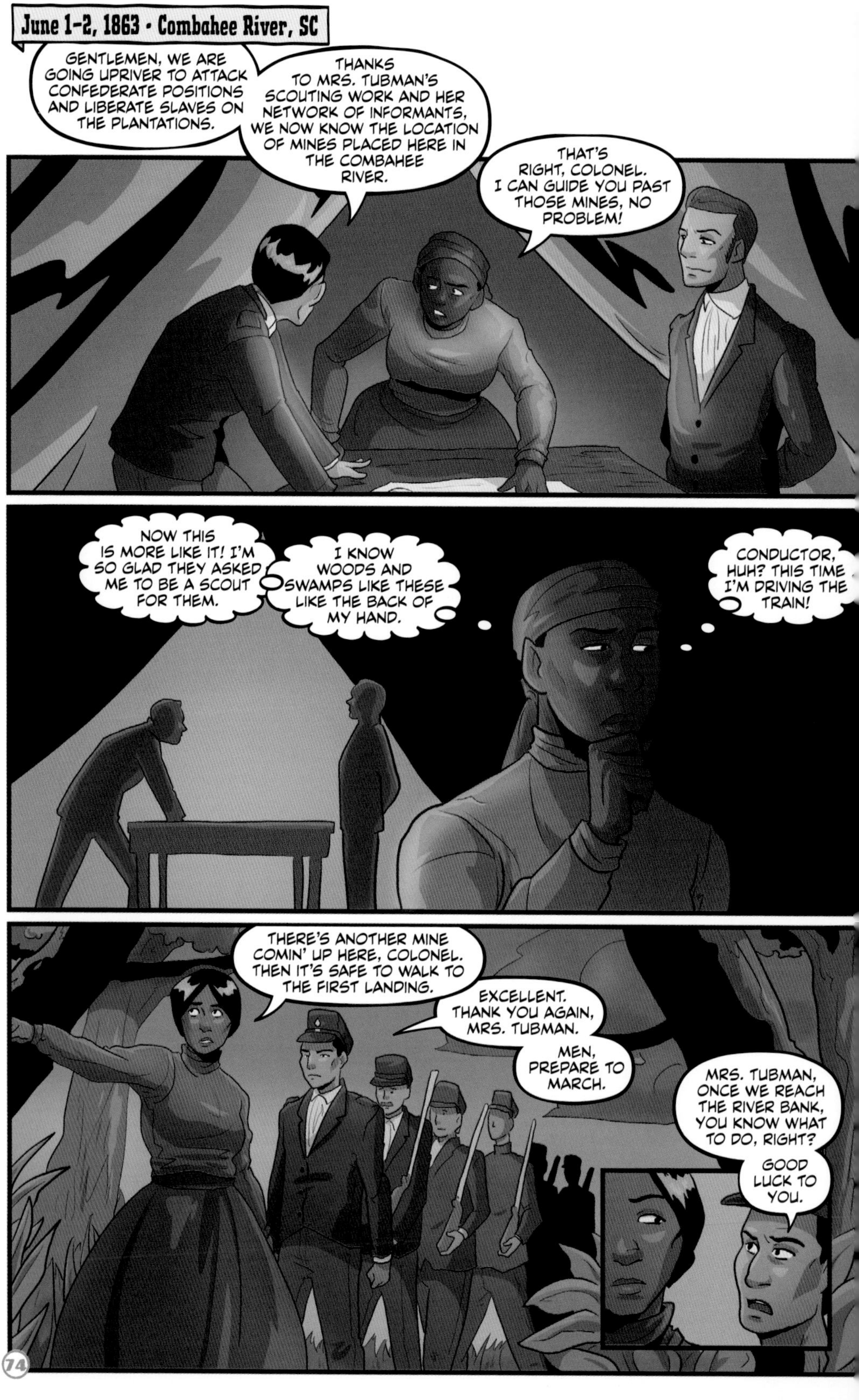
June 1-2, 1863 • Combahee River, SC
GENTLEMEN, WE ARE GOING UPRIVER TO ATTACK CONFEDERATE POSITIONS AND LIBERATE SLAVES ON THE PLANTATIONS.
THANKS TO MRS. TUBMAN'S SCOUTING WORK AND HER NETWORK OF INFORMANTS, WE NOW KNOW THE LOCATION OF MINES PLACED HERE IN THE COMBAHEE RIVER.
THAT'S RIGHT, COLONEL. I CAN GUIDE YOU PAST THOSE MINES, NO PROBLEM!
NOW THIS IS MORE LIKE IT! I'M SO GLAD THEY ASKED ME TO BE A SCOUT FOR THEM.
I KNOW WOODS AND SWAMPS LIKE THESE LIKE THE BACK OF MY HAND.
CONDUCTOR, HUH? THIS TIME I'M DRIVING THE TRAIN!
THERE'S ANOTHER MINE COMIN' UP HERE, COLONEL. THEN IT'S SAFE TO WALK TO THE FIRST LANDING.
EXCELLENT. THANK YOU AGAIN, MRS. TUBMAN.
MEN, PREPARE TO MARCH.
MRS. TUBMAN, ONCE WE REACH THE RIVER BANK, YOU KNOW WHAT TO DO, RIGHT?
GOOD LUCK TO YOU.

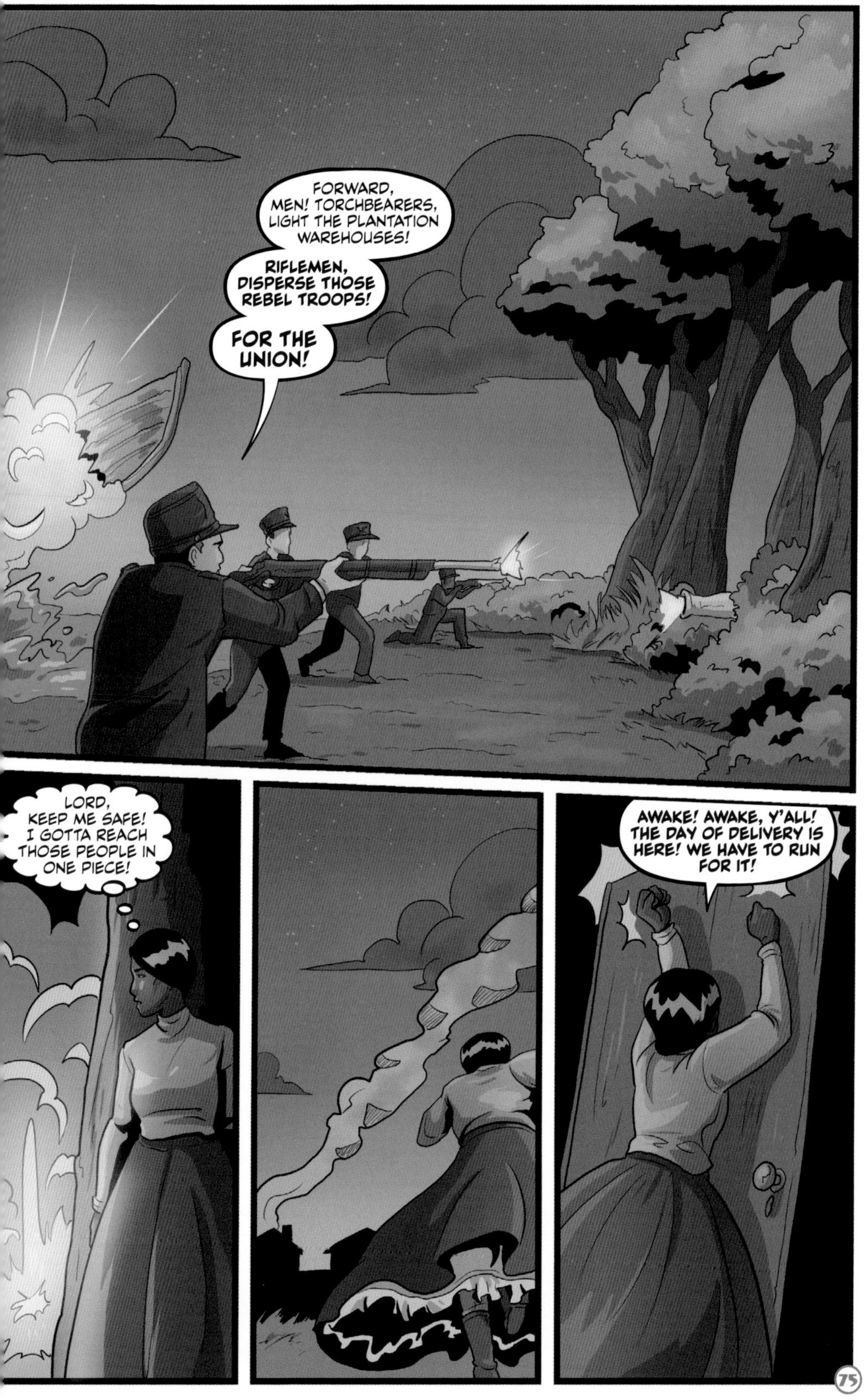
FORWARD, MEN! TORCHBEARERS, LIGHT THE PLANTATION WAREHOUSES!
RIFLEMEN, DISPERSE THOSE REBEL TROOPS!
FOR THE UNION!
LORD, KEEP ME SAFE! I GOTTA REACH THOSE PEOPLE IN ONE PIECE!
AWAKE! AWAKE, Y'ALL! THE DAY OF DELIVERY IS HERE! WE HAVE TO RUN FOR IT!

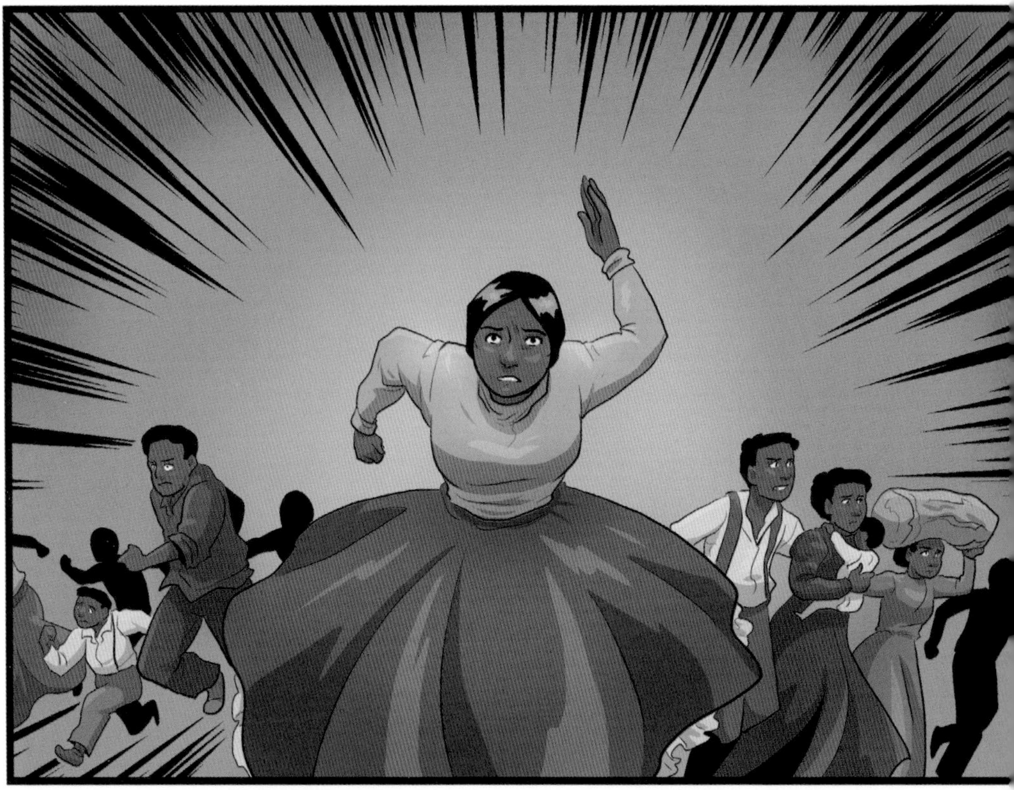

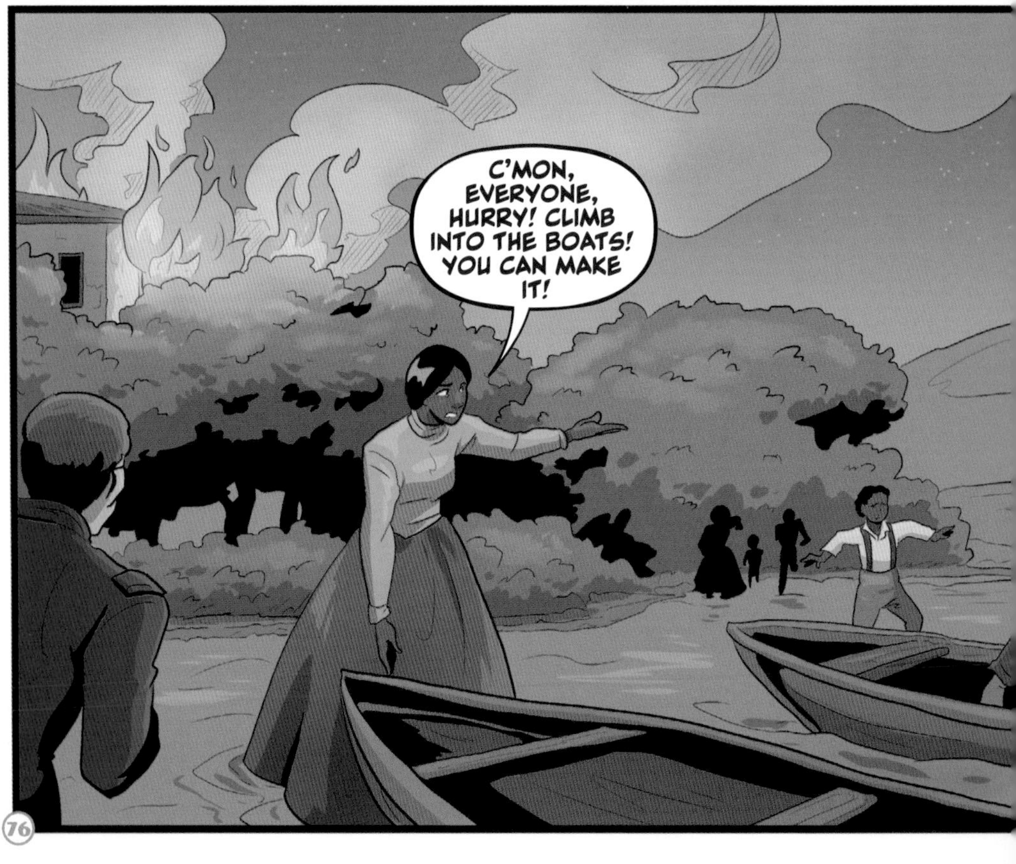
C'MON, EVERYONE, HURRY! CLIMB INTO THE BOATS! YOU CAN MAKE IT!

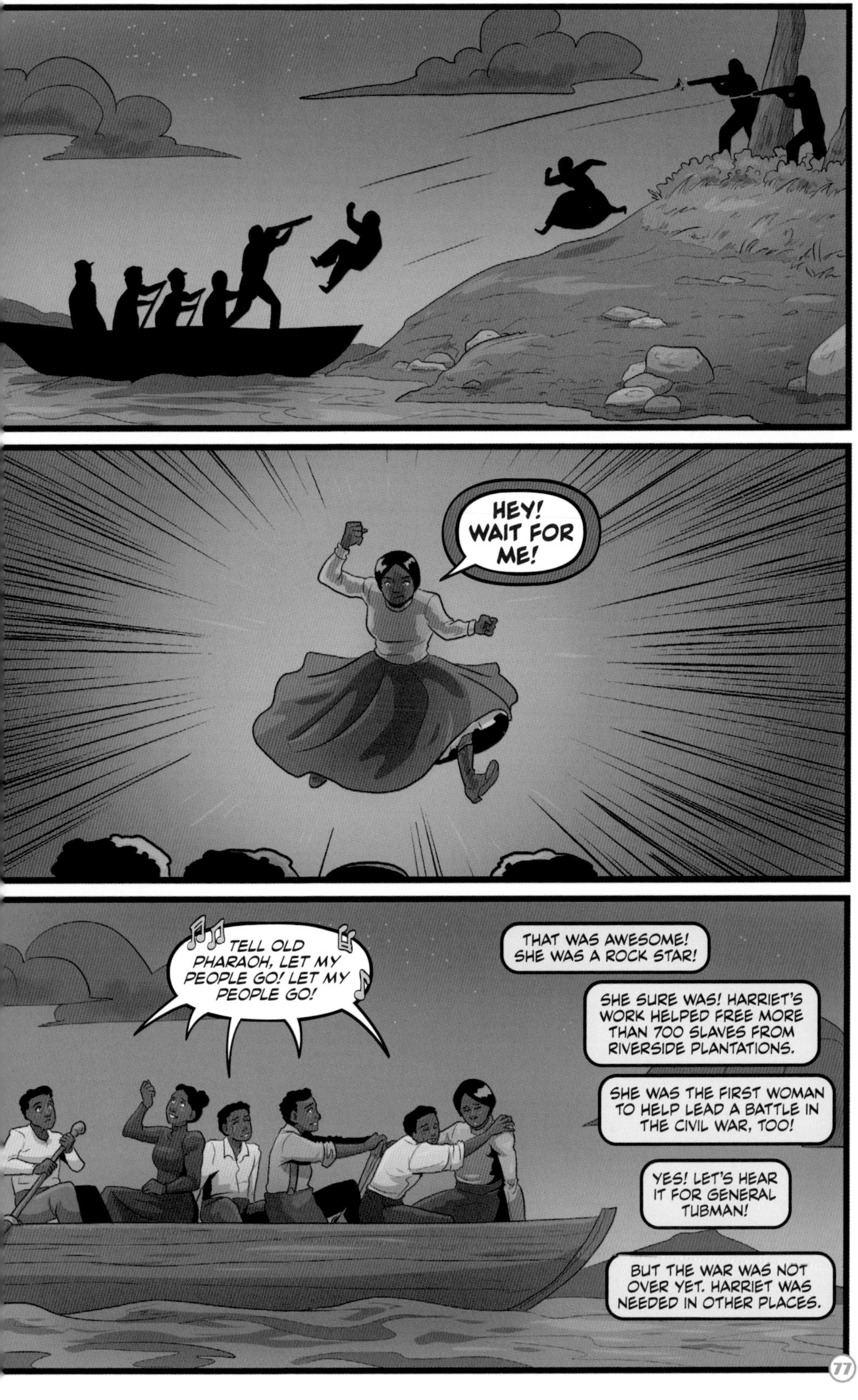
HEY! WAIT FOR ME!
TELL OLD PHARAOH, LET MY PEOPLE GO! LET MY PEOPLE GO!
THAT WAS AWESOME! SHE WAS A ROCK STAR!
SHE SURE WAS! HARRIET'S WORK HELPED FREE MORE THAN 700 SLAVES FROM RIVERSIDE PLANTATIONS.
SHE WAS THE FIRST WOMAN TO HELP LEAD A BATTLE IN THE CIVIL WAR, TOO!
YES! LET'S HEAR IT FOR GENERAL TUBMAN!
BUT THE WAR WAS NOT OVER YET. HARRIET WAS NEEDED IN OTHER PLACES.

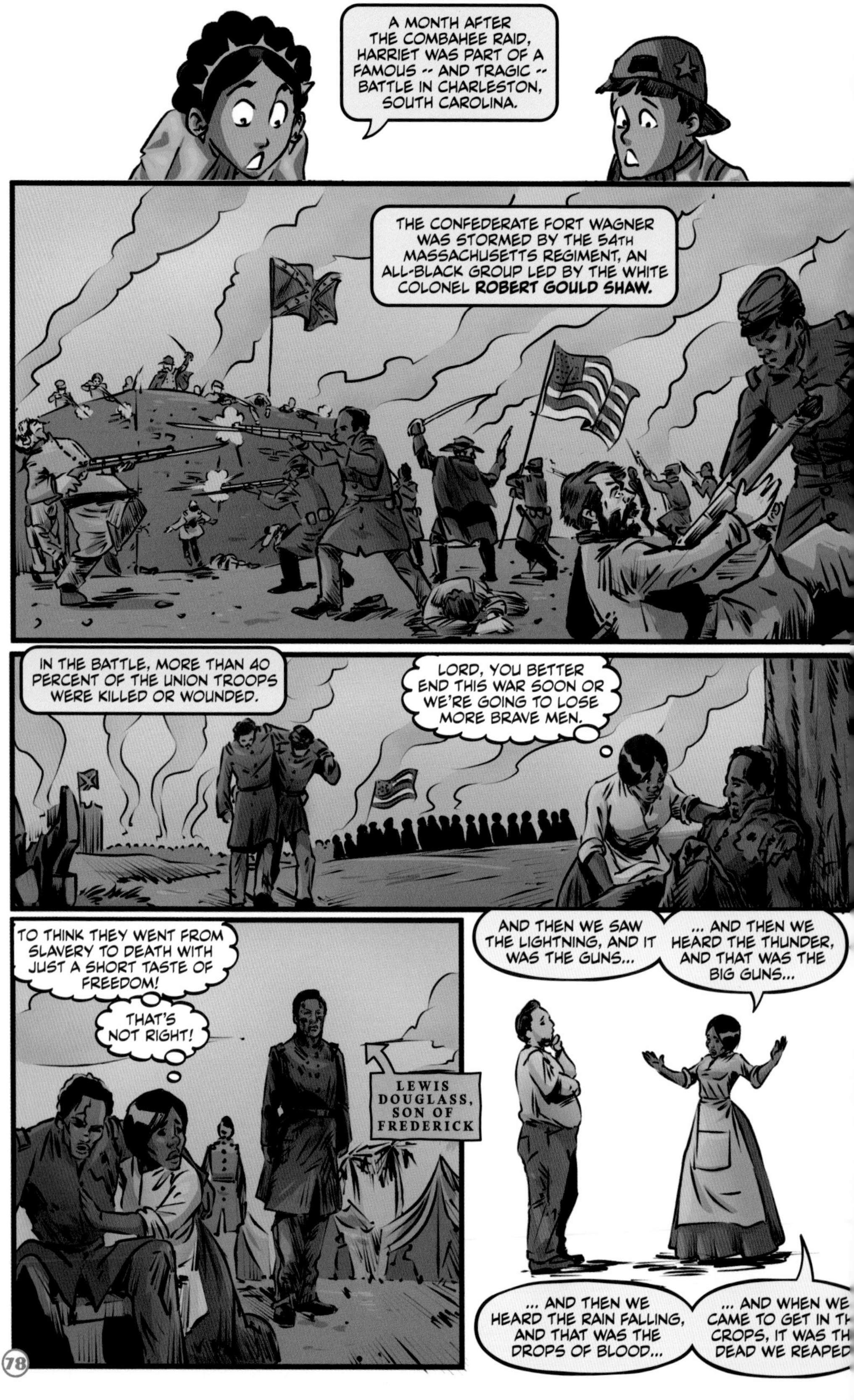

A MONTH AFTER THE COMBAHEE RAID, HARRIET WAS PART OF A FAMOUS -- AND TRAGIC -- BATTLE IN CHARLESTON, SOUTH CAROLINA.
THE CONFEDERATE FORT WAGNER WAS STORMED BY THE 54TH MASSACHUSETTS REGIMENT, AN ALL-BLACK GROUP LED BY THE WHITE COLONEL **ROBERT GOULD SHAW.**
IN THE BATTLE, MORE THAN 40 PERCENT OF THE UNION TROOPS WERE KILLED OR WOUNDED.
LORD, YOU BETTER END THIS WAR SOON OR WE'RE GOING TO LOSE MORE BRAVE MEN.
TO THINK THEY WENT FROM SLAVERY TO DEATH WITH JUST A SHORT TASTE OF FREEDOM!
THAT'S NOT RIGHT!
LEWIS DOUGLASS, SON OF FREDERICK
AND THEN WE SAW THE LIGHTNING, AND IT WAS THE GUNS...
... AND THEN WE HEARD THE THUNDER, AND THAT WAS THE BIG GUNS...
... AND THEN WE HEARD THE RAIN FALLING, AND THAT WAS THE DROPS OF BLOOD...
... AND WHEN WE CAME TO GET IN TH CROPS, IT WAS TH DEAD WE REAPED

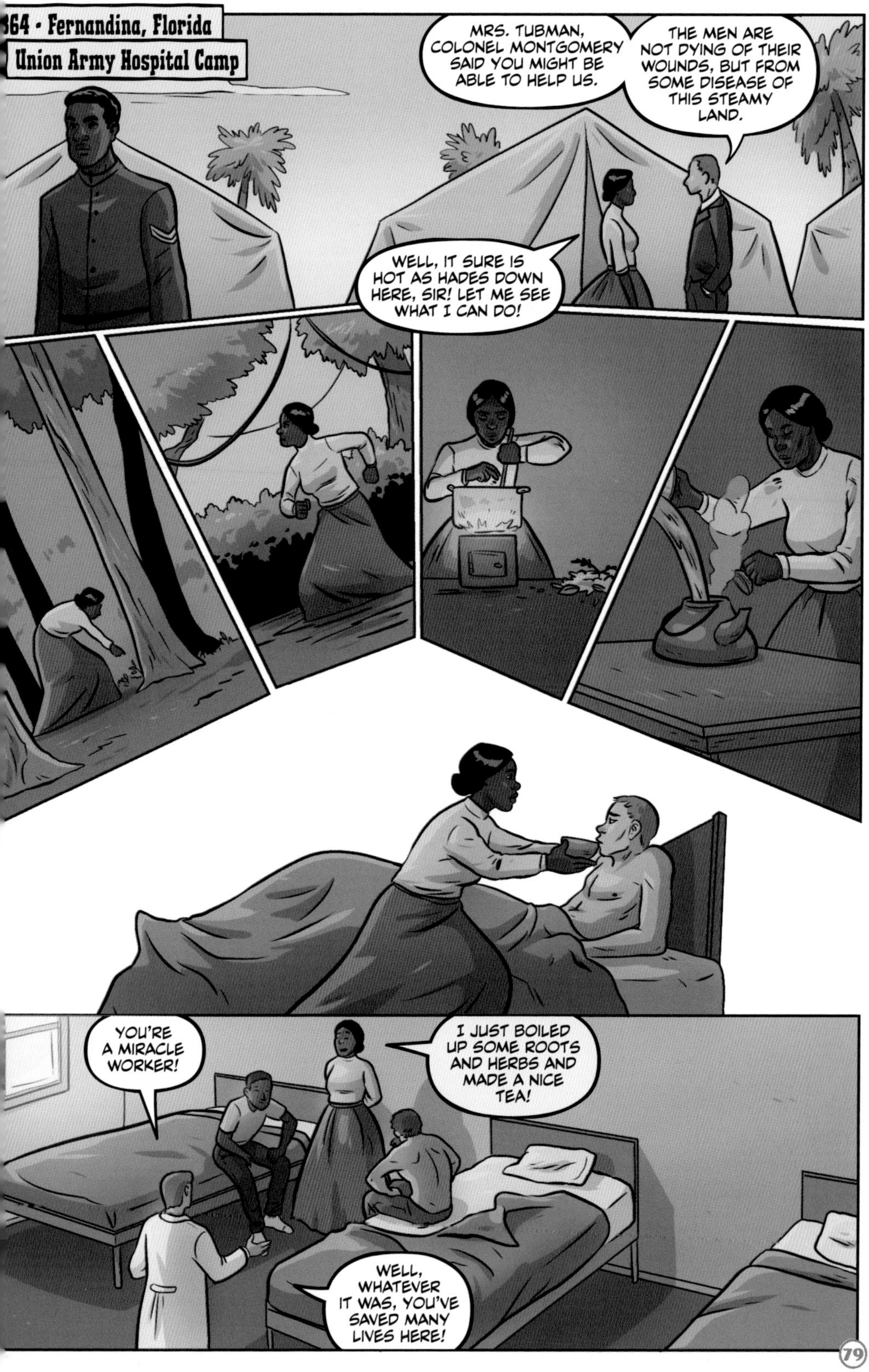
364 • Fernandina, Florida
Union Army Hospital Camp
MRS. TUBMAN, COLONEL MONTGOMERY SAID YOU MIGHT BE ABLE TO HELP US.
THE MEN ARE NOT DYING OF THEIR WOUNDS, BUT FROM SOME DISEASE OF THIS STEAMY LAND.
WELL, IT SURE IS HOT AS HADES DOWN HERE, SIR! LET ME SEE WHAT I CAN DO!
YOU'RE A MIRACLE WORKER!
I JUST BOILED UP SOME ROOTS AND HERBS AND MADE A NICE TEA!
WELL, WHATEVER IT WAS, YOU'VE SAVED MANY LIVES HERE!

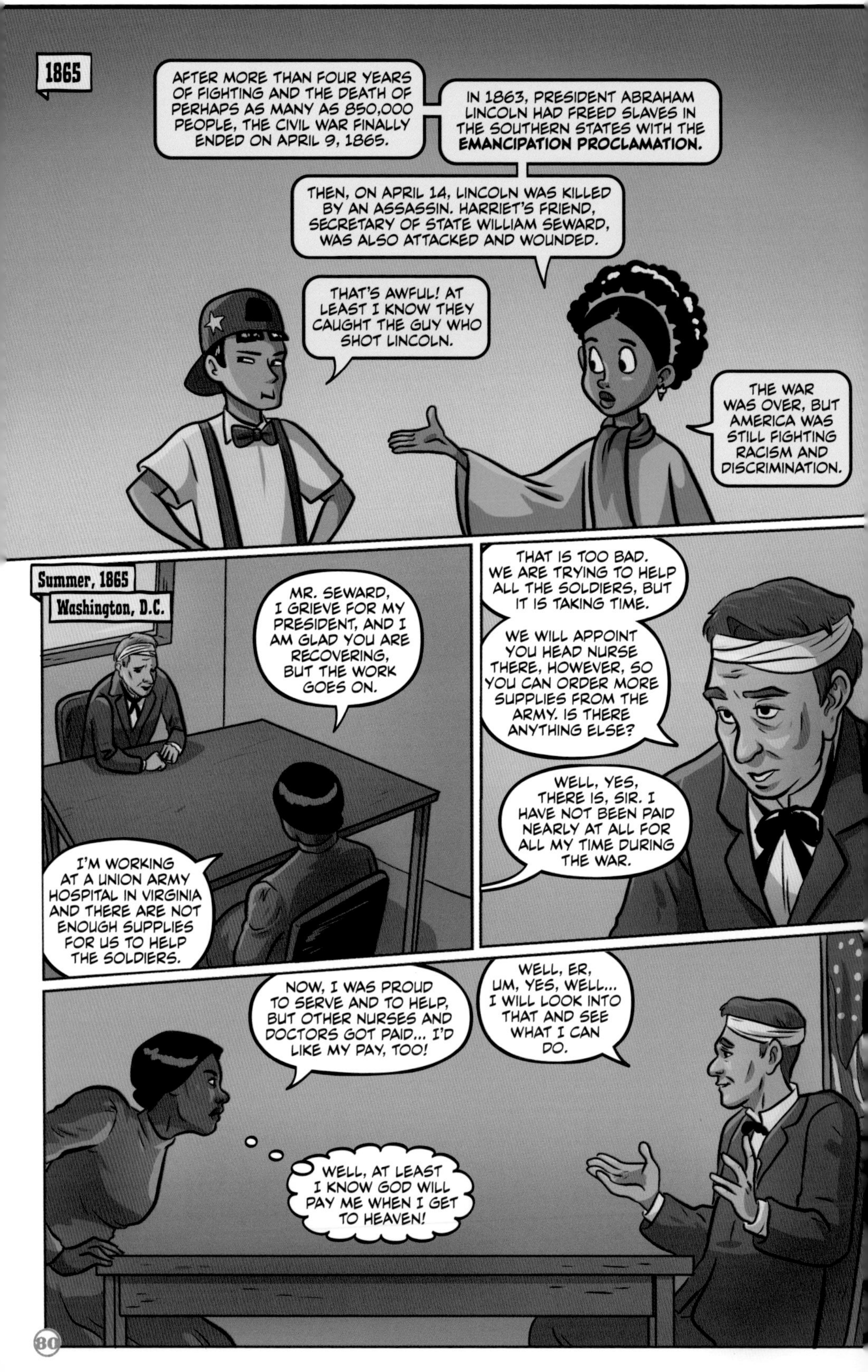

AFTER MORE THAN FOUR YEARS OF FIGHTING AND THE DEATH OF PERHAPS AS MANY AS 850,000 PEOPLE, THE CIVIL WAR FINALLY ENDED ON APRIL 9, 1865.

IN 1863, PRESIDENT ABRAHAM LINCOLN HAD FREED SLAVES IN THE SOUTHERN STATES WITH THE **EMANCIPATION PROCLAMATION.**

THEN, ON APRIL 14, LINCOLN WAS KILLED BY AN ASSASSIN. HARRIET'S FRIEND, SECRETARY OF STATE WILLIAM SEWARD, WAS ALSO ATTACKED AND WOUNDED.

THAT'S AWFUL! AT LEAST I KNOW THEY CAUGHT THE GUY WHO SHOT LINCOLN.

THE WAR WAS OVER, BUT AMERICA WAS STILL FIGHTING RACISM AND DISCRIMINATION.

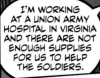
Summer, 1865
Washington, D.C.

MR. SEWARD, I GRIEVE FOR MY PRESIDENT, AND I AM GLAD YOU ARE RECOVERING, BUT THE WORK GOES ON.

THAT IS TOO BAD. WE ARE TRYING TO HELP ALL THE SOLDIERS, BUT IT IS TAKING TIME.

WE WILL APPOINT YOU HEAD NURSE THERE, HOWEVER, SO YOU CAN ORDER MORE SUPPLIES FROM THE ARMY. IS THERE ANYTHING ELSE?

WELL, YES, THERE IS, SIR. I HAVE NOT BEEN PAID NEARLY AT ALL FOR ALL MY TIME DURING THE WAR.

I'M WORKING AT A UNION ARMY HOSPITAL IN VIRGINIA AND THERE ARE NOT ENOUGH SUPPLIES FOR US TO HELP THE SOLDIERS.

NOW, I WAS PROUD TO SERVE AND TO HELP, BUT OTHER NURSES AND DOCTORS GOT PAID... I'D LIKE MY PAY, TOO!

WELL, ER, UM, YES, WELL... I WILL LOOK INTO THAT AND SEE WHAT I CAN DO.

WELL, AT LEAST I KNOW GOD WILL PAY ME WHEN I GET TO HEAVEN!

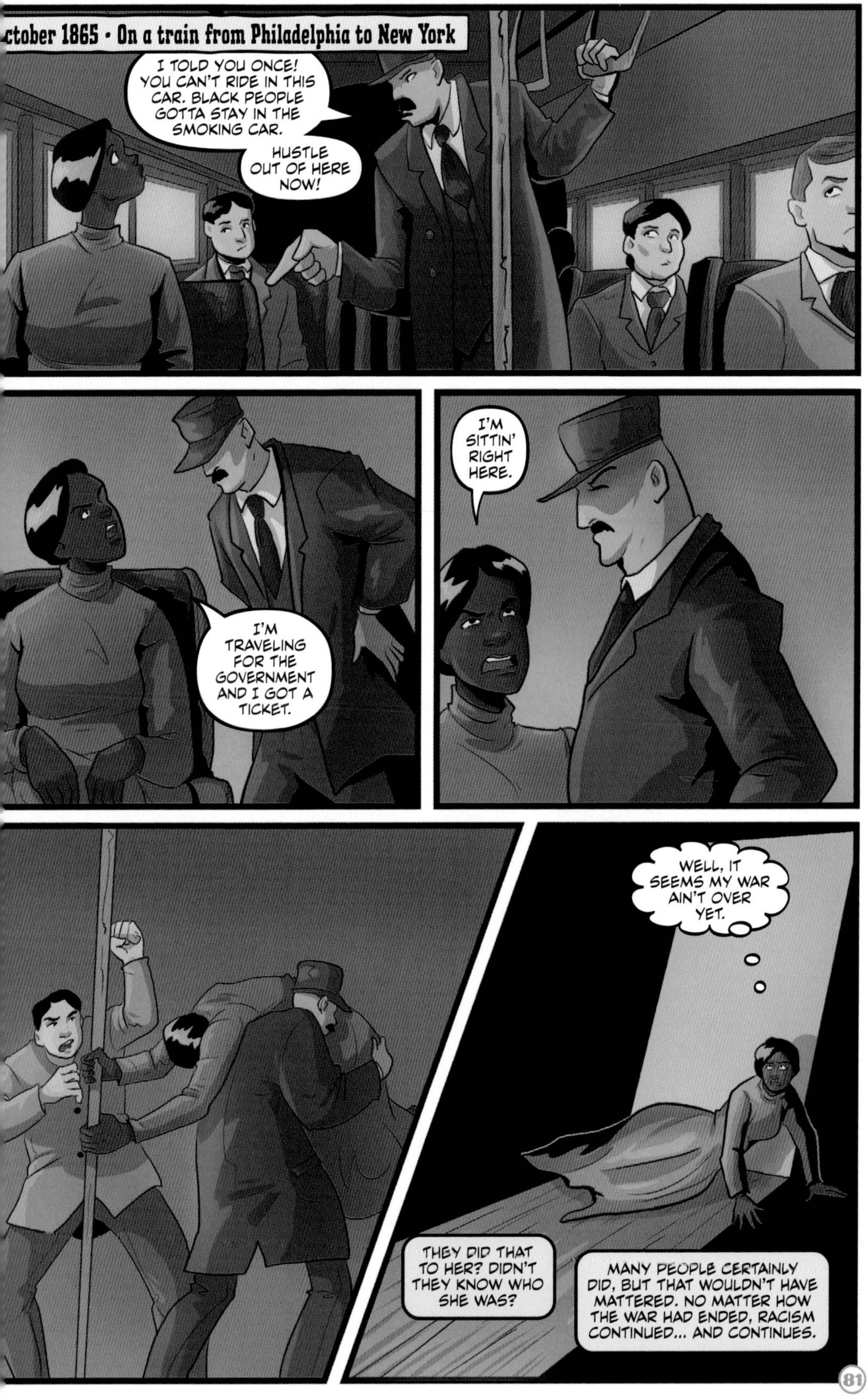
ctober 1865 • On a train from Philadelphia to New York
I TOLD YOU ONCE! YOU CAN'T RIDE IN THIS CAR. BLACK PEOPLE GOTTA STAY IN THE SMOKING CAR.
HUSTLE OUT OF HERE NOW!
I'M TRAVELING FOR THE GOVERNMENT AND I GOT A TICKET.
I'M SITTIN' RIGHT HERE.
WELL, IT SEEMS MY WAR AIN'T OVER YET.
THEY DID THAT TO HER? DIDN'T THEY KNOW WHO SHE WAS?
MANY PEOPLE CERTAINLY DID, BUT THAT WOULDN'T HAVE MATTERED. NO MATTER HOW THE WAR HAD ENDED, RACISM CONTINUED... AND CONTINUES.

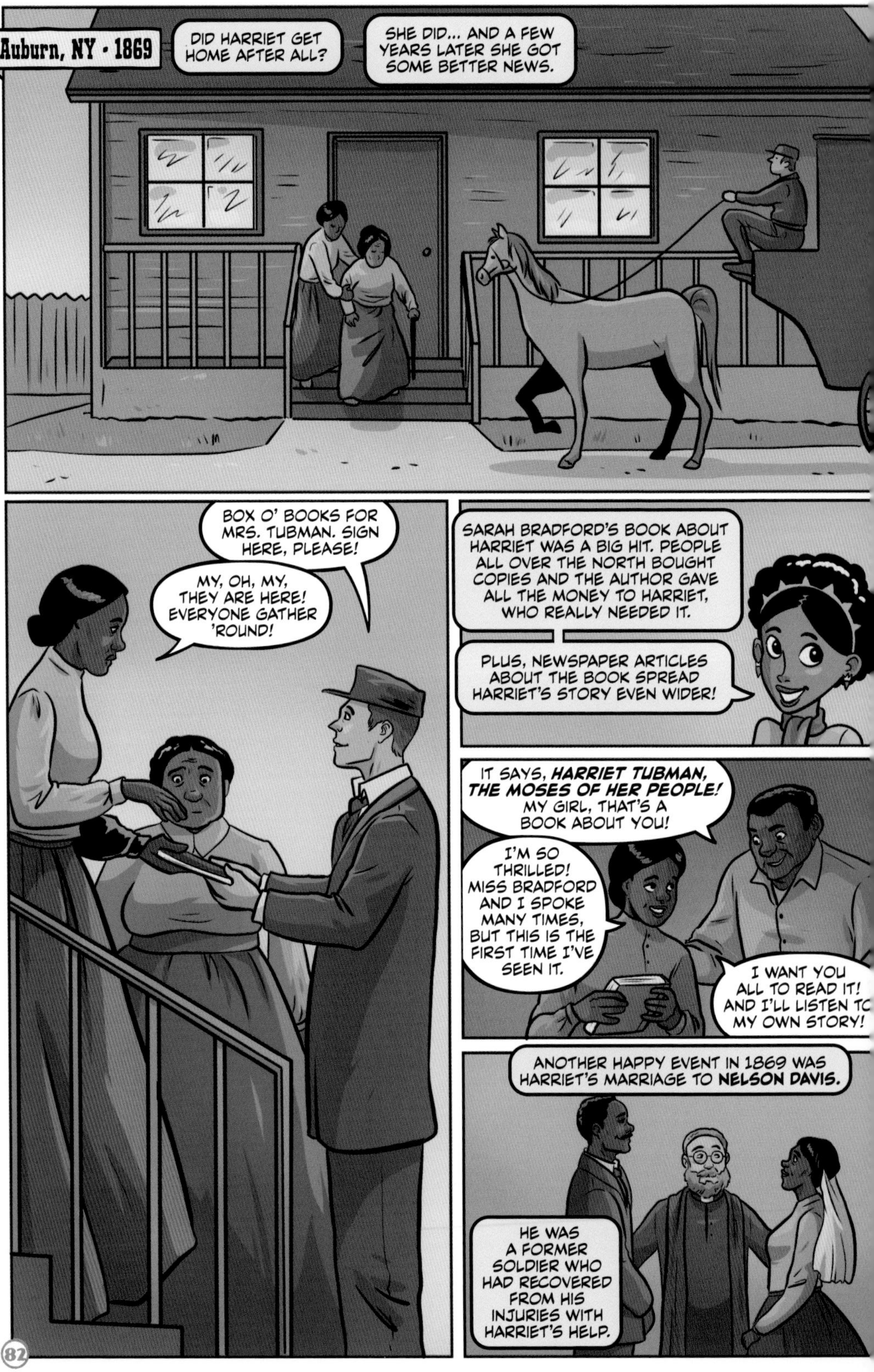
Auburn, NY • 1869
DID HARRIET GET HOME AFTER ALL?
SHE DID... AND A FEW YEARS LATER SHE GOT SOME BETTER NEWS.
BOX O' BOOKS FOR MRS. TUBMAN. SIGN HERE, PLEASE!
MY, OH, MY, THEY ARE HERE! EVERYONE GATHER 'ROUND!
SARAH BRADFORD'S BOOK ABOUT HARRIET WAS A BIG HIT. PEOPLE ALL OVER THE NORTH BOUGHT COPIES AND THE AUTHOR GAVE ALL THE MONEY TO HARRIET, WHO REALLY NEEDED IT.
PLUS, NEWSPAPER ARTICLES ABOUT THE BOOK SPREAD HARRIET'S STORY EVEN WIDER!
IT SAYS, ***HARRIET TUBMAN, THE MOSES OF HER PEOPLE!*** MY GIRL, THAT'S A BOOK ABOUT YOU!
I'M SO THRILLED! MISS BRADFORD AND I SPOKE MANY TIMES, BUT THIS IS THE FIRST TIME I'VE SEEN IT.
I WANT YOU ALL TO READ IT! AND I'LL LISTEN TO MY OWN STORY!
ANOTHER HAPPY EVENT IN 1869 WAS HARRIET'S MARRIAGE TO **NELSON DAVIS.**
HE WAS A FORMER SOLDIER WHO HAD RECOVERED FROM HIS INJURIES WITH HARRIET'S HELP.

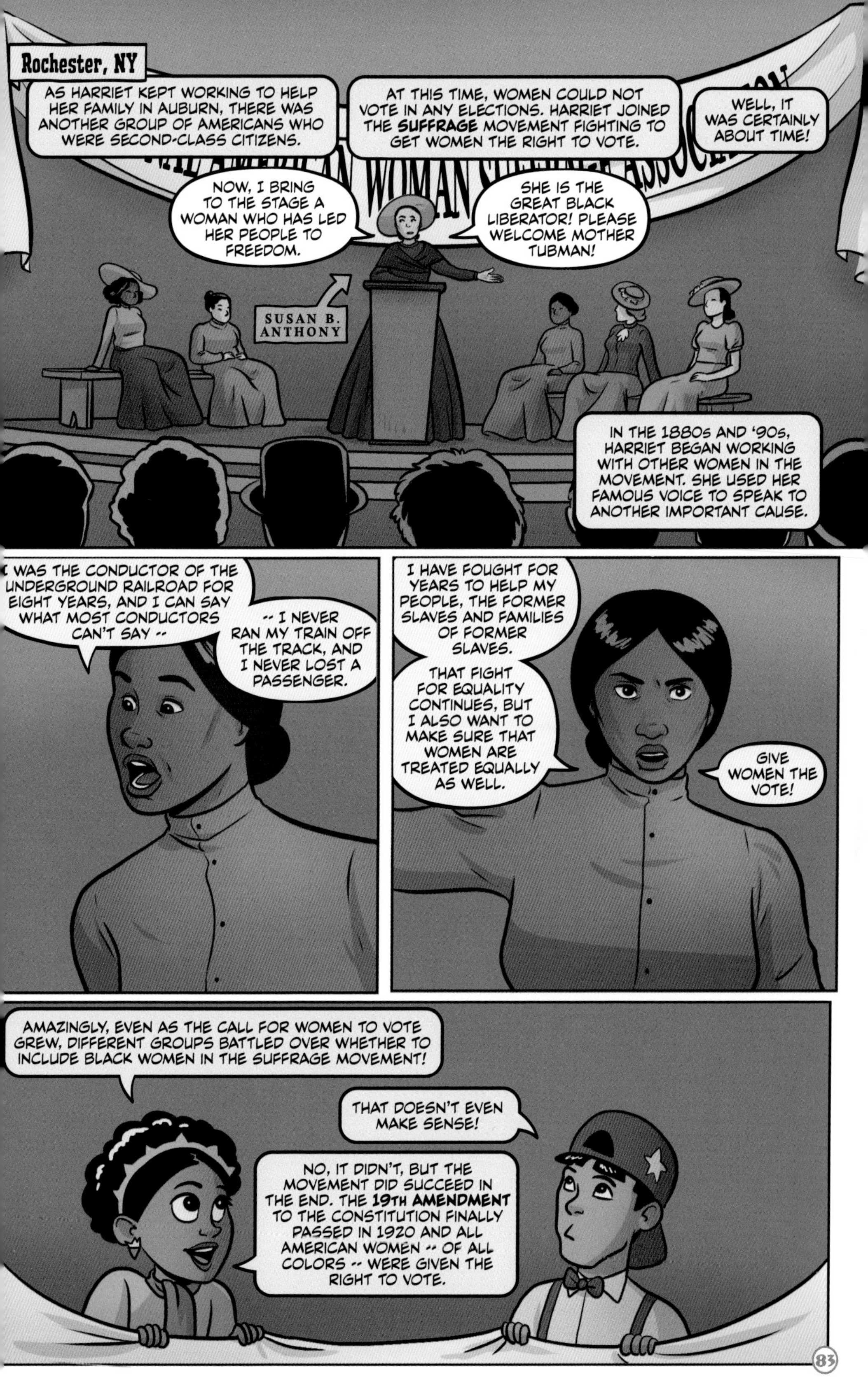

Rochester, NY
AS HARRIET KEPT WORKING TO HELP HER FAMILY IN AUBURN, THERE WAS ANOTHER GROUP OF AMERICANS WHO WERE SECOND-CLASS CITIZENS.
AT THIS TIME, WOMEN COULD NOT VOTE IN ANY ELECTIONS. HARRIET JOINED THE **SUFFRAGE** MOVEMENT FIGHTING TO GET WOMEN THE RIGHT TO VOTE.
WELL, IT WAS CERTAINLY ABOUT TIME!
NOW, I BRING TO THE STAGE A WOMAN WHO HAS LED HER PEOPLE TO FREEDOM.
SHE IS THE GREAT BLACK LIBERATOR! PLEASE WELCOME MOTHER TUBMAN!
SUSAN B. ANTHONY
IN THE 1880s AND '90s, HARRIET BEGAN WORKING WITH OTHER WOMEN IN THE MOVEMENT. SHE USED HER FAMOUS VOICE TO SPEAK TO ANOTHER IMPORTANT CAUSE.
WAS THE CONDUCTOR OF THE UNDERGROUND RAILROAD FOR EIGHT YEARS, AND I CAN SAY WHAT MOST CONDUCTORS CAN'T SAY --
-- I NEVER RAN MY TRAIN OFF THE TRACK, AND I NEVER LOST A PASSENGER.
I HAVE FOUGHT FOR YEARS TO HELP MY PEOPLE, THE FORMER SLAVES AND FAMILIES OF FORMER SLAVES.
THAT FIGHT FOR EQUALITY CONTINUES, BUT I ALSO WANT TO MAKE SURE THAT WOMEN ARE TREATED EQUALLY AS WELL.
GIVE WOMEN THE VOTE!
AMAZINGLY, EVEN AS THE CALL FOR WOMEN TO VOTE GREW, DIFFERENT GROUPS BATTLED OVER WHETHER TO INCLUDE BLACK WOMEN IN THE SUFFRAGE MOVEMENT!
THAT DOESN'T EVEN MAKE SENSE!
NO, IT DIDN'T, BUT THE MOVEMENT DID SUCCEED IN THE END. THE **19TH AMENDMENT** TO THE CONSTITUTION FINALLY PASSED IN 1920 AND ALL AMERICAN WOMEN -- OF ALL COLORS -- WERE GIVEN THE RIGHT TO VOTE.

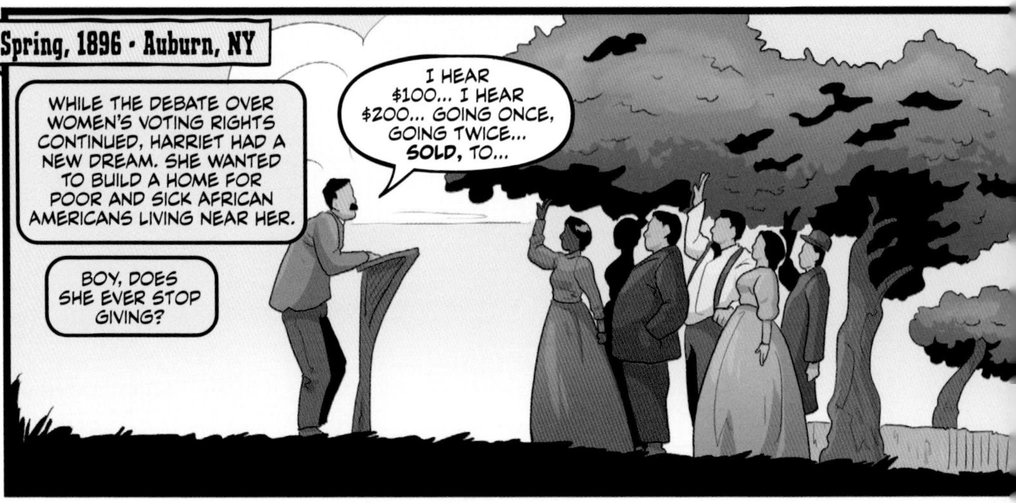
Spring, 1896 - Auburn, NY
WHILE THE DEBATE OVER WOMEN'S VOTING RIGHTS CONTINUED, HARRIET HAD A NEW DREAM. SHE WANTED TO BUILD A HOME FOR POOR AND SICK AFRICAN AMERICANS LIVING NEAR HER.
BOY, DOES SHE EVER STOP GIVING?
I HEAR $100... I HEAR $200... GOING ONCE, GOING TWICE... **SOLD,** TO...

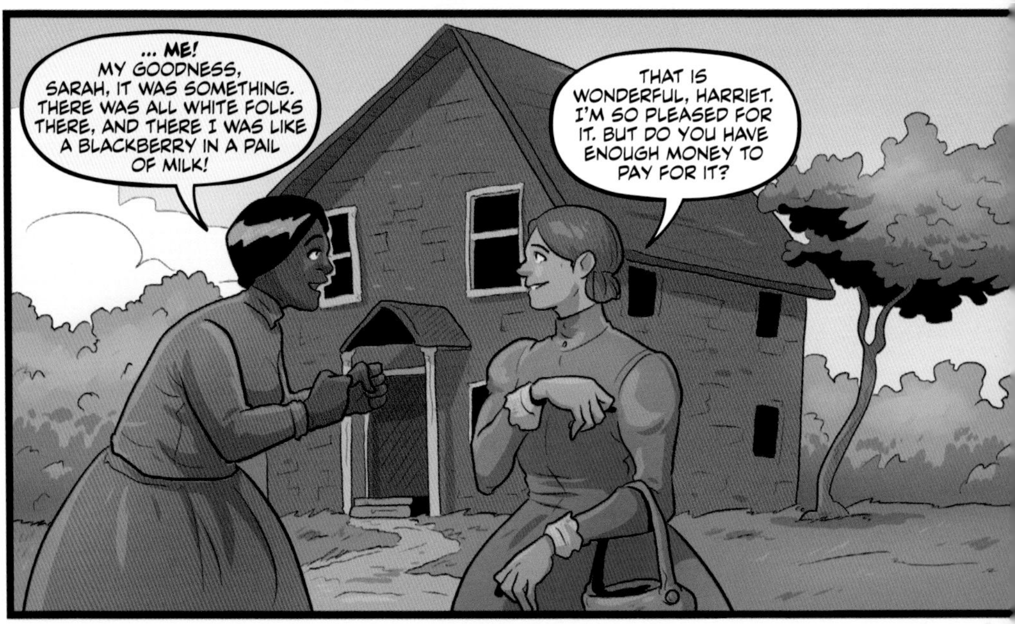
... **ME!** MY GOODNESS, SARAH, IT WAS SOMETHING. THERE WAS ALL WHITE FOLKS THERE, AND THERE I WAS LIKE A BLACKBERRY IN A PAIL OF MILK!
THAT IS WONDERFUL, HARRIET. I'M SO PLEASED FOR IT. BUT DO YOU HAVE ENOUGH MONEY TO PAY FOR IT?

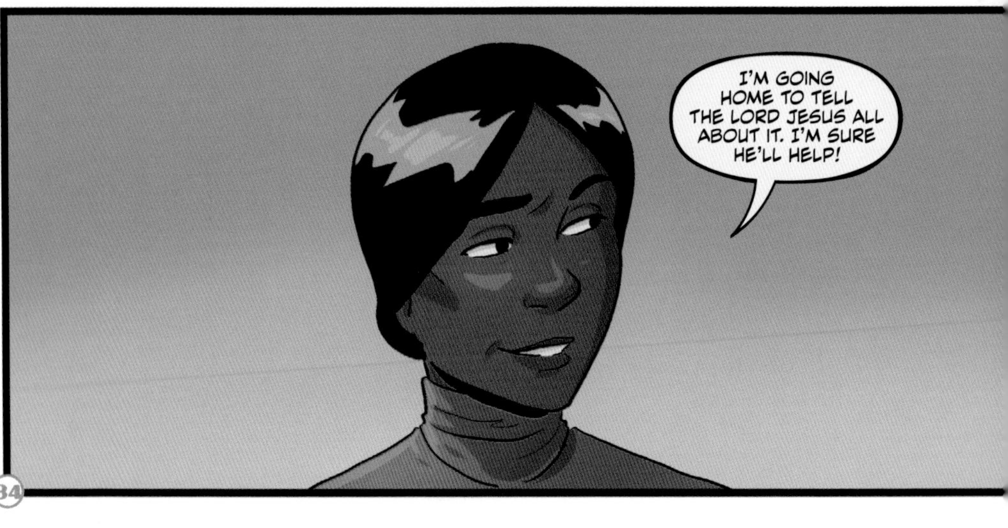
I'M GOING HOME TO TELL THE LORD JESUS ALL ABOUT IT. I'M SURE HE'LL HELP!

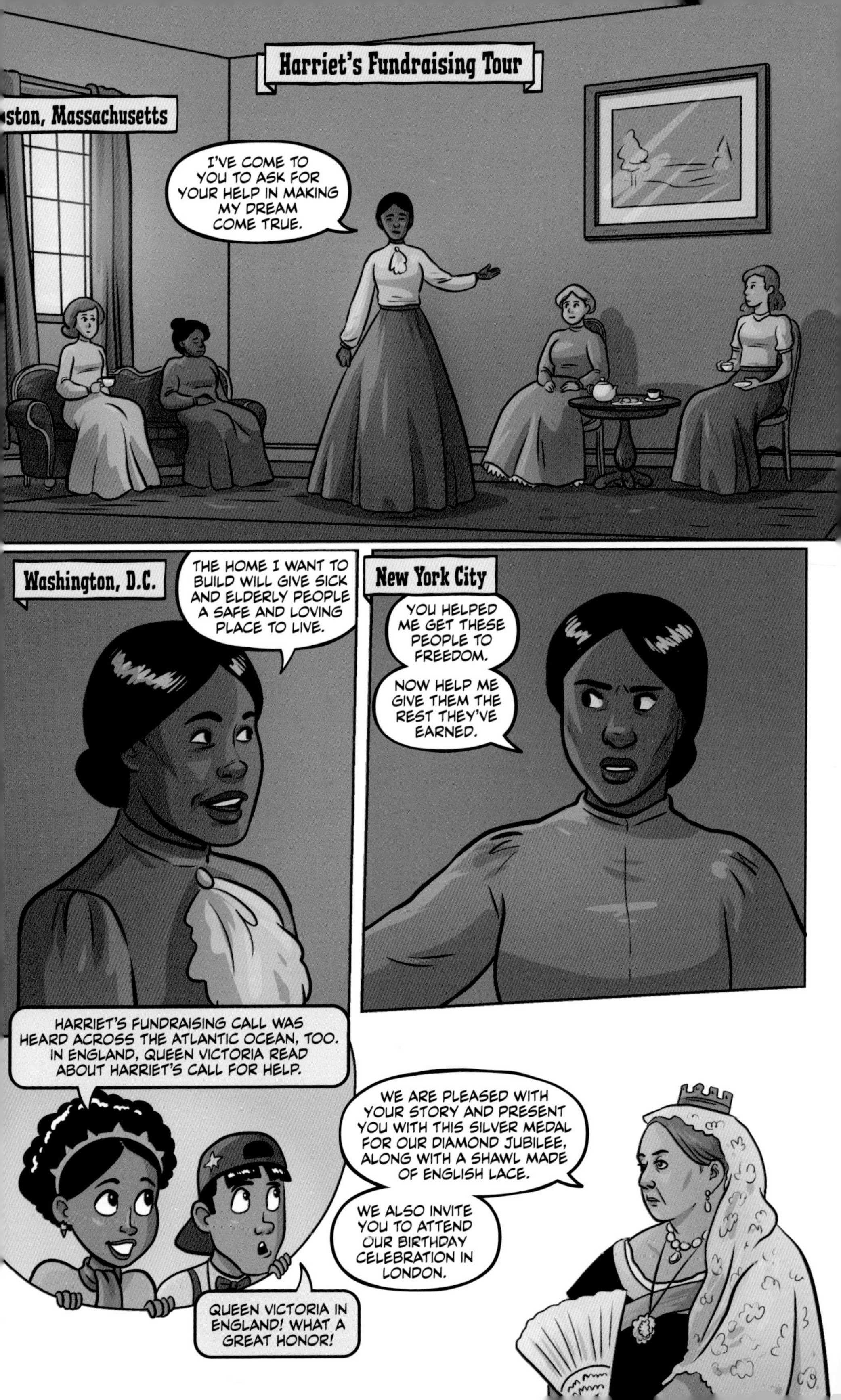
Harriet's Fundraising Tour
ston, Massachusetts
I'VE COME TO YOU TO ASK FOR YOUR HELP IN MAKING MY DREAM COME TRUE.
Washington, D.C.
THE HOME I WANT TO BUILD WILL GIVE SICK AND ELDERLY PEOPLE A SAFE AND LOVING PLACE TO LIVE.
New York City
YOU HELPED ME GET THESE PEOPLE TO FREEDOM.
NOW HELP ME GIVE THEM THE REST THEY'VE EARNED.
HARRIET'S FUNDRAISING CALL WAS HEARD ACROSS THE ATLANTIC OCEAN, TOO. IN ENGLAND, QUEEN VICTORIA READ ABOUT HARRIET'S CALL FOR HELP.
WE ARE PLEASED WITH YOUR STORY AND PRESENT YOU WITH THIS SILVER MEDAL FOR OUR DIAMOND JUBILEE, ALONG WITH A SHAWL MADE OF ENGLISH LACE.
WE ALSO INVITE YOU TO ATTEND OUR BIRTHDAY CELEBRATION IN LONDON.
QUEEN VICTORIA IN ENGLAND! WHAT A GREAT HONOR!

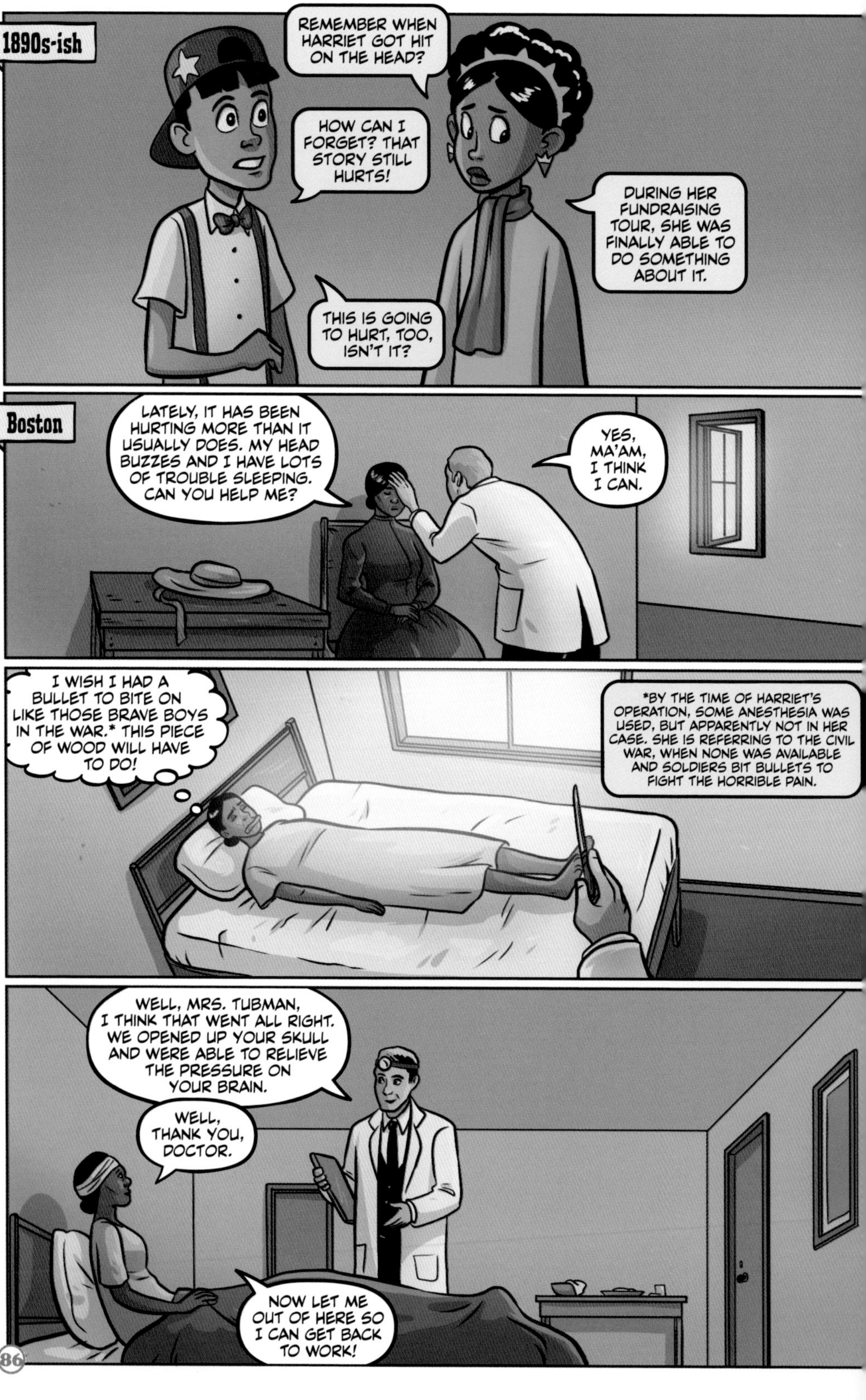
1890s-ish
REMEMBER WHEN HARRIET GOT HIT ON THE HEAD?
HOW CAN I FORGET? THAT STORY STILL HURTS!
DURING HER FUNDRAISING TOUR, SHE WAS FINALLY ABLE TO DO SOMETHING ABOUT IT.
THIS IS GOING TO HURT, TOO, ISN'T IT?
Boston
LATELY, IT HAS BEEN HURTING MORE THAN IT USUALLY DOES. MY HEAD BUZZES AND I HAVE LOTS OF TROUBLE SLEEPING. CAN YOU HELP ME?
YES, MA'AM, I THINK I CAN.
I WISH I HAD A BULLET TO BITE ON LIKE THOSE BRAVE BOYS IN THE WAR.* THIS PIECE OF WOOD WILL HAVE TO DO!
*BY THE TIME OF HARRIET'S OPERATION, SOME ANESTHESIA WAS USED, BUT APPARENTLY NOT IN HER CASE. SHE IS REFERRING TO THE CIVIL WAR, WHEN NONE WAS AVAILABLE AND SOLDIERS BIT BULLETS TO FIGHT THE HORRIBLE PAIN.
WELL, MRS. TUBMAN, I THINK THAT WENT ALL RIGHT. WE OPENED UP YOUR SKULL AND WERE ABLE TO RELIEVE THE PRESSURE ON YOUR BRAIN.
WELL, THANK YOU, DOCTOR.
NOW LET ME OUT OF HERE SO I CAN GET BACK TO WORK!

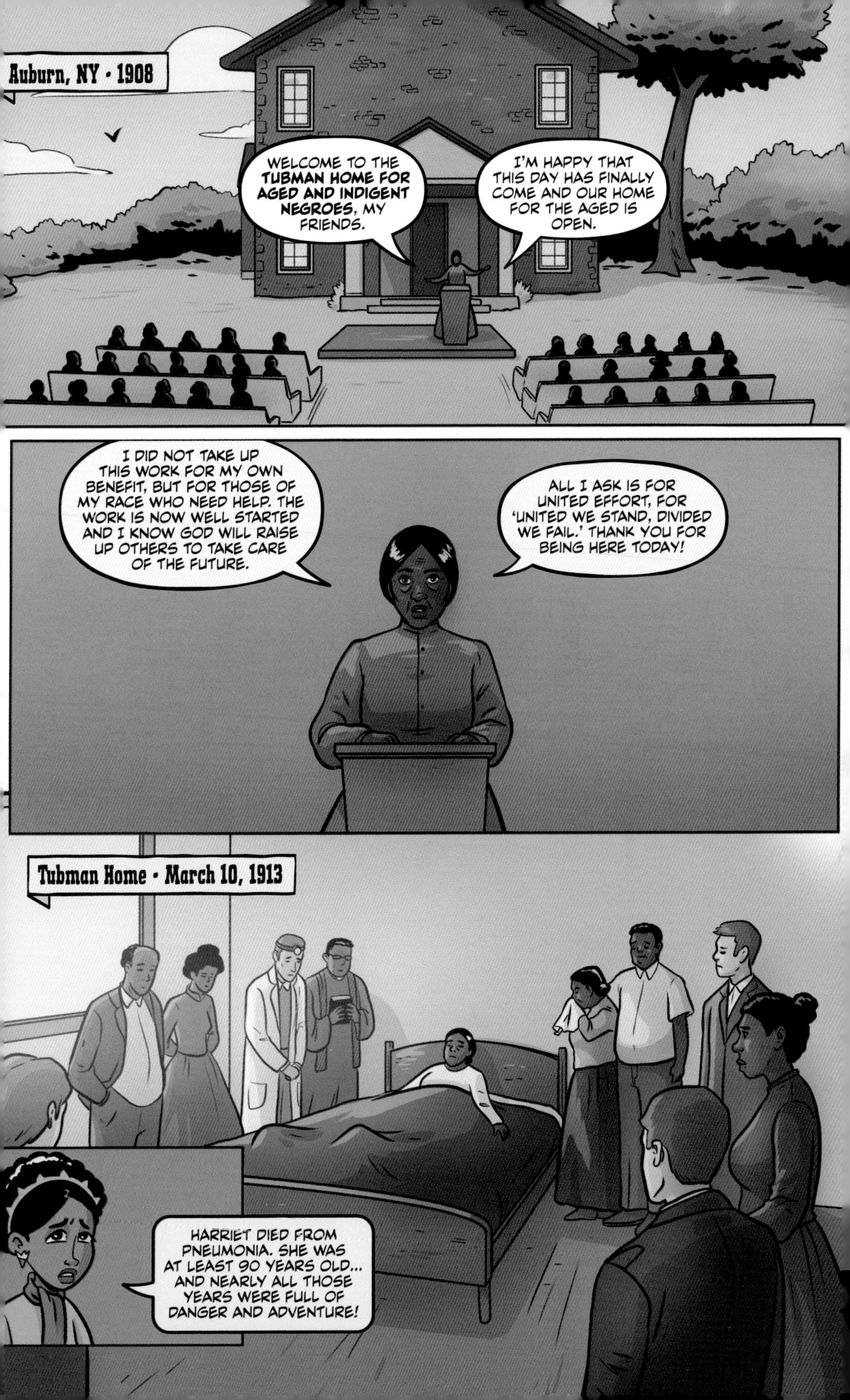
Auburn, NY • 1908
WELCOME TO THE TUBMAN HOME FOR AGED AND INDIGENT NEGROES, MY FRIENDS.
I'M HAPPY THAT THIS DAY HAS FINALLY COME AND OUR HOME FOR THE AGED IS OPEN.
I DID NOT TAKE UP THIS WORK FOR MY OWN BENEFIT, BUT FOR THOSE OF MY RACE WHO NEED HELP. THE WORK IS NOW WELL STARTED AND I KNOW GOD WILL RAISE UP OTHERS TO TAKE CARE OF THE FUTURE.
ALL I ASK IS FOR UNITED EFFORT, FOR 'UNITED WE STAND, DIVIDED WE FAIL.' THANK YOU FOR BEING HERE TODAY!
Tubman Home • March 10, 1913
HARRIET DIED FROM PNEUMONIA. SHE WAS AT LEAST 90 YEARS OLD... AND NEARLY ALL THOSE YEARS WERE FULL OF DANGER AND ADVENTURE!

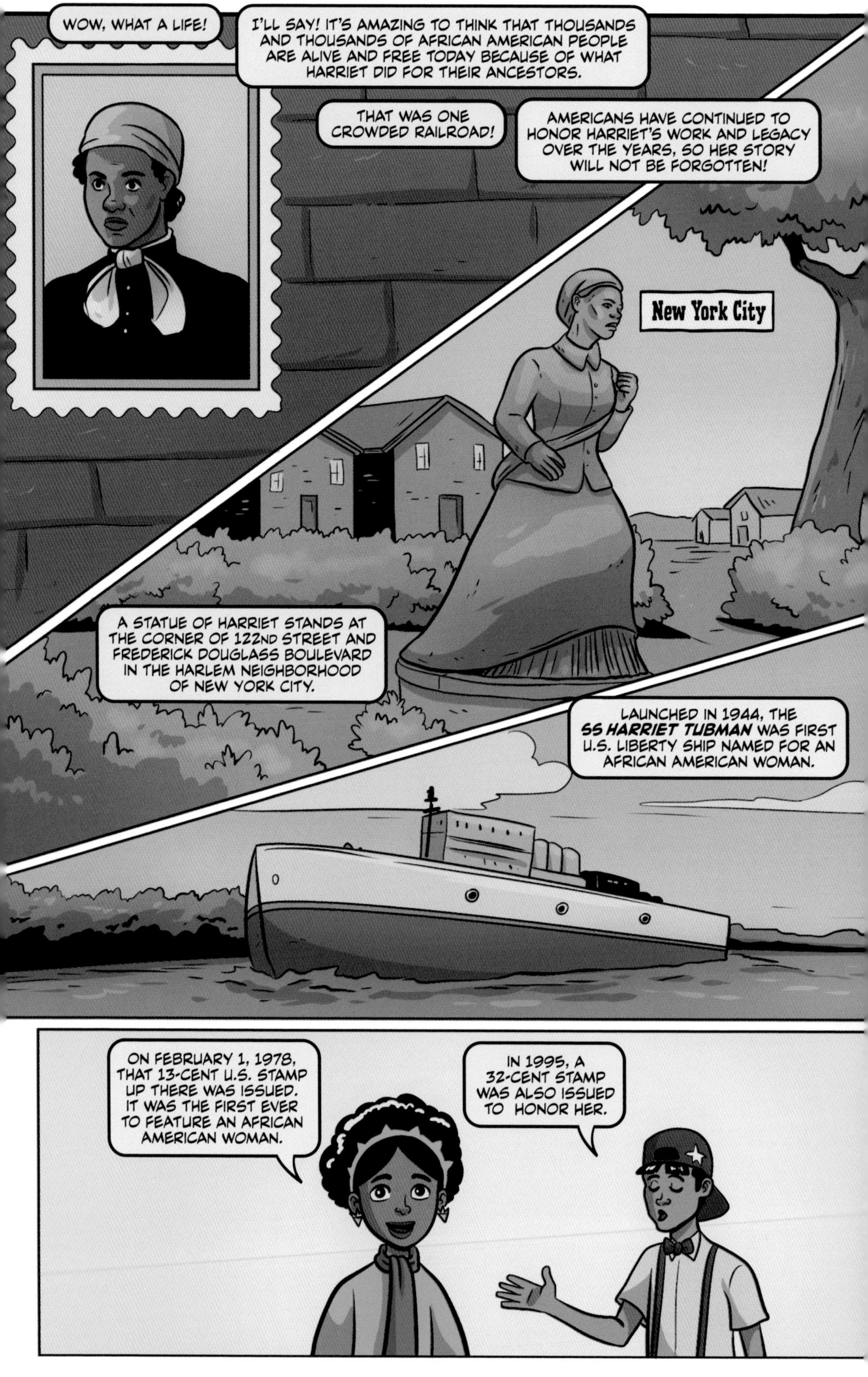

WOW, WHAT A LIFE!
I'LL SAY! IT'S AMAZING TO THINK THAT THOUSANDS AND THOUSANDS OF AFRICAN AMERICAN PEOPLE ARE ALIVE AND FREE TODAY BECAUSE OF WHAT HARRIET DID FOR THEIR ANCESTORS.
THAT WAS ONE CROWDED RAILROAD!
AMERICANS HAVE CONTINUED TO HONOR HARRIET'S WORK AND LEGACY OVER THE YEARS, SO HER STORY WILL NOT BE FORGOTTEN!
New York City
A STATUE OF HARRIET STANDS AT THE CORNER OF 122ND STREET AND FREDERICK DOUGLASS BOULEVARD IN THE HARLEM NEIGHBORHOOD OF NEW YORK CITY.
LAUNCHED IN 1944, THE ***SS HARRIET TUBMAN*** WAS FIRST U.S. LIBERTY SHIP NAMED FOR AN AFRICAN AMERICAN WOMAN.
ON FEBRUARY 1, 1978, THAT 13-CENT U.S. STAMP UP THERE WAS ISSUED. IT WAS THE FIRST EVER TO FEATURE AN AFRICAN AMERICAN WOMAN.
IN 1995, A 32-CENT STAMP WAS ALSO ISSUED TO HONOR HER.

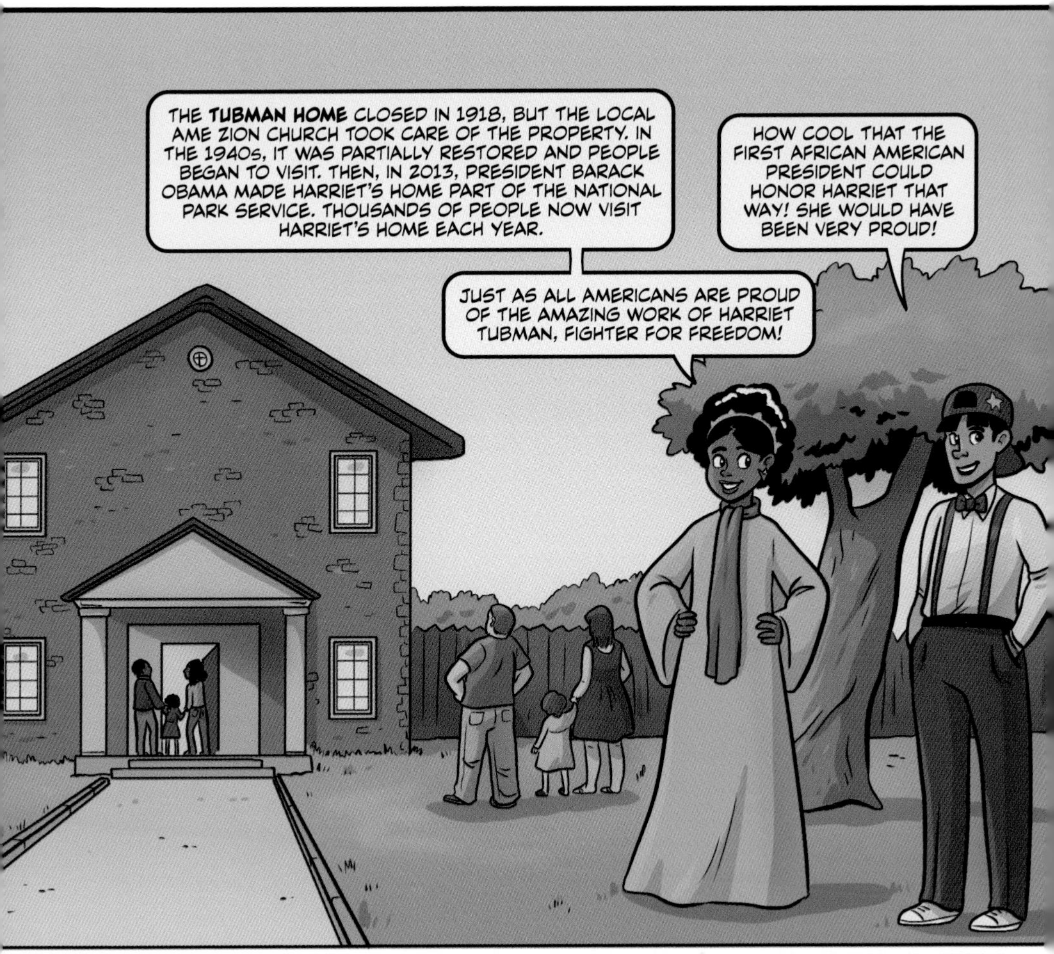
THE **TUBMAN HOME** CLOSED IN 1918, BUT THE LOCAL AME ZION CHURCH TOOK CARE OF THE PROPERTY. IN THE 1940s, IT WAS PARTIALLY RESTORED AND PEOPLE BEGAN TO VISIT. THEN, IN 2013, PRESIDENT BARACK OBAMA MADE HARRIET'S HOME PART OF THE NATIONAL PARK SERVICE. THOUSANDS OF PEOPLE NOW VISIT HARRIET'S HOME EACH YEAR.
HOW COOL THAT THE FIRST AFRICAN AMERICAN PRESIDENT COULD HONOR HARRIET THAT WAY! SHE WOULD HAVE BEEN VERY PROUD!
JUST AS ALL AMERICANS ARE PROUD OF THE AMAZING WORK OF HARRIET TUBMAN, FIGHTER FOR FREEDOM!

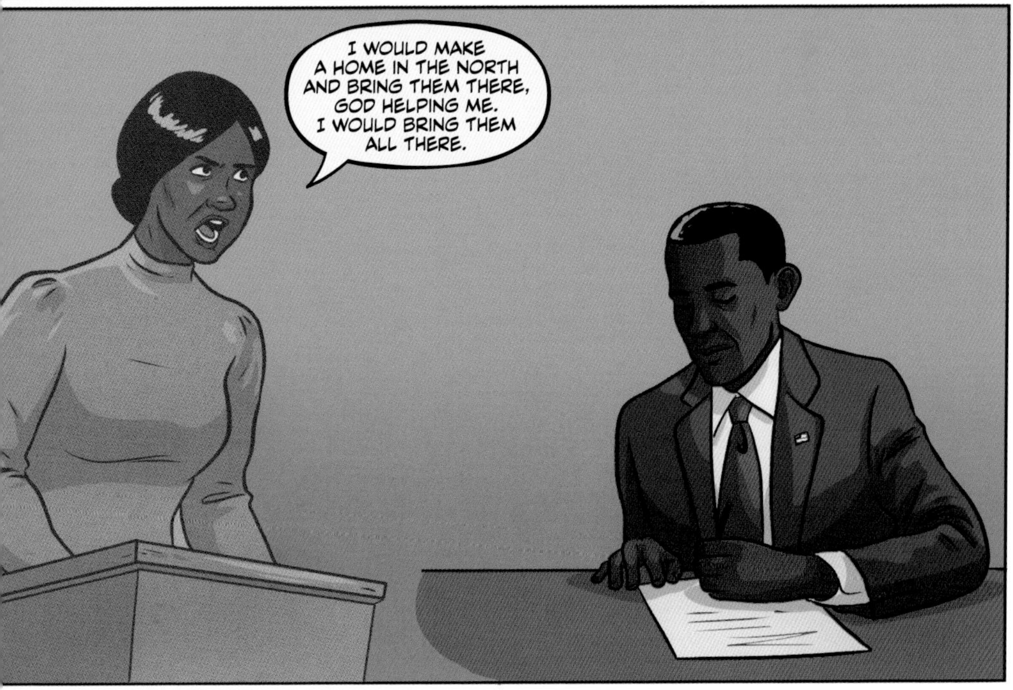
I WOULD MAKE A HOME IN THE NORTH AND BRING THEM THERE, GOD HELPING ME. I WOULD BRING THEM ALL THERE.

FEMALE FREEDOM FIGHTERS

JANE ADDAMS (1860-1935) was a lifelong fighter for the rights of poor people and immigrants. She created a series of settlement houses in major American cities. At such places, poor people could get help, take classes, or have fun.

A native of Guatemala, **RIGOBERTA MENCHÚ (1959-PRESENT)** won the Nobel Peace Prize in 1992 for her work fighting for the rights of native people in her country.

ELIZABETH CADY STANTON (1815-1902), along with Susan B. Anthony, Harriet, and many other women, was a key leader in the suffrage and antislavery movements in the 19th century.

In 1985 **WILMA MANKILLER (1945-2010)** became the first and only woman to be elected chief of the Cherokee Nation. In that role, she became a national voice for Native American and women's rights.

Born in Pakistan, **MALALA YOUSAFZAI (1997-PRESENT)** was a student in a land where women were not encouraged to study. Terrorists shot her in the head in 2012 to prevent her from going to school, but she survived... and kept going. Her fearlessness and determination to tell her story earned her the 2014 Nobel Peace Prize.

IDA B. WELLS-BARNETT (1862-1931) was an African American writer and journalist who focused attention on the horrible crime of lynching. She later helped found the *National Association for the Advancement of Colored People (NAACP)*, a leading civil rights group.

HARRIET TUBMAN IS NOT THE ONLY WOMAN IN HISTORY WHO RISKED HER LIFE TO FIGHT FOR THE FREEDOM OF OTHERS. HERE ARE OTHER BRAVE WOMEN YOU SHOULD KNOW ABOUT!

HARRIET TUBMAN TIMELINE

ca. **1822**	Araminta "Minty" Ross is born a slave in Maryland.
ca. **1835**	"Minty" suffers a serious head injury while defending another slave.
1844	Minty marries John Tubman, a free black man.
1849	She escapes from her plantation and arrives in Philadelphia, renaming herself Harriet Tubman.
1850	Harriet returns to Maryland to help her niece escape, her first work as a "conductor" on the Underground Railroad.
1850-1860	Harriet makes multiple trips south to free other slaves, perhaps more than 300 people in total.
1861	She volunteers to act as a nurse as the Civil War begins.
1863	After serving as a spy and a scout, Harriet helps lead an attack in South Carolina that frees 700 slaves.
1865	She is badly injured when thrown from a train by a racist conductor.
1869	Harriet remarries, to Nelson Davis. The same year, a biography of Harriet is published to wide acclaim.
1898	Harriet begins speaking on the cause of women's right to vote.
1903	Harriet donates her property to create a hospital for poor people.
1913	Harriet dies of pneumonia at 93 years old. She receives military honors at her funeral.

GLOSSARY

ABOLITION: The ending of something, in this case slavery.

ASHANTI: People who live in or are from southern Ghana in Africa.

CONTRABAND: Goods stolen from an enemy in war.

CONVICTION: In this meaning, having a strong belief in the rightness of a cause or movement.

DIAMOND JUBILEE: A celebration held to mark the 60th anniversary of an important event. (In this case, it means Queen Victoria's reign over Great Britain.)

FAITH: Believing in something without physical or visual proof.

FUGITIVE: A person escaping from the law.

PLANTATION: A large farm, usually with many acres of crops.

SECEDE: To officially withdraw from a political group or organization.

SUFFRAGE: The right to vote.

QUAKER: A member of the *Society of Friends*, a Christian religious group that preaches peacefulness and support for human rights.

WAGES: Money earned for performing a job.

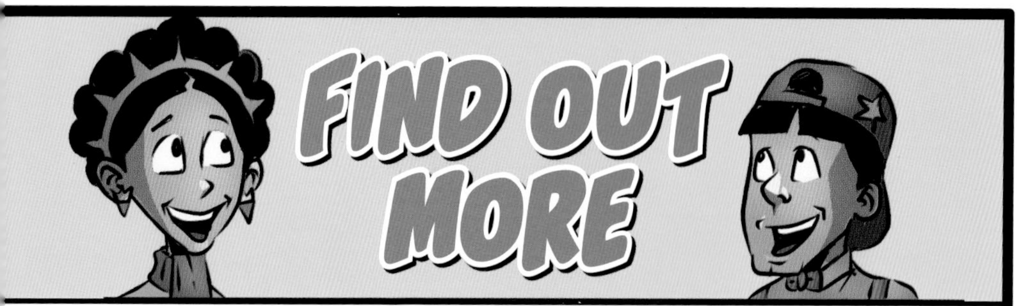
FIND OUT MORE

BOOKS

Bradford, Sarah Hopkins. *Harriet, the Moses of Her People.* Public Domain. (Kindle edition referenced for this book.)

Clinton, Catherine. *Harriet Tubman: The Road to Freedom.* New York: Little, Brown and Company, 2004.

Larson, Kate Clifford. *Bound for the Promised Land: Harriet Tubman: Portrait of an American Hero.* New York: Random House, 2004.

Levine, Ellen. *If You Traveled on the Underground Railroad.* New York: Scholastic Inc., 1988.

McDonough, Yona Zeldis. *What Was the Underground Railroad?* What Was? series. New York: Penguin Group, 2013.

McDonough, Yona Zeldis. *Who Was Harriet Tubman?* Who Was? series. New York: Penguin Group, 2002.

Weatherford, Carole Boston, illustrated by Kadir Nelson. *Moses: When Harriet Tubman Led Her People to Freedom.* New York: Hyperion Books for Children, 2006.

WEBSITES

Harriet Tubman National Historical Park
https://www.harriettubmanhome.com
Official website of the National Historical Park that surrounds Harriet's home in Auburn, New York.

National Park Service: Harriet Tubman
https://www.nps.gov/people/harriet-tubman.htm
More information about Harriet Tubman, commemorative parks, and monuments.

Smithsonian National Museum of African American History & Culture
https://nmaahc.si.edu
Located in Washington, D.C., the 19th museum of the Smithsonian Institution opened in 2016.

Tubman Museum
https://www.tubmanmuseum.com
Located in Macon, Georgia, the museum features African American art, history, and stories.

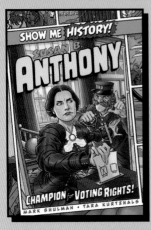
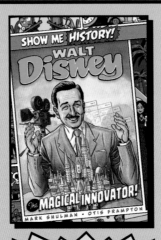

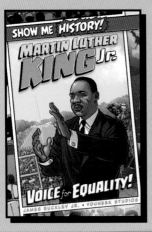